Righteous Armies, Holy Cause

RIGHTEOUS ARMIES, HOLY CAUSE

Apocalyptic Imagery and the Civil War

Terrie Dopp Aamodt

Mercer University Press
MMII

ISBN 0-86554-738-6
MUP/H554

First Edition.

The paper used in this publication meets the minimum
requirements of American National Standard for
Information Sciences— Permanence of Paper for Printed
Library Materials, ANSI Z39.48-1984.

Library of Congress Cataloging-in-Publication Data

Aamodt, Terrie Dopp, 1954-
  Righteous armies, holy cause : apocalyptic imagery and the Civil War / by Terrie Dopp
Aamodt.
     p. cm.
Includes bibliographical references and index.
  ISBN 0-86554-738-6 (alk. paper)
  1. United States—History—Civil War, 1861-1865—Religious aspects—Christianity I.
Title.
  BR526 .A22 2002
  973.7'1—dc21

2002004818

Table of Contents

List of Illustrations

ACKNOWLEDGMENTS

This volume owes a lot to a lot of books. First they piqued what seemed like idle curiosity; eventually they led to something more purposeful. Something Garry Wills wrote put me on the track to this study. In the introduction to his book on the Declaration of Independence, *Inventing America*, Wills discusses the Civil War and Julia Ward Howe's "Battle Hymn of the Republic." His remarks made me realize I had always taken for granted the incantatory power of her lines without thinking about their context or their meaning to the first people who sang them. Trailing Julia Ward Howe soon led me to Edmund Wilson's *Patriotic Gore*, which thoroughly explicates Howe's poem and many other apocalyptic Northern utterances. My biggest surprise came when I started reading Confederate texts. I had not anticipated the extent and intensity of the apocalyptic references residing there. More recently it has been intriguing to view all of the primary texts in light of the extensive, thoughtful work on apocalypticism as well as Civil War religion published in the 1990s.

This book also owes a lot to a lot of people. Cecelia Tichi and Earl Kent Brown guided the initial concept into an American Studies dissertation at Boston University, and Patricia Hills has provided encouragement. The pedagogical example of William Vance made me want to include visual art in the project, a life-changing decision as it turned out. Bill Marion, Hope Cushing, and Sylvia Nosworthy always knew what needed saying or doing. More recently, I have benefited from the knowledge and advice of Roy Branson, David Trim, Kendra Haloviak, Robert Ellison, and LuAnn Venden Herrell. Lee Johnston and Violet Maynard-Reid have helped me track down many sources. The Walla Walla College Faculty Development Committee provided a research grant for the project. Andrew Manis and Marc Jolley of Mercer University Press have been consistently encouraging during the transformation of the manuscript into a book.

I owe a lot to the direct and indirect contributions of my family: my parents, Matthew and Janice Dopp, who gave everything from a vocabulary to proofreading skills; my husband, Larry, who set me up with a Radio Shack TRS-80 and cassette tape storage when everyone else was still lugging a Kaypro to the library (the TRS-80 landed me a role in a

Huntington Library photograph illustrating the latest in information-gathering technology) and has since made my laptop's wireless connection to a campus network hum efficiently; my children, Erica and Alex, whose lively ways have led me to a more balanced life than I would otherwise be capable of, and whose cheerful, quiet toleration of my lapses into tunnel vision leave me in their debt.

PREFACE

Edmund H. Sears, a Northern apologist during the Civil War, enjoyed telling a story he had read in a newspaper, the *Louisville Journal.* Union troops were marching through a Kentucky town with regimental and national flags waving. Just then a rainbow appeared, and "a little boy, seeing it, ran to his mother, exclaiming, 'Mother, God is a Union man! he has just hung out in the sky the red, white and blue.'" Without blinking, Sears comments "there is no courage like that which springs from the consciousness that God is on our side."[1] Many Confederate supporters held an identical opinion.

In the first half of the nineteenth century, American Protestants had eagerly sought the millennium. The Civil War came just as the religious stage had been thoroughly set to prepare combatants on both sides for a conflict vast enough to propel the country to the threshold of the Apocalypse and eternity. It did not take long for the nation's civil troubles to grow to a magnitude apparently worthy of a time-ending event. The intensity of expectation helps to explain the war's ferocity and duration.

Christians on both sides shared assumptions about the roles of God and humans in history. Divine involvement was expected and repeatedly identified. As he watched the public respond to the war, Abraham Lincoln pointed out in 1862: "In great contests each party claims to act in accordance with the will of God. Both may be, and one must be, wrong. God cannot be for and against the same thing at the same time."[2] Lincoln continued to brood on that topic until he delivered his second inaugural address in 1865: "Both read the same Bible, and pray to the same God; and each invokes His aid against the other."[3] Lincoln's ability to establish a critical distance between himself and the events of the war was rare.

---

[1]Edmund H. Sears, "Signs in the Sky–Beautiful Incident," *The Monthly Religious Magazine* 27 (April 1862): 267.

[2]Quoted in *The Literary Works of Abraham Lincoln*, ed. Carl Van Doren (New York: Readers Club, 1942) 221.

[3]Lincoln, "Second Inaugural Address, March 4, 1865," in Abraham Lincoln, "First Inaugural Address, March 4, 1861," in *The Collected Works of*

History is filled with cataclysmic events that trigger religious responses. The Civil War, however, was unusual for the congruity of interpretations on both sides. The combatants had, after all, imbibed the same spiritual brew for over two hundred years. More remarkable still is the tendency of Civil War apocalypticism to function as a powerful aesthetic device in visual, literary, and polemical contexts; in the productions of accomplished painters, facile cartoonists, poets, song lyricists, novelists, slaves, slave owners, and preachers. Both the enormity of the event and the extent of a shared, or at least overlapping, religious culture enabled both Unionists and Confederates to view their soldiers as righteous armies and their goals as the same holy cause. The war's failure to bring a quick victory to either side transformed the role of apocalyptic interpretation in American culture. Cataclysms proceed, but congruity in their interpretation is the stuff of history.

Abraham Lincoln, ed. Roy P. Basler (New Brunswick NJ: Rutgers University Press, 1953) 8:333.

Figure 1: *Cotopaxi* (1862). Frederic Edwin Church. (The Detroit Institute of Arts, Founders Society Purchase, Robert H. Tannahill Foundation Fund, Gibbs-Williams Fund, Beatrice W. Rogers and Richard A. Manoogian Fund)

Figure 2: *View of the Capitol of the United States, After the Conflagration in 1814* (1817). Alexander Lawson. (Library of Congress)

Figure 3: *The Fifteenth Amendment, Celebrated May 19, 1870* (1870). (This item is reproduced by permission of the Huntington Library, San Marino, California.)

Figure 4: *Worship of the North.* Adalbert Volck. (Library of Congress)

Figure 5: *The Outbreak of the Rebellion in the United States 1861.* (Library of Congress)

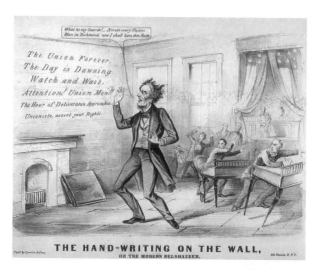

Figure 6: *The Handwriting on the Wall, or The Modern Belshazzer* (1862). Currier and Ives. (This item is reproduced by permission of the Huntington Library, San Marino, California.)

Figure 7: *Breaking that "Backbone."* (Library of Congress)

Figure 8: *Proclamation of Emancipation.* L. Franklin Smith. (This item is reproduced by permission of the Huntington Library, San Marino, California.)

Figure 9: *Stonewall Jackson's Camp* (1863). Adalbert Volck. (Library of Congress)

Figure 10: *Lincoln Crushing the Dragon of Rebellion (1862)*. David Gilmour Blythe. (Museum of Fine Arts, Boston. M. and M. Karolik Collection)

Figure 11: *Old Virginia Home.* David Gilmour Blythe. (© The Art Institute of Chicago, all rights reserved.)

Figure 12: *Tracks of the Armies* (1862). Adalbert Volck. (Library of Congress)

Figure 13: *Aurora Borealis* (1865). Frederick E. Church. (Smithsonian American Art Museum, gift of Eleanor Bladgett.)

Figure 14: *Evening Gun, Fort Sumter* (1864-1865). John Gadsby Chapman, after Conrad Wise Chapman. (The Museum of the Confederacy, Richmond, Virginia. Photography by Katherine Wetzel.)

Figure 15: Charleston, S. C. View of Ruined Buildings
Through the Porch of the Circular Church, 150 Meeting St.
(April 14, 1865). (Library of Congress)

1

Battle Poems, Storms, and Volcanoes: Icons of the Apocalypse

In April 1865 Herman Melville attended the annual exhibition at the National Academy of Design in New York. He particularly noted a painting by Sanford Robinson Gifford, a landscape painter who had served in the New York Seventh Regiment with Melville's cousin Henry Gansevoort. The painting, titled *The Coming Storm*, was owned by Edwin Booth, the great Shakespearean actor and brother of John Wilkes Booth. It depicted glowering black thunderclouds moving in on the Catskill mountains. As Melville looked at the painting, he thought about the way the painter had made nature symbolic, and the way the purchaser had identified with the message the painting embodied: "All feeling hearts must feel for him / Who felt this picture. Presage dire– / Dim inklings from the shadowy sphere / Fixed him and fascinated here."

Melville, as well as other perceptive viewers, could participate in assigning significance to this image from nature. No one, of course, is better equipped to understand its depths than a theatrical soul steeped in Shakespeare: "A demon-cloud like the mountain one / Burst on a spirit as mild / As this urned lake, the home of shades, / But Shakespeare's pensive child." By the time the Confederate armies surrendered, the war had developed into the dimensions of Shakespearean tragedy, perhaps best embodied in the faces of Abraham Lincoln and Robert E. Lee as they posed for Matthew Brady in early April. The pages of Shakespeare and the baffling fury of internecine carnage force people to admit hard truths about mankind, and perhaps about God as well, Melville notes in his poem: "No utter surprise can come to him / Who reaches Shakespeare's core; / That which we seek and shun is there– / Man's final lore."[1]

During the Civil War, scenes from nature, such as Gifford's storm portrayal, resonated both with their painters and their viewers as meaningful connections between the natural world and human events. Since God was assumed to rule over both, even by many Americans with just a casual connection to Christianity, natural phenomena and the movements of armies could be seen as the harmonious outworkings of a divine plan, or, failing that, they could at least be seen as symbolic events carried out with divine knowledge.

Herman Melville was deeply skeptical that God might take sides and countenance the unspeakable violence of civil war,[2] but his somber views of its events, translated into the poems of *Battle-Pieces and Aspects of the War* (1866), were steeped in biblical imagery and a Calvinist sensibility. Melville could not shake the conviction that the war was significant beyond the terrible, matter-of-fact present. As his biographer Edwin Havilland Miller noted about *Battle-Pieces*, "Whenever [Melville] killed off God, He rose again."[3] Perhaps this was the only way to explain the inexplicable.

Fighting a civil war requires uncanny depths of commitment and resolve. The initial impulse to leap into the fight and end the strife quickly and decisively lasts about as long as the interval between the first advance and the first retreat. In a perverse way, though, the slaughter itself sustains the engines of war: every death demands justification, which can only be obtained by ultimate victory. Citizens in Richmond and Washington, DC watched every day as apparently endless lines of ambulances creaked through the streets with their groaning cargo, populating hundreds of military hospitals with tens of thousands of maimed young men, America's future. Residents of every Northern and Southern town braced themselves for the next somber telegram or published list of battle victims. The war came, and the war had to be explained.

---

[1]Herman Melville, "The Coming Storm," *Battle-Pieces and Aspects of the War* (New York: Harper and Brothers, 1866) 143. See the appendix for the complete text of this poem and other quoted poems.

[2]Stanton Garner, *The Civil War World of Herman Melville* (Lawrence: The University Press of Kansas, 1993) 75.

[3]Edwin Havilland Miller, *Melville* (New York: George Braziller, 1975) 314.

The heat, smoke, and gore of battle continually encourage graphically realistic attempts to portray the carnage. At the same time, combatants often attach deeper meaning to wartime events, reaching for explanations that outpace the capacity of literal language. War's ability to make the familiar unrecognizable and terrifying has led participants again and again to find parallels with biblical language of ultimate destruction. A recurring motif for American mythmakers, particularly in times of crisis or national self-doubt, has been the Apocalypse.[4] This association occurred repeatedly in American history from the Revolution through World War I. Nowhere is this pattern more evident than in cultural responses to the Civil War, which fed both on the millennial fervor that had fired the first half of the nineteenth century and on the tendency of Northerners and Southerners alike to predict a special destiny for America. As Phillip Paludan has described it, "Since the nation was God's nation, corruption of it was a cosmic catastrophe."[5] The process of interpreting cataclysmic events in terms of the earth's violent end explained the otherwise inexplicable and placed America in a special role of prophetic fulfillment.

The ability to see such significance in the war was too broad to correspond with the assumption that apocalyptic judgment was "the myth of the North."[6] A significant body of apocalyptic literature appeared in the South during the Civil War. Furthermore, themes of the end of the world pervade the songs and oral history of Southern slaves. One reason for the startling similarity between Northern and Southern attitudes toward the Apocalypse is that antagonists on all sides shared a common perception of the significance of America in the world. Each saw itself as the righteous combatant, the prophetic antitype of Old Testament Israel; each also feared that the final judgment might prove it unworthy. During the war, Unionists and Confederates alike sought to be on God's side as prophecy unfolded. Despite the vast differences in the events leading to

---

[4]Ernest Lee Tuveson, *Redeemer Nation* (Chicago: University of Chicago Press, 1958) 199.

[5]Phillip Paludan, "Religion and the American Civil War," *Religion and the American Civil War*, ed. Randall M. Miller, et al. (New York: Oxford University Press, 1998) 22.

[6]Edmund Wilson, *Patriotic Gore* (New York: Farrar, Straus, and Giroux, 1962; reprint, Boston: Northeastern University Press, 1984) 91. Throughout his analysis of Julia Ward Howe's "Battle Hymn of the Republic," Wilson maintains that apocalyptic literature during the Civil War was a Northern phenomenon.

apocalyptic responses from North and South during the war, their content and tone are remarkably similar.

Clearly, at least some Americans were primed to apply apocalyptic interpretations to the war that erupted in 1861; the aftermath of the Millerite movement and the development of other premillennial groups had prepared at least a few people to expect a cataclysm, and the minuscule group of intense abolitionists, regardless of theological orientation, were primed to witness slavery reap destruction.[7] More unexpected is the extent of apocalyptic interpretation outside of these fervent groups. Postmillennialists, whose reformist zeal and millennial optimism had begun to wane in the 1840s and 1850s, read current events in the light of imminent apocalypse with remarkable ease.[8] Even liberal freethinkers, the popular press, and more casually religious citizens made meaning from the language of apocalypse. As Edmund Wilson has pointed out, "The minds of nations at war are invariably dominated by myths," and this fact has provided meaningful explanations of events that would otherwise have been too horrifying to explain.[9] Thousands of years of Jewish and Christian apocalyptic belief have created a general pattern: in times of moral and cultural disintegration, beleaguered believers turn to prophecies of the end for coherence, meaning, and hope. They become the cultural currency of minuscule, oppressed minorities. During the Civil War, combatants on all sides were able to adopt the vocabulary and outlook of the minuscule, oppressed minority. Apocalyptic explanations of the war's significance not only became an argumentative tool of the

---

[7]Stephen D. O'Leary, *Arguing the Apocalypse: A Theory of Millennial Rhetoric* (New York: Oxford University Press, 1994) 130 brings these two widely divergent groups together by pointing out that both groups sensed an imminent cataclysm. He concludes: "In a sense, one may say that the Millerites were correct in predicting an apocalyptic rupture of history; their prophecy proved to be off by only a generation" (131).

[8]James Moorhead has pointed out that nineteenth-century postmillennialism was able to accommodate both progressive and apocalyptic modes, and furthermore, "much of the cultural power of postmillennialism came from its evocation of cataclysmic images of the End whose energy was then harnessed in service to the incremental construction of an evangelical empire." "Apocalypticism in Mainstream Protestantism, 1800 to the Present," in *The Encyclopedia of Apocalypticism,* ed. Bernard McGinn, et al. (New York: Continuum, 1998) 3:83. Moorhead discusses the apocalyptic preoccupations of the four largest Northern Protestant denominations during the Civil War era in *American Apocalypse: Yankee Protestants and the Civil War 1860–1869* (New Haven: Yale University Press, 1978).

[9]Wilson, *Patriotic Gore,* 91.

pulpit and religious tracts, but they also swept through the general population in poetic language, verbal images, and visual iconography, becoming an aesthetic preoccupation as well as a rhetorical strategy.

American apocalyptic thought permeated the religious awakenings in the first half of the nineteenth century. These revivals created a sense of urgency: "Old men dreamed dreams and young men saw visions. And they all worked in a fury of passion lest the 'great and terrible day of His wrath' should overtake them unprepared."[10] The events of the Civil War galvanized the use of this imagery, which was still fresh in the minds of many Americans.[11]

Because the theological explanation of the significance of the Civil War seemed crucial to both Union and Confederate apologists and because it enriched the wartime vocabulary, it moved beyond argument to propaganda. Apocalyptic references appeared in topical fiction, poetry, songs, and drawings. They represented a pervasive cultural phenomenon from Unionist, Confederate, and slave viewpoints.

The revolutionary possibilities of Civil War apocalyptic rhetoric explain its popularity during a time of cultural upheaval. It justified entering the war and motivated adherents to continue the prolonged conflict. The aesthetic power of apocalyptic imagery enabled some participants to tiptoe on the deliciously dangerous edge between the sublime and the terrible while envisioning the punishments God would rain on his followers if they were unfaithful. The images also suggested the hope of ultimate victory and regeneration that underlay the lurid symbols of the end. Each group envisioned a radically different world made by the war. To Unionists it promised the purgation of the last great sin—slavery—that kept the United States from fulfilling its millennial promise. To Confederates it held out the hope of removing the corruption that had infiltrated the national government since the Constitutional Convention adjourned. To slaves it meant forsaking the

---

[10]Timothy L. Smith, *Revivalism and Social Reform: American Protestantism on the Eve of the Civil War* (New York: Harper & Row, 1957) 237.

[11]See William A. Clebsch, "Baptism of Blood: A Study of Christian Contributions to the Interpretation of the Civil War in American History" (Ph.D. diss., Union Theological Seminary, New York, 1957). Some of this material later appeared in *Church History* 30/2 (June 1961): 212–22 and was then published as *Christian Interpretations of the Civil War* (Philadelphia: Fortress Press, 1969).

bondage of their world in favor of the freedom they would experience as new Children of Israel.

The varieties of Civil War apocalypticism shared the ability to pull what had been seen as a premillennial antebellum preoccupation into the cultural mainstream. Christian apologists and innovative artists shared an essentially Protestant apocalyptic vocabulary, a rhetorical strategy of warning followed by the promise of victory for the faithful and the hope of eternal peace after the war and time itself ended. The flexibility of apocalyptic interpretations as they were adapted to current events and changes in the cultural climate kept them intact and refreshed during the first three years of the war. By contrast, the last year of the conflict yielded ever higher body counts and a loss of hope that not even the suppleness of conventional apocalypse could overcome. After the war liberal Protestants, fundamentalists, and artists formed increasingly divergent expectations about the end of the world.

Some examples of Civil War art forms illustrate the power of apocalyptic imagery as an aesthetic device. For decades this imagery had been present in revivalist language, and its particular application to the North/South conflict was nearly as old. Of all the forces that led to sectional strife, abolitionist literature made some of the earliest and most pointed references to the apocalypse. For example, an abolitionist poem published in 1843 detected signs of Doomsday on the horizon:

> There's a cloud, blackening up the sky!
> East, west, and north its curtain spreads;
> Life to its muttering folds your eye!
> Beware! For, bursting on your heads,
> It hath a force to bear you down;—
> 'Tis an insulted people's frown.[12]

Writers on both sides were able to assign contemporary meaning to ancient texts. During the war the Southern poet James R. Randall went back to Jewish apocalyptic texts of the intertestamental period to undergird his "Battle-Cry of the South." The headnote he chose to accompany the poem is taken from Maccabees I: "Arm yourselves and be

---

[12]"A Word from a Petitioner" *Anti-Slavery Poems,* ed. John Pierpoint (Boston: Oliver Johnson, 1843) 12. Similar imagery may be found in a sermon by Orestes Brownson, *Babylon is Falling,* 2nd ed. (Boston: I. R. Butts, 1837).

valiant men, and see that ye be in readiness.... For it is better for us to die in battle than to behold the calamities of our people and our sanctuary."

Appealing to stark images that dramatize the South's long odds, Randall's poem balances Confederate extremity with a sense of divine certainty:

> Brothers! The thunder-cloud is black,
> And the wail of the South wings forth;
> Will ye cringe to the hot tornado's rack,
> And the vampires of the North?
> Strike! Ye can win a martyr's goal,
> Strike! With a ruthless hand–
>
> Strike! With the vengeance of the soul
> For your bright, beleaguered land!
> To arms! To arms! For the South needs help,
> And a craven is he who flees–
> For ye have the sword of the Lion's Whelp,
> And the God of the Maccabees![13]

The significance of the black cloud of war and evil is not just a figment of criticism or artistic expression. During the Civil War the most striking interpretations of storm clouds as apocalyptic images came from the general public. An example is the response to a landscape painting, *Cotopaxi*, by Frederic E. Church (Figure 1).[14] The culmination of South American expeditions undertaken in 1853 and 1857, this 1862 painting was regarded as Church's best work. A contemporary critic, Louis D. Noble, described the painting in detail and gave his judgment: "Of all Mr. Church's pictures, this is certainly the most remarkable for magnificence of light.... This is, all in all, Church's finest painting."[15] The art historian David Huntington describes this painting and Church's 1860 *Twilight in the Wilderness* as significant depictions of the Apocalypse, part of

---

[13]James R. Randall, "The Battle-Cry of the South," *War Poetry of the South*, ed. William Gilmore Simms (New York: Richardson, 1867) 37 (see appendix).

[14]Courtesy of The Detroit Institute of Arts.

[15]Louis D. Noble, "Cotopaxi: A Picture by Frederic E. Church," 1862 manuscript published in Katherine Manthorne, *Creation & Renewal: Views of Cotopaxi by Frederic Edwin Church*, (Washington, DC: National Museum of American Art, 1985) 64.

Church's effort to make a theological statement via natural landscape. According to Huntington, Church created the "iconology for the America of Manifest Destiny...[substituting] nature for civilization."[16] *Cotopaxi*, specifically, was "an icon of the American religion of 1862, and its creator was a prophet with a brush."[17]

The painting may be viewed as apocalyptic because of the destruction implied by the smoking volcano and millennial by the promise of new life suggested by the early morning sun shining through the smoke, transforming the landscape. The compositional studies for *Cotopaxi* were done in the opening days of the Civil War, a time when Church was preoccupied by the nation's troubles.[18] Of the many studies and canvases of Cotopaxi produced by Church between 1853 and 1867, the 1862 canvas is the first to depict the threat of desolation brought about by volcanic eruption, and it was perhaps intended as "an omen to his countrymen of the error of their present actions."[19]

The response of the viewers to Church's painting illustrates the willingness of the American public to see the Civil War in apocalyptic terms. When the painting was first exhibited in New York in March 1863, the crowds who flocked to view it immediately identified the picture with their national calamities.[20] The striking affinity these viewers saw between

---

[16]David C. Huntington, *The Landscapes of Frederic Edwin Church* (New York: George Braziller, 1966) x–xi.

[17]Ibid., 16.

[18]For a detailed study of the development of this painting in relation to the Civil War, see David Huntington, "Church and Luminism: Light for America's Elect," *American Light: The Luminist Movement 1850–1875*, ed. John Wilmerding (Washington, DC: National Gallery of Art, 1980) 155–90.

[19]Katherine Manthorne, *Creation and Renewal: Views of Cotopaxi by Frederic Edwin Church* (Washington, DC: Smithsonian Institution Press, 1985) 50. Here Manthorne also points out that Church was not unique in using volcanic imagery to make a statement about the war; James Hamilton's *The Last Days of Pompeii* (1864) shows the final destruction of Pompeii, accompanied by lurid lighting and showers of ash and rock. Manthorne notes that Hamilton paired this painting with *The Foundering* (1863) showing a sinking Confederate ship.

[20]The public response to this painting has been extensively documented by David Huntington, *American Light*, ed. Wilmerding, 180-82. The author notes in particular the religious imagery used to describe the painting in the *New York Times*, 17 March 1863 and argues a parallel between Church's painting and a sermon by Horace Bushnell, *Reverses Needed: A Discourse Delivered on the Saturday after the Disaster of Bull Run* (Hartford: L. E. Hunt, 1861).

the painting and current events establishes it as one of the primary metaphors of the war; it "accomplishes in pictorial terms what 'The Battle Hymn of the Republic' and 'The Gettysburg Address' accomplish in song and speech."[21] Like "Battle Hymn," this painting demonstrates the power of apocalyptic imagery in two areas: the prospect of ultimate destruction balanced by the hope of redemption.

The examples of abolitionist and Confederate poetry, as well as Church's *Cotopaxi*, exemplify the wide range of aesthetic and intellectual forms that comprised apocalyptic imagery during the Civil War. A coherent understanding of the cultural evidence requires an intellectual framework based on sermons, pamphlets, essays, and visual texts. Popular literary material supplements this framework and indicates the extent of understanding and the breadth of acceptance of the idea. Apocalyptic fiction, poetry, and songs were designed to appeal to unifying religious and prophetic impulses, and these forms played an important part in shaping public perceptions of the war. Apocalyptic imagery appears in forms ranging from the fast-day sermon to the political cartoon. It was used by writers of serious and popular literature, poetry, songs, and political speeches, and by artists in paintings, drawings, and prints. References to the war's significance in the cosmic timetable laced journals and family correspondence.

The material available for analysis is vast. It is particularly rich in the North, which had more writers, more printing supplies, and more available artists during the war. Northern material used for this study includes sermons (primarily occasional), popular fiction, poetry, songs, soldiers' journals, political literature, paintings, drawings, and political cartoons. The Southern material analyzed here includes sermons, fiction, poetry, songs, prints, and diaries and family papers. Slave material consists primarily of songs and oral histories, accompanied by the commentary of whites who worked closely with slaves or freed slaves.

While apocalyptic imagery of the Civil War era ties into millennia of Jewish and Christian thought, it is also informed by its nineteenth-century context, which in the United States was predominantly Protestant. In nineteenth-century America, "apocalypse" had become less associated with its original meaning of "unveiling" and more closely tied to the end of the world prophesied in Scripture. (However, Civil War

---

[21]Huntington, *American Light*, ed. Wilmerding, 182.

participants continually "unveiled" mysterious biblical symbols by interpreting them as representations of current events.) The term had come to mean an imminent cosmic cataclysm in which God would destroy the ruling powers of evil and raise the righteous to life in a messianic kingdom. It was the dividing line between temporality and eternity. This catastrophic end was accompanied by the Last Judgment or the Day of Judgment, an event that would separate humanity into good and evil categories.

Apocalyptic thought is related to millennialism, since the thousand-year period of peace and prosperity known as the millennium is expected to accompany the end of the world. In the nineteenth century postmillennialists believed the Second Coming was still distant, after the millennium, but a period of conflict might take place just before the thousand-year period began.[22] Their premillennialist contemporaries saw the Second Coming as the moment when the beleaguered saints would be delivered into the millennium. Because the apocalypse is so closely tied to the concept of the Last Judgment, it is related to jeremiad rhetoric, with its tendency to call for repentance and to predict dire consequences if the warning is ignored.[23]

After the Civil War "apocalypse" increasingly came to mean a secular episode of earthly devastation, usually with no hope of renewal. It is necessary to distinguish between apocalyptic imagery resulting from Protestant prophetic interpretation and secular doom-saying. Because Calvinism was still pervasive at the time of the Civil War, literature was laced with the sense that God oversaw the world in general and the United States in particular. The war, according to many Christians, must have been sent from God. It could only be interpreted as punishment: either God was punishing the nation for allowing slavery to exist, or he was reproving worldly humanists for destroying a divine institution. But

---

[22]James Moorhead has described nineteenth-century postmillennialism as a balance between progressive and apocalyptic views of history: "believing that cataclysms of the book of Revelation described upheavals that the Church would face throughout history, not merely at the end of time, postmillennialists expected tumults as well as gradual progress as the Kingdom advanced." Moorhead attributes the success of nineteenth-century postmillennialism to its ability to enlist apocalyptic intensity in its "incremental construction of an evangelical empire." "Apocalypticism in Mainstream Protestantism, 1800 to the Present," *Encyclopedia of Apocalypticism*, 3:81, 83.

[23]See Sacvan Bercovitch, *The American Jeremiad* (Madison: University of Wisconsin Press, 1978).

slavery was not the only issue. Individuals who attempted to explain the war's horrors looked inside themselves and saw moral blights that needed removal. Or they looked at their opponents and saw political corruption. War became an instrument to punish wrongdoers and to remove impurities from the lives of the righteous.

Because supernatural forces were believed to be at work in this war, literature and art often portrayed the enemy as diabolically inspired. Devils, dragons, and evil angels urged on their allies or were crushed by their righteous opponents. Fiery war imagery took on cosmic significance. Battles were assumed to be the conflict of Armageddon, which by the mid-nineteenth century had become associated with the time of the end. The strife was expected to sift out the evildoers and also to test the faithful by filling them with a sense of urgency and encouraging them to repent of any individual or collective sin.

Apocalyptic writers of the mid-nineteenth century understood the effectiveness of the concept of the sublime for communicating their purpose. The affinity of their theology with this concept becomes clear upon examination of the term as defined by Edmund Burke in the eighteenth century: "Whatever is fitted in any sort to excite the ideas of pain, and danger, that is to say, whatever is in any sort terrible, or is conversant about terrible objects, or operates in a manner analogous to terror, is a source of the sublime; that is, it is productive of the strongest emotion which the mind is capable of feeling. I say the strongest emotion, because I am satisfied the ideas of pain are much more powerful than those which enter on the part of pleasure."[24]

The powerful psychological effect of the sublime, as described by Burke, explains the broad appeal of apocalyptic imagery. David Morgan has identified an American variant he terms "the evangelical sublime," fostered by Jonathan Edwards, which permeated religious expression in the eighteenth and nineteenth centuries.[25] American preachers and artists understood the persuasiveness of fear.

---

[24]Edmund Burke, *A Philosophical Inquiry into the Origin of Our Ideas of the Sublime and Beautiful* (London: 1759; reprint, New York: John B. Alden, 1885) 32.

[25]David Morgan, *Protestants and Pictures: Religion, Visual Culture, and the Age of American Mass Production* (New York: Oxford University Press, 1999) 131. Morgan maintains that American preachers often merged the sublime and its counterpart, the beautiful, to achieve a more positive effect. While this combination applies to apocalyptic imagery when it includes allusions to a glorious future, much Civil War imagery focuses on the sublime, awful present.

Apocalyptic imagery during the Civil War permeated American culture, and its extent may be observed in several ways. Theological writings establish the historical and intellectual milieu of the Civil War period. They serve as an index of ideas about the apocalypse and aid in establishing the varieties of apocalyptic thought that flourished during the period. For example, theological pronouncements indicate that people focused the inevitable threat of judgment sometimes on themselves and sometimes on their opponents. These statements were primarily persuasive and argumentative, and they followed a formal rhetorical structure.[26]

Some of the theological material under discussion also doubles as literature. It makes extensive use of visual imagery, rhythmic patterns, and allusions to aesthetic ideas. Henry Ward Beecher's sermons reflect his familiarity with the concept of the sublime, as is evident in his sermon in Glasgow in October of 1863:

> I have stood on the summit of the noblest mountains in Switzerland. I have seen whatever that country had to show me of mountain peak, of more than royal mountains of clouds of glaciers: I have seen the beauties of Northern Italy: I have seen the glories of the ocean: I have seen whatever Nature has to show of her sublimity on land and on sea: but the grandeur of the uprising of the Northern people, when the thunder of the first cannon rolled through their valleys and over their hills, was something beyond all these; nor do I expect till the judgment day fills me with wondering awe, to see such a sight again.[27]

Another clergyman whose prose had a distinct literary quality was the Methodist abolitionist Gilbert Haven. When discussing the role of General Grant at the close of the war, Haven recalled the conflict's opening days when the government refused to free slaves in newly conquered territory. Echoing poetic passages of the Old Testament, he employs literary devices while introducing a poetry quotation:

---

[26]See O'Leary, *Arguing the Apocalypse*, 5-11. O'Leary traces the relationship between the urgency of apocalyptic warnings and the messages' ability to survive disconfirmation.

[27]Henry Ward Beecher, *The American Rebellion* (Manchester, England: Union & Emancipation Society, 1864) 38.

We did not succeed, notwithstanding the light that shone at the mouth of the Mississippi; the government refused to speak the word of Liberty, and destruction came. That word appeared, and light broke dimly over the black and maddening waves. The waves still roared, and were troubled. The mountains shook with the swelling thereof. But a new creating spirit was brooding upon its turbulent depths. The influences of regeneration moved through the seething mass. The enemy arose and defeated the idea at the polls. It raged again in mobs and massacre; it was savage, unrelenting. The kings of the earth took counsel together against us. All that passed by wagged their heads, exclaiming,—

"She has gone down, our evil-boding star,
Beneath a hideous cloud of civil war,
Strife such as heathen slaughterers abhorred,
The lawless band who would call no man lord,
In the fierce splendor of her insolent morn,
She has gone down—the world's eternal scorn."[28]

Fiction, like the richly imaged apocalyptic sermons, sometimes served more than one function. For example, *Uncle Tom's Cabin* served as propaganda made memorable by powerful images. Literary authors gained something by using the devices of creative writing to proclaim their vision of the Apocalypse. The foundational Apocalypse, the book of Revelation, was written in highly poetic language. Its nonliteral quality helps to explain how people accept the repeated failure of apocalyptic predictions; they can be "disconfirmed without being discredited."[29] This poetic quality must be noted when analyzing apocalyptic literature. Visual and sound imagery are important, and they in turn lead to the identification of certain symbols that were commonly recognized.[30] Sound imagery is particularly important for poetry, songs, and the sermons of the "poetic preachers"; even in the original apocalypse,

---

[28]Gilbert Haven, "Grant," *National Sermons: Sermons, Speeches and Letters on Slavery and Its War* (Boston: Lee and Shepard, 1869) 401.

[29]Frank Kermode, *The Sense of an Ending: Studies in the Theory of Fiction* (New York: Oxford University Press, 1967) 8.

[30]The existence of these accepted symbols is certainly part of the reason for the widespread identification with the words of the "Battle Hymn."

sounds were significant: "Blessed is he that readeth, and they that hear the words of this prophecy, and keep those things which are written therein; for the time is at hand" (Rev. 1:3).[31] Acknowledging the poetic component of apocalyptic material can lead to a fuller understanding of its dual function: exhorting its adherents to reform and providing hope during setbacks.

The longest foreground of apocalyptic imagery related to the Civil War begins in the writings of Revolutionary-era critics of slavery. The most memorable abolitionist literature after *Uncle Tom's Cabin* centered on the person and legend of John Brown. A subsequent but equally compelling set of images grew around the defense of Confederate righteousness, embodied in the descriptions of the Confederate victory at the First Battle of Manassas. As prewar abolitionism infiltrated Unionist thinking, a set of images corresponding to the South's Manassas accounts developed around the story of the battle of Antietam. The ensuing depiction of the conflict as a holy war required righteous heroes. A number of leaders were described in apocalyptic terms, including Winfield Scott, W. T. Sherman, Leonidas Polk, Robert E. Lee, and Albert Sidney Johnston among others, but the two outstanding embodiments of apocalyptic imagery were Abraham Lincoln, the "Moses" of the North, and the Southern Cromwell, General Thomas J. Jackson. The Civil War endured long enough to bring an end even to the Apocalypse, or at least to the comparatively unified apocalyptic interpretation that sustained the combatants for most of the war. Rhetorical and aesthetic apocalypses diverged after the Civil War. Since then there has been no shortage of catastrophes, real and imagined, but attempts to describe them in

---

[31]Adela Yarbro Collins, *Crisis and Catharsis: The Power of the Apocalypse* (Philadelphia: The Westminster Press, 1984) 144 points out that the aural effect of Revelation was very important. It was probably communicated largely by reading aloud in the churches, and it represented a call to action through emotional involvement, via both the poetic quality of the language and the audible cadences and emphases supplied by the public reader.

apocalyptic terms have varied from fundamentalist biblical literalism to the secular pessimism of literature and film. Millennial hope no longer underlies the apocalyptic fears of writers and artists; it no longer cements religious and literary culture.

2

THE ROAD TO ARMAGEDDON
SLAVERY AND THE NORTH

Northern apocalyptic rhetoric of the Civil war traces its origins to the earliest days of the Republic, and in the intervening decades, it was closely tied to the slavery issue. The national sin of slavery was held responsible for national catastrophes, and a notable visual record of this response emerged from the War of 1812.

In 1814 hopeful-but-not-very-confident Americans had to deal with twin humiliations. One was the braggadocio of British soldiers who claimed to have feasted on the remnants of President Madison's dinner just after he and the First Lady had fled the White House in unseemly haste on 24 August. After their meal, the British troops set fire to the Executive Mansion. The other embarrassment was the specter of the charred ruins of the unfinished Capitol, the eagerly anticipated temple of democracy, also torched by British troops during the War of 1812. Such humiliating setbacks had to be explained, particularly when they happened to a young nation believed by many Americans to have an intimate relationship with God. One explanation took the form of an 1817 print by Alexander Lawson (Figure 2).[1] In his view, the burning of the Capitol was divinely ordained: angelic figures in the sky look down at the ruined building and the slave coffle in the lower right corner. The white gentleman who looks at the slaves over his shoulder appears by his gesture to be connecting them to the ruins in front of him. In other words, Lawson believed America could not expect to prosper as long as it retained slavery. For many years, the warnings of Lawson and others like him fell on deaf ears.

Postmillennial visions filled the spiritual sight of most Northern Protestants (and thus the majority of Americans) before the Civil War.

---

[1]Courtesy of the Library of Congress.

The expectation of general progress meshed well with their emphasis on social reform, and it harmonized with Manifest Destiny and nation-building politics. While slavery did not fit neatly into the picture, most Northern ministers hesitated to repudiate the institution entirely, even, as George Frederickson has pointed out, after denominational splits on the issue.[2] On the other hand, apocalyptic themes permeated the sermons of a few Protestant clergymen, premillennialist groups, and abolitionists; these individuals did not hesitate to identify slavery as a crucial national problem. Their numbers remained small for decades, but their voices grew increasingly strident and urgent. Their point of view became the basis for Northern apocalyptic interpretations of the Civil War, and eventually postmillennialists tended to fall into line.[3]

Notable more for intensity than popular success, the opponents of slavery virtually held cult status until the 1850s, characterized as fanatics by an unsympathetic general public. To these individuals, the Revolution had ended prematurely by failing to eliminate slavery. The resulting sense of collective guilt found expression in jeremiad rhetoric, which predicted an outbreak of God's wrath against the great national sin. Even passive support for slavery was sinful. Northerners who held this belief determined to be on God's side when the inevitable revolution would destroy the nation's last, greatest sin and usher in the millennium. For more than twenty years, this line of thought preoccupied the abolitionists, who exemplified the cultural climate where apocalyptic thought has traditionally flourished: they were a tiny minority ignored, even oppressed, by society at large. Harriet Beecher Stowe, with her publication of *Uncle Tom's Cabin* in 1852, made this apocalyptic interpretation of slavery resonate with the general public. In the last few years before the Civil War erupted in 1861 an increasingly large slice of the body politic adopted the stance of the oppressed minority. Such a climate made it possible for John Brown's quixotic raid in 1859 to be taken seriously.

This antislavery path from the margins to the center traversed nearly a century of American history. The tendency of Americans to see cosmic significance in national events was already deeply ingrained during the

---

[2]George Frederickson, "The Coming of the Lord: The Northern Protestant Clergy and the Civil War Crisis" *Religion and the American Civil War,* ed. Miller et al., 115.

[3]James Moorhead notes that postmillennialism "adapted remarkably well" to the sudden disappearance of social progressivism in 1861. "Apocalypticism" *Encyclopedia of Apocalypticism,* 3:85.

Revolutionary War.[4] For a century and a half, American Puritans had explained events large and small by seeing spiritual significance and symbolism in them, and this tendency continued into the new nation's first crisis. The Reverend Samuel Hopkins, a disciple of Jonathan Edwards and the pastor of the First Congregational Church in Newport, Rhode Island for thirty-three years, applied this thinking to slavery. Newport's prominence as a slave-trading seaport led Hopkins to a public crusade against the evils of the trade. The outcome of the Revolution, he eventually came to believe, would depend upon the fate of slavery.

Hopkins's crusade began even before the Revolution, when he became one of the first Congregational ministers to speak out against the evils of slavery, leading fundraising drives to free slaves and promoting African colonization for them. In 1776 he made his first published statement about slavery, using the events of the war to emphasize his point. In an address dedicated to the Continental Congress, Hopkins created a dialogue designed to prove it was America's duty as a Christian nation to emancipate all slaves.

Meeting an increasingly popular argument, Hopkins charged that justifying slavery for missionary purposes was merely a rationalization: "If the Europeans and Americans had been as much engaged to Christianize the Africans as they have been to enslave them…[Africa] would have been full of gospel light."[5] Hopkins proceeded to argue that slavery was anti-Christian, a "seven-headed monster."[6] If a so-called Christian nation harbored slavery, it could not succeed in a righteous struggle for independence. In fact, war reversals could be attributed directly to the continued tolerance of slavery. To hope for a quick resolution of the conflict would defy God's plan for the American colonies: "And if we continue in this evil practice and refuse to let the oppressed go free, under all this light and admonition suited to convince and reform us, and while God is evidently correcting us for it as well as

---

[4]Nathan O. Hatch, "The Origins of Civil Millennialism in America: New England Clergymen, the War with France, and the Revolution," *William and Mary Quarterly* 31/3 (1974): 407–30. Hatch sees civil millennialism growing out of "the politicizing of Puritan millennial history" (429); New England clergymen, he points out, explained the conflict as a cosmic interpretation between God's elect and Antichrist (407).

[5]Samuel Hopkins, *A Dialogue Concerning the Slavery of the Africans*, (Norwich CT: Judah P. Spooner, 1776; reprint, Robert Hodge, 1785) 19.

[6]Ibid., 20.

for other sins, have we any reason to expect deliverance from the calamities we are under?"[7]

Slavery was contradictory to American principles of freedom, Hopkins maintained; furthermore, his country's precarious position in the war resulted from its failure to relieve oppression. If the former colonies persisted in their obstinacy, he warned, "God will yet withdraw his kind protection from us, and punish us yet seven times more."[8] In another tract, in language even more direct, he addressed the owners specifically. Slaveholders, he declared, would be responsible if Americans lost the war.[9]

The successful conclusion of the Revolution with slavery intact led Hopkins to modify his position only slightly. God's judgment against America had been withheld on this occasion, he explained, because the Northern states had begun to emancipate their slaves. The continuing participation in the Africa/West Indies slave trade by some New Englanders, however, meant America was likely to repeat the experience of the Jews as described in Jeremiah 34. The Jews, concerned about the military threat from the Babylonian king Nebuchadnezzar, had emancipated their slaves at God's command. When the danger receded, they once again enslaved the people they had just freed. Using the familiar Puritan technique of pointing out analogies between his country and Old Testament Israel, Hopkins warned that if New England repeated Israel's mistake and ignored God, and if "we escape the destruction which came on the inhabitants of Jerusalem, or evils that shall be as great, it must be ascribed to mere, sovereign, distinguishing, mercy, which we have no reason to expect."[10] Hopkins also established a precedent by labeling slavery a "national sin." The existence of this sin, "a sin which righteous Heaven has never suffered to pass unpunished in this world," made eventual retribution inevitable.[11] This belief became a rallying point for abolitionists up to the eve of the Civil War.

---

[7]Ibid., 57.

[8]Ibid., 59.

[9]Hopkins, "Address to Owners," *The Works of Samuel Hopkins, D. D.*, ed. Edwards Amasa Parks (Boston: Doctrinal Tract and Book Society, 1852) 2:594.

[10]Hopkins, "Dialogue," 71 (appendix, 1785).

[11]Hopkins, "A Discourse Upon the Slave Trade and the Slavery of Africans," *The Works of Samuel Hopkins* (Boston: Doctrinal Tract and Book Society, 1852) 2:614–15.

In addition to shaping views on the role of slavery in American history, Hopkins also reinforced and refined the New Light theology he had inherited from Jonathan Edwards, including the doctrine of the millennium.[12] Although Hopkins believed the final struggle between good and evil, the Second Coming, and the rescue of God's faithful people would occur at the end of the millennium, he saw another period of strife and tumult at the *beginning* of the thousand-year period. This version of postmillennialism, along with a strain of premillennialism that emerged in the mid-nineteenth century, provided a ready explanation for the increasingly ominous atmosphere in a country accustomed to regarding itself as a nation favored by God. This ability of postmillennialists as well as premillennialists to see a great battle occurring before the millennium brought apocalypticism into the cultural mainstream and helps to explain public response to the events leading up to the Civil War. Although Hopkins does not discuss slavery specifically in his book on the millennium, his abolitionist writings helped the two issues to become associated.[13]

The connection between slavery and the righteous wrath of God against his chosen nation was not unique to orthodox Protestant theologians of the Revolutionary era. It appeared again after the Revolutionary War in *The Columbiad,* Joel Barlow's epic prophecy of American destiny. In the poem Barlow foresees the beginning of the millennium in America and the end of conflict and prejudice; Hesper, the guardian of America, predicts an era when all racial injustice will disappear. Promises for the future, however, do not satisfy Atlas, who in Book VIII blasts the West for what it has done to the inhabitants of the continent under his charge, Africa. If slavery should continue, Atlas warns, America will endure severe punishment. Earlier remonstrances will seem insignificant if America does not change her ways:

---

[12]See Hopkins, "A Treatise on the Millennium," in *Works,* 2:234–364. Reiner Smolinski describes the utopian extent of Edwards' postmillennialism in "Apocalypticism in Colonial North America" in *Encyclopedia of Apocalypticism,* 3:61.

[13]It is not coincidental that a "Hopkins revival" occurred after 1850, with new editions of both his theological and abolitionist writings. These included *Works,* already referred to, and a separate collection of his abolitionist tracts titled *Timely Articles on Slavery,* ed. Edwards Amasa Parks (Boston: Congregational Board of Publication, 1854). The Rev. Parks wrote a biography of Hopkins titled *Memoir of the Life and Character of Samuel Hopkins, D. D.* (Boston: Doctrinal Tract and Book Society, 1852).

Nor shall these pangs atone the nation's crime;
Far heavier vengeance, in the march of time,
Attends them still; if still they dare debase
And hold inthrall'd the millions of my race;
A vengeance that shall shake the world's deep frame,
That heaven abhors and hell might shrink to name.
Nature, long outraged, delves the crusted sphere
And molds the mining mischief dark and drear;
Europa too the penal shock shall find,
The rude soul-selling monsters of mankind.

If this dire warning is not enough, Atlas goes on to appeal to slaveholders' self-interest. Slavery enslaves masters ("tyrants are never free"), and all masters will eventually be tyrants. "Would you not be slaves...then be not masters," Atlas cautions slaveholders.[14] Similar warnings and exhortations were to fuel several decades of abolitionist rhetoric later in the century.

With expectations of divine judgment already in place, some observers were primed to identify final retribution against slaveholders during the next national trauma, the War of 1812. While the violation of the nation's capital by the British puzzled believers in an ever-ascendant American destiny, Jesse Torrey found slavery responsible. Inserted into the front of his 1817 book on slavery is the extra illustration print by Alexander Lawson described at the beginning of this chapter.[15]

Torrey was not a radical abolitionist; he believed in the gradual emancipation of slaves and in a colonization program for free blacks. His primary concern in the book seems to be the protection of white slaveholders from divine retribution. Torrey says that up to this time slaveowners survived only because of "divine forbearance." The "dangerous disease" of slavery must be eradicated before divine patience expires, because it is "an incontrovertible theorem, that the sentinels of Divine justice, are seldom trespassed upon, without regular and appropriate retribution."[16]

---

[14]Joel Barlow, *The Columbiad* (Philadelphia: Fry and Kammerer, 1807) 8:261–70, 345, 353–54.

[15]Jesse Torrey, *A Portraiture of Domestic Slavery in the United States* (Philadelphia: published by author, 1817).

[16]Ibid., iii–iv.

Although Christian writers identified many reasons for eliminating slavery, the ultimate justification for emancipation or abolition always came down to the same issue: America must renounce slavery in order to escape divine punishment. Torrey asserted this idea in images that became the working vocabulary for apocalyptic abolitionists: "Unconditional slavery is contrary to the precepts of religion, moral justice, and the abstract, natural and political rights of man. It is a *black*, accumulating, *threatening-thundercloud*, in our moral horizon, the sudden explosion of which, might produce dangerous and fatal consequences."[17] This image of a great black cloud was appropriate to the language of the Apocalypse and became doubly significant for Americans as a symbol of literal, earthly warfare.

The predictions of the Apocalypse were not the only sources of a sense of foreboding and guilt arising from human bondage. Slavery also lent a taint of hypocrisy to past American claims of freedom and equality. While he was president, and just a few months after his father died, John Quincy Adams wrote a sonnet on what would have been his father's ninety-first birthday. In the poem he recognizes that the freedom his father fought for was not yet complete:

Day of my father's birth, I hail thee yet.
What though his body moulders in the grave,
Yet shall not Death th' immortal soul enslave;
The sun is not extinct—his orb has set.
And where on earth's wide ball shall man be met,
While time shall run, but from thy spirit brave
Shall learn to grasp the boon his Maker gave.
And spurn the terror of a tyrant's threat.
Who but shall learn that freedom is the prize
Man still is bound to rescue or maintain;
That nature's God commands the slave to rise,
And on the oppressor's head to break his chain.
Roll, years of promise, rapidly roll round,
Till not a slave on this earth be found![18]

---

[17]Ibid.,18.

[18]John Quincy Adams, *Memoirs of John Quincy Adams*, ed. Charles Francis Adams (Philadelphia: J. B. Lippincott & Co., 1874–77) 7:164. Embarrassed by the quality of his poetry, Adams wrote this poem in shorthand in his journal: "I record it thus that it may

Adams regrets that his father's principles are not being followed consistently in America. The elder Adams's work had not yet been completed, and the nation would not be true to the memory of its Founding Fathers until the slavery issue had been resolved. In this poem John Quincy Adams expresses the thinking of many emancipationists and abolitionists: moral laxity was hastening the approach of the Apocalypse.

Only three years after Adams wrote this sonnet, a similar uneasiness pervaded William Lloyd Garrison's first antislavery address. This speech, generally considered the opening salvo of the long war of abolitionism, was delivered on the Fourth of July in 1829. Garrison was disturbed that patriotic orators freely used the metaphors of the Revolution to assure themselves that Americans were still created equal. Attempting to open the eyes of his countrymen, he proclaimed that American politics were "rotten to the core."[19]

Garrison emphasized two principles noted earlier by Barlow, Torrey, and Adams that were to become central themes of the abolitionist message: America was playing false to the Declaration of Independence, and this sin would result in dire national punishment. For Garrison, slavery was "a gangrene preying upon our vitals, an earthquake rumbling under our feet, a mine accumulating materials for a national catastrophe. [It ought to make the Fourth of July] a day of fasting and prayer."[20] The day's patriotic festivities did not conceal the great lie of American freedom: "I am ashamed of my country. I am sick of our unmeaning declamation in praise of liberty and equality, of our hypocritical cant about the unalienable rights of man."[21] To Garrison, slavery was a national sin committed equally by North and South. A victory against slavery would be worth any amount of fighting, and a defeat would create a cataclysm resembling those described in apocalyptic biblical passages:

---

be legible only to myself, or to a reader who will take the trouble to pick it out of the short-hand. If it were better poetry I would have written it at full length."

[19]William Lloyd Garrison, "Fourth of July Address, 1829," *William Lloyd Garrison*, ed. George M. Frederickson, Great Lives Observed Series (Englewood Cliffs: Prentice-Hall, 1968) 11–21.

[20]Ibid.,12.

[21]Ibid.,15.

Woe to the safety of this people! The nation will be shaken as if by a mighty earthquake. A cry of horror, a cry of revenge, will go up to heaven in the darkness of midnight, and re-echo from every cloud. Blood will flow like water,—the blood of guilty men and of innocent women and children. Then will be heard lamentations and weeping, such as will blot out the remembrance of the horrors of St. Domingo. The terrible judgments of an incensed God will complete the catastrophe of republican America.[22]

Other abolitionists hurried to reinforce Garrison's logic, and their rhetorical intensity made up for their numerical insignificance. Their failure to enlist their countrymen in large numbers becomes evident in the shrillness of the language that pervades their poetry and hymns. In one poem, W. B. Tappan spies a bloodstain resembling Lady Macbeth's on the national flag. With revivalistic fervor, Tappan exhorts all those who have profited from slavery to restore freedom to the slaves and retrieve a sense of national mission:

> Lift up your brother from the dust,
> And speak his long crush'd spirit FREE!
> That millions, by your av'rice curst,
> May sharers in your blessings be:
> Then to the universe wide spread
> Your glorious stars without a stain;
> Bend from your skies, illustrious dead!
> The land ye won is free again.[23]

Another poem, "The Thunder-Cloud," not only indicates a sense of national guilt but also declares that this particular sin will receive a swift and vengeful response from God. It contains the storm-cloud imagery that abolitionists used to symbolize the end of the world, and it hints at repentance:

---

[22]Ibid., 19. Garrison is referring to the strong fear that the atrocities of Santo Domingo in the 1790s would be repeated in America.

[23]W. B. Tappan, "Blood is on the 'Star-Spangled Banner,'" *Freedom's Lyre*, ed. Edwin Francis Hatfield (New York: S. W. Benedict, 1840; reprint, Miami: Mnemosyne Pub. Co., 1969) 186–87. (See appendix.)

Thy thunder pealeth o'er us,
God of the earth and sky!
And o'er the gloomy heavens,
The clouds roll dark and high;
But oh! there lieth brooding
A cloud more dark and dread,
Above our guilty nation,
In fearful portent spread.

Extend a little longer
Thy mercy, O our God!
And touch our flinty bosoms,
With thy dissolving grace,
That we may hate our vileness,
And weep before thy face.[24]

Another song associates God's wrath and judgments against slavery with the end of the world: "The end will come, it will not wait, / Bonds, yokes and scourges have their date; / Slavery itself must pass away, / And be a tale of yesterday."[25] This chain of events—sin, guilt, judgment, punishment, and the end of the world—became a primary emphasis of antebellum abolitionist rhetoric for more than two decades.

To abolitionists, the sequence leading from sin to ultimate destruction inevitably polarized the conflict into a struggle between absolute good and absolute evil. They increasingly associated their opponents with diabolical forces, and they freely adopted images of dragons, devils, and monsters borrowed from Scripture and other sources. The following poem, written several years after the poems quoted above, shows the effects of the prolonged struggle on the abolitionists. Their foes are thoroughly wicked and their friends are on the defensive; the "flushed dragon of Oppression" is stalking the earth and wringing drops of blood from the oppressed. The conflict pits Satan against God's bold warriors:

---

[24]Miss Chandler, "The Thunder-Cloud," *Freedom's Lyre*, ed. Hatfield, 203–204. (See appendix.)

[25]"The Day is at Hand," *Songs of the Free, and Hymns of Christian Freedom*, comp., Maria Chapman (Boston: I. Knapp, 1836) 98–99. (See appendix.)

Fearlessly onward have the nobler souls
In Freedom's host the tide of battle borne;
And on them rain the fiery darts, which pour
From the mailed legions of the maddened foe.
Malignant Hate, by holy walls entrenched,
Masked Treachery, and unblenching Scorn, hurl forth
Their dreadless malisons in Religion's name
To blast our vanguard in their bold career.[26]

The willingness of the abolitionists to associate their opponents with diabolism, together with the presence of many proslavery individuals in mainstream Protestant denominations, prompted Northern churches to approach the slavery issue with caution. In fact, before the Civil War no major denomination supported immediate emancipation.[27] An ironic situation developed: "infidel" abolitionists renounced the churches but continued to rely on biblical imagery as they gradually gained a presence in the national conscience.

In addition to fastening labels of diabolism on their opponents, the abolitionists also claimed that *Christian* slavery was a manifestation of Antichrist, "the diametric opposite to Christianity, under the Christian name, claiming to be the doctrine of the Bible, a divine institution."[28] Furthermore, they tended to associate national calamities with specific national sins. Echoing Samuel Hopkins, James Renwick Willson associated a string of disasters in 1836 with the tolerance of slavery. These misfortunes were a mere signal of what could happen next: "Other judgments will follow if the oppressor persevere in outraging the rights of

---

[26]George S. Burleigh, "Our First Ten Years in the Struggle for Liberty," *Liberty Bell* 5 (1843): 45–46; 48. (See appendix.)

[27]John R. McKivigan, *The War Against Proslavery Religion: Abolitionism and the Northern Churches, 1830–1865* (Ithaca NY: Cornell University Press, 1984) 15. McKivigan points out that even after sectional schisms in the Methodist and Baptist churches in the 1840s and 1850s, Northern churches allowed border-state slaveowners to remain members and absolved slaveholders of individual guilt. Justification of the extreme behavior of the abolitionists may be found in Henry Wilson, *History of the Rise and Fall of the Slave Power in America,* 3 vols. (Boston: J. R. Osgood, 1873–1877) 3:718. Wilson maintains that it took nearly ten years for Garrison to abandon his attempts to work within organized denominations.

[28][C. Bowen], *The Bible in the Present Crisis* (New York: S. Toucey, c. 1863) 49.

man…the storm which gathers and lowers in the horizon…will be found charged with great powers of destruction."[29]

As the antislavery struggle intensified it attracted individual Northern clergymen, if not entire denominations. One of the most successful manipulators of biblical imagery for the cause of abolition, on both propagandistic and aesthetic levels, was the outspoken Methodist clergyman Gilbert Haven. Several events in 1856 prompted him to identify his era with the upheaval predicted in the apocalyptic books of the Bible. Believing that Preston Brooks's attack on Charles Sumner in May could presage an attempt to destroy civil liberties, Haven saw a fearful struggle approaching when, "through the tearing asunder of the national ties perhaps, through the flames of awful war, through blood up to the horses' bridles, we may have to wade to the peaceful glories of a Republic of universal freedom."[30] Haven prophesied eventual victory for the North, followed by prosperity "even if over those Southern valleys of the plain a dead sea of tribulation shall continue to roll."[31] A few months later, however, when his countrymen elected James Buchanan to the presidency, Haven turned from promises of triumph to prophecies of punishment: "The greatest crimes that ever broke away from hell, and emerged on this fair earth, are being defiantly committed by the rulers of this nation."[32] Ordinary citizens were also implicated, since they had put their rulers in place. They were all subject to the wrath of God. America was a tyrant before the rest of the world, and its glory was gone. "Clouds and darkness are round about us," he warned. "The air is pierced with lightning, and shaken by mutterings of avenging thunder."[33] The collective guilt of America invited perpetual torment: "We are all partakers in Pilate's crime. The innocent blood he has shed is on us and our children. It will be demanded of us, drop for drop, by the God of justice…. [American slavery] is a system the smoke of whose torment blackens all our sky. No such organized iniquity exists elsewhere on the earth."[34]

---

[29]James Renwick Willson, *Tokens of the Divine Displeasure* (Newburgh NY: Charles U. Cushman, 1836) 45.

[30]Gilbert Haven, "The State Struck Down," *National Sermons* (Boston: Lee & Shepard, 1869) 86.

[31]Ibid., 86.

[32]Haven, "The National Midnight," *National Sermons*, 90.

[33]Ibid., 98.

[34]Ibid., 112.

In this passage Haven combines several images that were to recur frequently in the apocalyptic rhetoric of the antislavery movement. Haven alludes to the Crucifixion by saying that Americans are inheriting Pilate's penalty because they have repeated his offense of shedding innocent blood. By echoing Isaiah 34 and Revelation 19 near the end of the passage, Haven also associates America's punishment with the fate of the wicked at the Last Judgment.

A similar reference to judgment may be found in an early abolitionist hymn:

> The Lord will come! the earth shall quake,
> The hills their fixed seat forsake;
> And, withering, from the vault of night
> The skies withdraw their feeble light.
> ....
> The Lord will come! a dreadful form,
> With wreath of flame and robe of storm.
> Master and slave alike shall find
> An equal judge of human kind.[35]

These lines suggest what will happen when tyranny gives way to apocalyptic equality; when placed on an equal basis with slaves, masters will have many reasons to call for the rocks to fall on them. The ironic comparison between the lowly first advent of Christ and his majestic return parallels a comparison between the lowly slave of the present and the triumphant, heaven-bound ex-slave of the future.

The tendency of traditional apocalyptic rhetoric to contrast the dreadful present of the most oppressed segment of society with a triumphant, ascendant immediate future resonated with the abolitionists. Not only did they see themselves in this position, but they found the slaves there as well. This identification appears again and again as abolitionists associated the slaves with the Hebrews in Egypt, implying that they too might be God's chosen people, a New Israel, passing through a time of tribulation in preparation for future glory. An abolitionist song from the 1830s describes an exodus of slaves led by Christ himself:

---

[35]Reginald Heber, "Advent of Christ," *Songs of the Free*, ed. Maria Chapman (Boston: I. Knapp, 1836) 9–11. (See appendix.)

They come—the nation of the FREED!
Who leads their march? Beneath his wheel
Back rolls the sea, the mountains reel!
Before their tread the trump is blown,
Who speaks in thunder, and 'tis done!
. . . .
Even for this hour thy heart's blood streamed!
They come!—the host of the redeemed!
What flames upon the distant sky?
'Tis not the comet's sanguine dye,
'Tis not the lightning's quivering spire,
'Tis not the sun's ascending fire.[36]

This poem combines imagery from the Exodus, the Crucifixion, and the Second Coming.[37] One reason for the popularity of apocalyptic imagery becomes evident here; it is an effective way of invoking the awe-inspiring, terror-striking power of the sublime. The heavenly phenomenon described in this poem is subsequently depicted as an explosion of multiple rainbows across the sky. It is a powerful use of visual imagery to demonstrate the significance of the antislavery struggle, and it points to the imminent end of the world. The sense of a rapidly approaching consummation of these issues motivated abolitionists to continue their activities. As long as they could remain convinced of the eternal significance of their cause, they would continue to fight.

Visual artists also found many themes in the religious and political issues that preoccupied the nation in the 1840s and 1850s. Many Hudson River School painters devoted major works to themes of biblical contexts

---

[36]"Restoration of Israel," *Songs*, ed. Chapman, 17–19. (See appendix.) The heavenly wheel that disrupts the earth in this poem finds a counterpart in an engine of Satan described in another poem: "That slavery is in fact the devil's grand engine / To crush the souls of men. Oh, my friend, is it not / The ante-type of that monstrous car of Juggernot, / Whose pond'rous wheels for generations past have roll'd / In blood." Daniel Holmes, *Dialogue on Slavery* (Dayton: Gazette Book and Job Rooms, 1854) 16.

[37]This combination was not unusual in apocalyptic rhetoric of this period. The plagues of Egypt and the subsequent deliverance of the Israelites were compared with similar events in Revelation. Similarly, the earthquake and the act of salvation associated with the crucifixion were used as parallels with the disturbances and eventual redemption at the end of the world.

or apocalyptic renderings of natural phenomena allegorizing current events. Asher B. Durand's 1851 canvas *God's Judgment Upon Gog* combined both aspects in a powerful visual statement.[38] Durand pushes the visual rendition of sublime imagery to a fever pitch in this canvas of towering cliffs, black clouds, lightning bolts, and a tantalizing glimpse of a beautiful pastoral, even millennial scene in the distance.

In addition to powerful poetic and visual attempts to capture the spirit of the times, the prose of informative writing also drew upon similar descriptive devices as antislavery rhetoric intensified. In an 1854 sermon Theodore Parker used diabolical imagery from Revelation to describe slavery: "Slavery has privately emptied her seven vials of wrath upon the nation—committing seven debaucheries of human safeguards of our Natural Rights. That is not enough—there are other seven to come. This Apocalyptic Dragon, grown black with long-continued deeds of shame and death, now meditates five further steps of crime [the spread of slavery to free territories, etc.]."[39] Parker described a debauched, slumbering America about to suffer a fate similar to the peers of Noah. The Old Testament Flood story provided yet another way of combining past events with future predictions, but its modern counterpart would be a deluge of fire, not water. In this sermon Theodore Parker, an abolitionist, a Transcendentalist, and a close associate of Ralph Waldo Emerson, assumes the Calvinist vocabulary of a Puritan preacher as he thunders out this apocalyptic message saturated with imagery from the Book of Revelation. Parker, and Julia Ward Howe a few years later, demonstrate the ease with which liberal intellectuals adopted a rhetorical mode usually associated with biblical literalists.

Numerous references to Old Testament figures and Puritan doomsayers throughout abolitionist rhetoric indicate these mid-nineteenth-century zealots were assuming a prophetic role toward America. It was prophetic both because it predicted what could be expected from the future and also because it proclaimed a warning, a call

---

[38]Angela Miller has noted this tendency comprehensively in *The Empire of the Eye: Landscape Representation and American Cultural Politics, 1825–1875* (Ithaca: Cornell University Press, 1993) 107–136. In a doctoral dissertation, Gail Husch has focused particularly on the apocalyptic themes of visual art during the peak of abolitionism and sectional strife: "'Something Coming': Prophecy and American Painting, 1848–1854" (Ph.D. diss., University of Delaware, 1992).

[39]Theodore Parker, *A Sermon on the Dangers Which Threaten the Rights of Man in America* (Boston: Benjamin B. Mussey, 1854) 50–51.

to repentance. Great sins called for divine retribution. George B. Cheever, a combative Presbyterian clergyman and reformer, noted this when he pointed out the enormity he saw in his nation's sin: "This is the deep damnation of our guilt. The offense cries up to heaven. By stealing children from their birth, we are A NATION OF MEN-STEALERS, and we renew, perpetuate and increase the guilt from generation to generation."[40] Abolitionists easily assumed their prophetic role, but their ability to turn the public away from the great national sin went about as unheeded as the pleadings of Old Testament doomsayers. Not until Harriet Beecher Stowe unleashed the aesthetic power of fiction on the problem in the 1850s did a significant part of the American public begin to heed the abolitionists' message.

Abolitionist rhetoric of the 1850s seems to parallel the initial burst of zeal that launched the organized effort to end slavery. The second surge in what had become a prolonged struggle grew out of several factors: the increasingly militant resistance of Southerners, particularly Southern churches, to the concept of abolition; the Fugitive Slave Law (1850); the Kansas-Nebraska Act (1854); and the Dred Scott decision (1857). A literary event also contributed to the escalation in the verbal warfare: the publication of *Uncle Tom's Cabin* in 1852. This book transformed abolitionism from a fanatical cult to a regional institution. It infuriated the South and strengthened support of slavery in that region. Within a few months several replies to the book were issued, each claiming to show the *true* picture of slavery as it actually existed in the South.[41]

Harriet Beecher Stowe was astonished by the reaction to her book. Since she had, she thought, taken pains to depict slaveowners as "amiable, generous, and just...[having] the noblest and most beautiful traits of character, [and having] admitted fully their temptations, perplexities, and difficulties," she expected Southerners to appreciate her sympathy.[42] She also expected abolitionists to reject the book as too

---

[40]George B. Cheever, *The Fire and Hammer of God's Word Against the Sin of Slavery* (New York: American Abolition Society, 1858) 7.

[41]The most popular of these books was Mary Eastman's *Aunt Phillis' Cabin; or, Southern Life as It Is* (Philadelphia: Lippincott, Grambo & Co., 1852; reprint, New York: Negro University Press, 1968). This book contends that slavery is God's way of punishing Ham and his descendants.

[42]Harriet Beecher Stowe, *Uncle Tom's Cabin* (Boston: Houghton Mifflin Co., 1878); Preface reprint "The Story of 'Uncle Tom's Cabin'" *Old South Leaflets, 82* (Boston: Directors of the Old South Work, 1897). In this passage Stowe also comments that one

charitable toward slaveholders. Instead, she learned that John Greenleaf Whittier, an outspoken abolitionist, had written to Garrison shortly after the book was published to exult: "What a glorious work Harriet Beecher Stowe has wrought! *Thanks* for the Fugitive Slave Law! Better for slavery that law had never been enacted, for it gave occasion for 'Uncle Tom's Cabin!'"[43] Because the book was not written for abolitionists, Whittier sensed that it would arouse a larger army to prepare for global warfare. The efforts of the abolitionists, he reflected, had been "conflicts and skirmishes which are preparing the way for the great battle of Armageddon,—the world-wide, final struggle between freedom and slavery."[44] The publication of *Uncle Tom's Cabin* would attract the sympathy of readers who had been indifferent to the radical activities of anti-slavery societies.

Whittier also must have noticed that Stowe directed her book especially to Northerners, to awaken their sensibilities to the inhumanity of slavery (particularly the Fugitive Slave Law) and to depict slavery as it actually existed. *Uncle Tom's Cabin* is filled with allusions to a fast-approaching Judgment that will assign the greater share of guilt to the North. This approach is vintage New England Puritan jeremiad rhetoric—the prophetic voice rebuking the community of believers from within, balancing dire predictions of doom with promises of bliss for the repentant. This fact reconciles an apparently puzzling disparity between the preface to the first edition of *Uncle Tom's Cabin*, in which the author refers to the present as a time when "the hand of benevolence is everywhere stretched out" (a sure sign that the millennium had nearly arrived), and the novel's conclusion, where all at once the Judgment is imminent. The two extremes each play a role in the language of the jeremiad, which demands humiliation and penitence from erring but salvageable believers while promising future rewards for returning to abandoned truths.

Stowe's use of Puritan rhetoric was not coincidental, nor was it merely a subconscious tribute to her culture. Vernon Parrington has

---

reader had predicted that the book would be "the great pacificator: it will unite both North and South" (9).

[43]John Greenleaf Whittier, quoted in Stowe preface, 9. The letter was written in May 1852, two months after the publication of *Uncle Tom's Cabin*. The passage quoted in Stowe's preface is the only source for this letter.

[44]Ibid.

remarked that "no more Puritan mind than Mrs. Stowe's ever contributed to the literature of New England,"[45] and it is evident that her ties to Puritanism were the result of careful research. Stowe noted and adapted the Puritan strain in the work of Samuel Hopkins, which significantly influenced the views expressed in *Uncle Tom's Cabin*. Stowe was thoroughly familiar with both his millennialist and abolitionist writings, and the first book she wrote after her two slavery novels was *The Minister's Wooing*, loosely based on Hopkins' life.[46]

In *The Minister's Wooing*, Hopkins preaches a sermon to his Newport, Rhode Island congregation of slave traders that drew from his actual published statements on slavery. He tells his audience that its post-Revolution distress is a sign of God's wrath, and that divine anger is directed against not just slave-traders, slave ship captains, and slaveholders, but also against "the legislatures who have authorized, encouraged, or even neglected to suppress [slavery] to the utmost of their power." All are "guilty of shedding rivers of blood."[47] In *Uncle Tom's Cabin*, Stowe spreads the blame beyond the legislature to the general population; the apparently sympathetic Northerner to whom her book is addressed may be more culpable than the calloused slave trader Haley. In "Select Incident of Lawful Trade," after the slave woman Lucy drowns herself because her sleeping child had been sold and spirited away from her, Stowe's indignation breaks into one of her periodic addresses to her audience, and she asks, "But who, sir, makes the trader? Who is most to blame? The enlightened, cultivated, intelligent man, who supports the system of which the trader is the inevitable result, or the poor trader himself?...In the day of a future Judgment, these very considerations may make it more tolerable for him than for you."[48]

---

[45]Vernon Louis Parrington, *Main Currents in American Thought*, 3 vols. (New York: Harcourt Brace Jovanovich, 1930) 2:371.

[46]For a description of Stowe's familiarity with the writings of Hopkins, see Lawrence Buell, "Calvinism Romanticized: Harriet Beecher Stowe, Samuel Hopkins, and *The Minister's Wooing*," *ESQ: A Journal of the American Renaissance* 24 (Fall 1978): 119–32; reprint, Elizabeth Ammons, ed., *Critical Essays on Harriet Beecher Stowe* (Boston: G. K. Hall, 1980) 259–75.

[47]Harriet Beecher Stowe, *The Minister's Wooing* (Boston: Houghton Mifflin, 1885) 242–43.

[48]Harriet Beecher Stowe, *The Annotated Uncle Tom's Cabin*, ed. Philip Van Doren Stern (New York: Paul S. Eriksson, 1964) 194. Subsequent references to this edition will be abbreviated *UTC*. Stowe also makes it plain that sometimes Northerners were directly

Although Stowe had long held moral objections against slavery, her first novel was triggered when the institution's effects crept north of the border states. Her primary targets in *Uncle Tom's Cabin* are the complacent, self-righteous Northerners who decry slavery but protect the institution through legislation and profit from it directly or indirectly. In her 1878 introduction she remarks that the atrocities of slavery she had witnessed had bothered her for many years but that she was able to quiet her conscience until the passage of the Fugitive Slave Law. This law brought the problem of slavery directly to New England, since it jeopardized the freedom of former slaves living and working there. Black families fled to Canada in the middle of winter, but what seemed "more dreadful" to Stowe was "the apparent apathy of the Christian world of the free North to these proceedings."[49] Divine retribution, she suggests, will be as sure as it will be swift.

The evils of slavery in *Uncle Tom's Cabin* are invariably identified and described by benevolent Southern masters and mistresses, whose good intentions seem to be derailed by circumstances beyond their control. Mrs. Shelby, Tom's first mistress, attributes her husband's financial problems to God's curse on slavery. She admits rationalizing the institution's inevitable evils by working within the system to give slaves a stable, Christian home. Even these efforts, she recognizes, have never removed the sense of guilt about slavery she acquired as a child.[50]

The varieties of Southern guilt and rationalization appear in a dialogue as Haley shepherds his merchandise southward on the riverboat.

---

involved in slavery as well. When a Northern Christian creditor cashes in on a bankrupt client's real estate, part of the property—a young girl and her mother—are put up for auction. When they are separated and the lecherous Legree buys only the girl, Stowe comments, "Two days after, the lawyer of the Christian firm of B. & Co., New York, send on their money to them. On the reverse of that draft, so obtained, let them write these words of the great Paymaster, to whom they shall make up their account in a future day: *'When he maketh inquisition for blood, he forgetteth not the cry of the humble!'"* (428).

[49]Stowe, "Story of 'Uncle Tom's Cabin,'" 5. The Fugitive Slave Law also drew comment from a satiric "defense" of slavery written in response to *Uncle Tom's Cabin*: "Were I to ransack the spheres, and collocate the dialects of worlds, I should fail to find language expressive of my admiration of thy law.... It is a new dispensation. It is an abrogation of all going before that is inconsistent with it. It is like the kingdom mentioned by old Daniel. It swallows up all other laws, and shall stand forever, a consummate and supermagnificent finality." Nicholas Brimblecomb [pseud.], *Uncle Tom's Cabin in Ruins!* (Boston: Charles Waite, 1853) 161.

[50]*Uncle Tom's Cabin*, 83.

A rustic drover piques Haley's conscience, a clergyman spells out the biblical defense of slavery, and a second clergyman, a slender young man, takes the opposite point of view. Then, before their eyes, a slave husband and wife are separated. The clergyman who opposes slavery responds first:

> "God will bring you into judgment for this."
> The trader turned away in silence.
> "I say, now," said the drover, touching his elbow, "there's differences in parsons, an't there? 'Cussed be Canaan' don't seem to go down with this 'un, does it?"
> Haley gave an uneasy growl.
> "And that ar arn't the worst on 't," said John; "mabbee it won't go down with the Lord, neither, when ye come to settle with Him, one o' these days, as all on us must, I reckon."[51]

In Stowe's romantic view, it was appropriate for the open, simple-hearted drover to come closer to the truth than his better-educated companions.

The most detailed confession of guilt and sense of doom comes from Augustine St. Clare, who describes his relationship to the institution of slavery to his Yankee cousin Ophelia, after he buys Tom from Haley. Many other owners agree with him, he insists, that "the land groans under [slavery]" and "bad as it is for the slave, it is worse, if anything, for the master."[52] The only thing preventing the South from suffering the fate of Sodom and Gomorrah, St. Clare tells Ophelia, is that most masters are more benevolent than the law requires.[53] He sees American slavery crumbling under a worldwide revolt among the oppressed masses. His religious background requires a religious explanation of the expected event: "The same thing is working in Europe, in England, and in this country. My mother used to tell me of a millennium that was coming, when Christ should reign, and all men should be free and happy. And she taught me, when I was a boy, to pray, 'thy kingdom come.' Sometimes I think all this sighing, and groaning, and stirring among the dry bones foretells what she used to tell me was coming. But who may abide the day

---

[51]Ibid.,186.
[52]Ibid., 308.
[53]Ibid., 298.

of His appearing?"[54] According to Stowe, few people would survive the Last Judgment. In her impassioned conclusion, she describes the world being shaken to its foundations, as if by an earthquake. This final convulsion is a result of the actions of all nations who have allowed injustice to exist within their borders. Her final words employ the jeremiad rhetoric of Hopkins and the abolitionists. She predicts dreadful events while still hopeful of ultimate reform:

> O, church of Christ, read the signs of the times! Is not this power the spirit of HIM whose kingdom is yet to come?...every time that you pray that the kingdom of Christ may come, can you forget that prophecy associates, in dread fellowship, the *day of vengeance* with the year of his redeemed?
> A day of grace is yet held out to us. Both North and South have been guilty before God; and the *Christian church* has a heavy account to answer. Not by combining together, to protect injustice and cruelty, and making a common capital of sin, is this Union to be saved,—but by repentance, justice and mercy; for, not surer is the eternal law by which the millstone sinks in the ocean, than that stronger law, by which injustice and cruelty shall bring on nations the wrath of Almighty God![55]

Stowe redoubles her efforts to read ultimate significance into contemporary events in her conclusion. She calls for overturning the economic conventions and social practices of a slaveholding society. This catastrophic upheaval is required, she insists, if the nation is to survive.

By employing a narrative frame, visual imagery, and imaginative appeal, Stowe awakened many Northerners to a sense of impending doom that they had never before taken seriously. Her fictions, combined

---

[54]Ibid., 308. In another part of the book, Stowe points out the contrast between Augustine's conscience-stricken view and the secular confidence of his brother Alfred: "We are breaking all humanizing ties, and making them brute beasts; and, if they get the upper hand, such we shall find them." "They shall never get the upper hand!" said Alfred.

"That's right," said St. Clare; "put on the steam, fasten down the escape-valve, and sit on it, and see where you'll land."

"Well," said Alfred, "we *will* see. I'm not afraid to sit on the escape-valve, as long as the boilers are strong, and the machinery works well.... I hope I shall be dead before this millennium of your greasy masses comes on." (Ibid., 349–50.)

[55]Ibid., 560–61.

with actual political events, created expectations of a major civil conflict of the revolutionary dimensions she describes at the end of her book. Stowe's book had a powerful popular impact because it functions both on a highly romantic plane and also on a level of self-proclaimed realism. She endeavored to establish verisimilitude in her account by comments in the book and additional statements after its publication. Along with her theme of judgment, she attempted to portray slavery as it actually existed.

To accentuate the story's realism, Stowe strove to create her strongest impressions with virtually photographic descriptive images. When she introduces Tom, she creates a "daguerreotype" for the readers, and nearly all the other main characters are created with this same consciously pictorial technique. She uses it even when describing something as fanciful as the road to Legree's plantation—her attempt to approximate hell.[56]

In her conclusion Stowe informs her readers that the incidents she described were drawn directly from reality; they are, "to a very great extent, authentic, occurring, many of them, either under her own observation, or that of her personal friends."[57] Reiterating the book's primary focus on a Northern audience, she claims that in order to depict actual slavery, she had decided "to exhibit it in a *living dramatic reality.*"[58]

Given the suspicion with which her primarily Christian audience eyed novels, Stowe seemed anxious to avoid the "fiction" label. When the novel's veracity was substantially denied by Southerners, she responded by issuing her *Key to Uncle Tom's Cabin* in 1854, a documentary collection designed to give her earlier fiction additional factual weight. In the introduction to the *Key*, she says the novel is disturbing and horrible to readers because it was drawn from fact; "In fictitious writing, it is possible to find refuge from the hard and the terrible, [but] no such resource is open in a work of fact."[59] The story of Uncle Tom, she insists, "more, perhaps, than any other work of fiction that ever was written, has been a collection and arrangement of real incidents."[60] She wanted her

---

[56]Ibid., 436.
[57]Ibid., 551.
[58]Ibid., 554.
[59]Harriet Beecher Stowe, *A Key to Uncle Tom's Cabin* (Boston: J. P. Jewett, 1854) iii.
[60]Ibid., 2.

first novel to be remembered as a work of journalism rather than a work of art.

Stowe uses a reportorial technique to recreate the reality of slave life from the slave's point of view, particularly in her depiction of slave religion. And this point is where the purposes of her fanciful vision of judgment and her detailed picture of reality coincide. She portrays slave religion in terms appropriate to a chosen people emerging from a convulsed society: the slave's favorite biblical passages describe the end of the world. Before Tom embarks on an apocalyptic journey to the heart of Louisiana darkness, he leads out in religious services for the Shelby slaves. These meetings are steeped in imagery of warfare and victory from the book of Revelation. The heroes of the slaves' songs die on the field of battle, are bound for Canaan, and are "going to glory."[61] The climax of their meeting occurs when "Mas'r George" reads to them from the book of Revelation. His rendition of the closing chapters is "often interrupted by such exclamations as 'The *sakes* now!' 'Only hear that!' 'Jest think ot't!' 'Is all that a comin' sure enough?'"[62]

Apocalyptic imagery is also associated with the description of Tom's death, an event described by Stowe biographer Joan Hedrick as "the Protestant equivalent of the Roman Catholic mass, a dramatic reenactment of the Crucifixion."[63] The ultimate sacrifice of this modernday type of Christ is associated with the end of the world in a manner that would reappear throughout the Civil War. The despairing Tom, who has already become a redemptive figure by submitting to his sale in order to keep the rest of the Shelby slave population intact, sees a vision of the dying Christ and sings a hymn about eternity: "The earth

---

[61] *UTC*, 76.

[62] Ibid., 77. Eva, the white female saint in *Uncle Tom's Cabin*, regarded the apocalyptic books of the Bible as her favorites; "she and her simple friend, the old child and the young one, felt just alike about it" (339). This imagery is of course important for the overall theme of the book, but it is powerful for Eva because "the soul awakes, a trembling stranger, between two dim eternities,—the eternal past, the eternal future. The light shines only on a small space around her; therefore, she needs must yearn towards the unknown" (339). This also suggests why this type of imagery was so popular during this period.

[63] Joan Hedrick, *Harriet Beecher Stowe: A Life* (New York: Oxford University Press, 1994) 215.

shall be dissolved like snow, / The sun shall cease to shine; / But God, who called me here below, / Shall be forever mine."[64]

In Stowe's novel, characters do not have to be conventional Christians to appreciate the Apocalypse. Simon Legree's quadroon slave Cassy epitomizes secular despair. Despite Cassy's religious upbringing, her life experience has suggested that a merciful God could not allow slavery and therefore must not exist. She is unable, however, to erase childhood beliefs entirely:

"You tell me," she said, after a pause, "that there is a God,—a God that looks down and sees all these things. May be it's so. The sisters in the convent used to tell me of a day of judgment, when everything is coming to light;—won't there be vengeance, then!...I've wished the houses would fall on me, or the stones sink under me. Yes! and, in the judgment day, I will stand up before God, a witness against those that have ruined me and my children, body and soul!"[65]

Although Cassy cannot imagine being saved herself, should God exist, she would at least relish bearing witness to the damnation of slaveholders. Factual slaves, as well as Stowe's fictional ones, tended to make their servitude a religious issue. Furthermore, slaves strongly associated their situation with the prophetic books of the Bible. While whites repeatedly told the slaves they were racially inferior and needed white protection, the single most persistent image in religious slave songs is that of "the chosen people."[66] One acute observer of slave religion, Thomas Wentworth Higginson, commanded a black regiment during the Civil War. He noticed that his black soldiers, recently freed from slavery, had been brought up on the books of Moses and Revelation. These books, says Higginson, "constituted their Bible; all that lay between, even the narratives of the life of Jesus, they hardly cared to read or hear."[67] The

---

[64]UTC, 493.

[65]Ibid., 464.

[66]Lawrence W. Levine, "Slave Songs and Slave Consciousness," Anonymous Americans: Explorations in Nineteenth-Century Social History, ed. Tamara K. Hareven (Englewood Cliffs NJ: Prentice-Hall, 1971) 111.

[67]Thomas Wentworth Higginson, Slave Life in a Black Regiment (Boston: Fields, Osgood & Co., 1870) 218.

language of their songs came from the same scriptural passages. Although Stowe's Tom had borrowed the hymns he sang from Methodist hymnals and other white sources, similar music was produced by slaves. One slave hymn recalled by an ex-slave deals with themes of judgment and heaven similar to those in the hymn Tom sang as he accepted the inevitability of his approaching death. The slave song, though, adds references to the Children of Israel:

> I am bound for the promised land
> No more, no more, I'll never turn back no more
> Come on moaner, come on moaner, come on before the judgment day
> Run away to the snow field, run away to the snow field, my time is not long
> Moses smote the water and the children they crossed over,
> Moses smote the water and the children they crossed over,
> Moses smote the water and the sea gave away.
> Quit this sinful army and your sins are washed away.[68]

The affinity for biblical accounts of the liberation of the children of Israel from bondage and for the symbols of ultimate freedom in Revelation was as old as the slaves' exposure to Christianity. These scriptural accounts influenced the revolts of both Nat Turner and Denmark Vesey, and they provided the theme for Harriet Beecher Stowe's second novel, *Dred of the Dismal Swamp* (1856), which was constructed around factual accounts of slave religion. In this novel Stowe provides an historical interlude complete with the description of Denmark Vesey's revolt and the subsequent escape to the swamp of his son Dred, and in an appendix she includes the confessions of Nat Turner, who was assisted by another slave named Dred.[69] She produced the book

---

[68]George P. Rawick, ed., *The American Slave: A Composite Autobiography* (Westport CT: Greenwood Press, 1972, 1979) 18:47. This song is from a group of ex-slave narratives pertaining to religion collected by Fisk University.

[69]Harriet Beecher Stowe, *Dred: A Tale of the Great Dismal Swamp* (Boston: Houghton, Mifflin and Co., 1889) 580–86. The abolitionists followed the Nat Turner case with fascination. In an interview recorded by Maria Chapman in 1837, an ex-slave revealed that slaves were forbidden to sing certain songs thought by whites to allude to Turner's rebellion. In the lines of one song, "A few more risings and settings of the sun, / Ere the winter will be over— / Glory, Hallelujah! / There's a better day a coming," whites

in a flurry of urgency dictated by the increasing tension between the North and the South and symbolized by the thrashing Charles Sumner received from Preston Brooks in the Senate in May 1856.[70] The sense of a rapidly approaching resolution of the slavery crisis is even stronger in *Dred* than in *Uncle Tom's Cabin*. In her preface, Stowe signals the urgency of the issue: "If ever a nation was raised up by Divine Providence, and led forth upon a conspicuous state, as if for the express purpose of solving a great moral problem in the sight of all mankind, it is this nation."[71] In her view, God is asking America whether slavery is moral, and America is about to answer. The slaves in this story are not saintly and long-suffering. They are angry, they sense the imminence of a conflict over their condition, and they are willing to participate with violence.

Stowe weaves into her story the familiarity both Turner and Vesey had with the prophetic books of the Bible. Dred is a hypnotic, nearly crazed figure and resembles "one of the wild old warrior prophets of the heroic ages."[72] He is thoroughly familiar with the Bible and knows how to capitalize on the other slaves' biblical knowledge.[73] Dred senses that the end of the world has nearly arrived. In the midst of Father Bonnie's camp-meeting revival, the newly reconverted worshipers are startled by a disembodied voice sounding down from the treetops: "I hate and despise your feast-days! I will not smell in your solemn assemblies; for your hands are defiled with blood, and your fingers are greedy for violence!…the day of the Lord is near in the valley of decision! The sun and the moon shall be dark, and the stars withdraw their shining; for the Lord shall utter his voice from Jerusalem, and the heavens and earth shall shake!"[74] Dred reveals why his outrage has gone to such lengths when he meets Harry, a mulatto slave, shortly after his "sermon." He condemns most of the people at the camp-meeting, including the clergy, for participating in the slave trade: "Hunters of men, their hands red with the

---

heard a call to rebellion. Interview with ex-slave Charity Bowery in *Liberty Bell* 1 (1839): 43.

[70]See Stowe's bitter reference to this incident in *Dred*, 519, when Edward Clayton is beaten by a ruffian wielding a gutta-percha cane.

[71]Ibid., iii–iv.

[72]Ibid., 207.

[73]Stowe comments that although the slaves are illiterate, "yet most completely have [the Bible] language and sentiment penetrated among them, giving a Hebraistic coloring to their habitual mode of expression" (Ibid., 221).

[74]Ibid., 275–76.

blood of the poor, all seeking unto the Lord!... Is this a people prepared for the Lord?" Eventually Dred energizes the genteel Harry to acknowledge revolt as the only recourse for frustrated slaves.

Whereas much of Stowe's message in *Uncle Tom's Cabin* was directed at the North, she focuses on Southern slaveowners in *Dred.* She describes how escalating tensions preclude tolerance and reasoned arguments. She even allows Dred to rage, Lear-like, during a savage storm: "The voice of the Lord shaketh the wilderness.... Hailstones and coals of fire!... Rend the heavens...avenge the innocent blood!"[75] Stowe comments that Dred displays a "fierce impatience" with the Almighty. This impatience is ominous: "Could Dred have possessed himself of those lightnings, what would have stood before him? but his cry...only went up to stand in waiting till an awful coming day!"[76] Dred indicates he is willing to give up his life, as Christ did, but his sacrifice is not the passive one made by Tom. He intends to die fighting, as Nat Turner and his own father, Denmark Vesey, had done, because a fighting death is better than a crawling life.[77]

Dred is not surprised when a cholera epidemic threatens the area; to him, it is one of the last plagues prophesied in Revelation. He delivers this message to a sympathetic white man, Edward Clayton, who is on his way to the plantation at Canema, where his fiancee's life is being threatened by the disease. Dred's language reveals his increased sense of urgency: "I saw the Lord coming with ten thousand of his saints! Before him went the pestilence, and burning coals went forth at his feet!... thrust in thy sharp sickle, and gather the clusters of the vine of the earth, for her grapes are fully ripe! Behold, the wine-press shall be trodden without the city, and there shall be blood even to the horses' bridles!"[78] Stowe makes her most direct warning to slaveowners after her description of a prayer Dred made shortly before he was shot and killed by slave hunters. The theme again is "How long, O Lord," and he asks the Lord how long he will wait before avenging the deaths of his people: "Behold under the altar the

---

[75]Ibid., 288.

[76]Ibid., 288.

[77]See Dred's appeal to Harry to stop trying to placate slaveowners and to join the struggle for freedom (Ibid., 359).

[78]Ibid., 392–93. Dred is quoting from Revelation 14.

souls of those they have slain!" (Rev 6:9). Stowe describes this prayer as "that inarticulate moaning which goes before the earthquake."[79]

The first jolt of that earthquake occurred when John Brown led his raid into Harpers Ferry on the night of 16 October 1859, and it intensified when he was executed for treason on 2 December. To many in both the North and the South, Brown's raid signaled the revolution prophesied when the abolitionists first disrupted America's conscience. The Harpers Ferry raid stirred Southern fears about how far Northerners were willing to go to destroy slavery, and it encouraged some Northerners to elevate Brown to near-sainthood. In the view of Edmund Clarence Stedman, the controversy was stirred up by a crazy man along with "eighteen other madmen."[80] The significance placed on the event in both the North and the South, however, was enormous.

Perhaps the element of the anti-heroic in Brown hastened his canonization by Northern abolitionists before the Civil War broke out. His audacious, sparsely staffed enterprise could only have come from a leader with a powerful sense of the morality and even the divine approval of his cause. Moncure Daniel Conway, a Transcendentalist supporter of abolition from Virginia, was certain the South recognized this special quality in Brown: "Slavery said, 'He is firm, truthful, intelligent,—the gamest man I ever saw',—then proceeded to hang him. Slavery would have hung him had it been Jesus Christ, because it must."[81] Although Brown typified the Old Testament prophets, his death led to comparisons with Christ. Brown himself claimed to be a redeemer rather than a revolutionary. During his pretrial questioning, he said he had resolved "not to act the part of an incendiary or ruffian, [but] to aid those suffering great wrong." Although he could be disposed of easily, he warned, "the end of [this Negro question] is not yet."[82]

Brown's stature was also enhanced by the timing of subsequent events. As one contemporary historian pointed out, Brown's greatness was due to "the fact that his 'martyrdom' was rapidly followed by, if it did

---

[79]Ibid., 524–25.

[80]Edmund Clarence Stedman, "How Old Brown Took Harper's Ferry," *The Poems of Edmund Clarence Stedman* (Boston: Houghton Mifflin, 1908) 3.

[81]Moncure Daniel Conway, *The Golden Hour* (Boston: Ticknor and Fields, 1862); reprint, *Addresses and Reprints 1850–1907* (Boston: Houghton Mifflin, 1909) 64.

[82]Thomas Drew, *The John Brown Invasion: An Authentic History of the Harper's Ferry Tragedy* (Boston: James Campbell, 1860) 24.

not, indeed, hasten, the shot on Sumter's walls. In some indefinable manner the Southern Rebellion came to be regarded as a fulfillment of his prophecies."[83] Brown's friends in the North were eager to make him a redemptive saint. Theodore Parker, one of the Secret Six conspirators who had aided Brown's mission, declared that "there have been few spirits more pure and devoted than John Brown's, and none that gave up their breath in a nobler cause."[84] Parker also tied Brown's mission to the "Sic Semper Tyrannis" emblem of Virginia. The tyrant in the emblem, according to Parker, should be white, and the figure standing on him and chopping off his head should be black. Parker saw in the Brown movement a reference back to the children of Israel and forward to a time of bloodshed: "All the great charters of Humanity have been writ in blood. I once hoped that of American Democracy would be engrossed in less costly ink; but it is plain, now, that our pilgrimage must lead through a Red Sea, wherein many a Pharoah will go under and perish."[85] The South, predicted Parker, having sown a wind would reap a whirlwind of revolution and destruction. The severity of atrocities perpetrated against the slaves would multiply when the slaves turned on their former masters. By watching their owners burn Negroes alive, the slaves had learned "how to fasten the chain, how to pile the green wood, how to set this Hell-fire of Slavery agoing." The slave could be depended upon to turn on his antagonists, and when he did, "the Fire of Vengeance" would be put out by "the white man's blood."[86]

Another writer who tied Brown's death to warfare was Herman Melville. He wrote the poem "The Portent (1859)" in 1865 as a "proem" to his postwar collection, *Battle-Pieces*.[87] Melville, recalling that in 1859 there had actually been a comet sighting, used the poem to elevate Brown to a cosmic symbol of the significance of the conflict:

---

[83]Ibid.

[84]Theodore Parker, *John Brown's Expedition* (Boston: The Fraternity, 1860) 18. For a detailed description of the activities of the Secret Six see Jeffrey Rossbach, *Ambivalent Conspirators: John Brown, The Secret Six, and a Theory of Slave Violence* (Philadelphia: The University of Pennsylvania Press, 1982).

[85]Parker, *Brown's Expedition*, 8.

[86]Ibid., 17.

[87]Garner, *Civil War World of Herman Melville*, 423. See also Robert Milder, "The Rhetoric of Melville's *Battle-Pieces*," *Nineteenth Century Literature* 44/2 (September 1989): 173–200.

Hanging from the beam,
Slowly swaying (such the law),
Gaunt the shadow on your green,
Shenandoah!
The cut is on the crown
(Lo, John Brown),
And the stabs shall heal no more.
Hidden in the cap
Is the anguish none can draw;
So your future veils its face,
Shenandoah!
But the streaming beard is shown
(Weird John Brown),
The meteor of the war.[88]

Melville notes the ironic proximity of Harpers Ferry to the Shenandoah Valley, which was ravaged during the war. Noting the judgment to be pronounced on the Shenandoah region and employing the image of the comet, a galactic sign of the end, Melville places this poem at the heart of an apocalyptic interpretation of the war. Although Melville was not a conventional Protestant, he found Calvinist predestination harmonious with his own fatalistic outlook, and he took an apocalyptic view of the world, especially during the Civil War.[89] An even more explicit image occurs at the end of Edmund Clarence Stedman's poem on John Brown. He warns the judge who had declared that "all such rebels" will receive Brown's fate:

But, Virginians, don't do it! for I tell you that the flagon,
Filled with blood of Old Brown's offspring, was first
        poured by Southern hands;
And each drop from Old Brown's life-veins, like the red gore of
        the dragon,

---

[88]Herman Melville, *Battle-Pieces and Aspects of the War* (New York: Harper & Brothers, 1866) 11.

[89]Stanton Garner notes that Melville believed the "preordained, predestined" fate of the world unfolded during the final months of the war, humbling and cleansing the nation (*Civil War World of Herman Melville*, 423).

> May spring up a vengeful Fury, hissing through your slaveworn
>   lands!
> And Old Brown
> Osawatomie Brown,
> May trouble you more than ever, when you've nailed his coffin
>   down![90]

John Brown lived on as a propaganda symbol in the song "John Brown's Body." It became the inspiration for Julia Ward Howe's "The Battle Hymn of the Republic" (see chapter 4), but it was also important on its own merits as an enormously popular marching song for Northern troops.[91] One of the earliest versions of this song was printed in broadside form, probably in 1860. It marks the beginning of the impulse to use John Brown as a metaphor for the Northern cause. His ties to blacks are not mentioned; rather, he is depicted as a soldier in heaven, who has "gone to be a soldier in the army of our Lord," and whose "pet lambs will meet him on the way."[92] Another version of the song was produced by members of the Massachusetts infantry. Many Massachusetts citizens identified closely with Brown, and the Massachusetts marching song emphasizes Brown's martyrdom. His rifle is "red with blood-spots turned to rust," and his soul, under the altar, cries out "How long, O Lord?" He becomes the leader of an army of martyrs who have fallen in the Northern cause. Their former associates in the Union's earthly army are still spreading God's wrath:

> Who rides before the army of martyrs to the word?
> The heavens grow bright as He makes bare his flaming sword,
> The glory fills the earth of the coming of the Lord—
> His soul is marching on!

---

[90]Stedman, "Old Brown," 8–9. This poem was written in November 1859, before Brown was executed.

[91]During the war one commentator noted that "The origin of this song is a mystery...it seems to have taken form insensibly.... The sublime cadences of that wild song, chanted by whole divisions, were the inspiration of the 'Army of the Union' when it went into battle.... The leaders of the Union army acknowledge its superhuman power for inspiriting the ranks. One of the most eminent of Department commanders has said that the song "'made heroes of all his men.'" See Orville James Victor, *History of American Conspiracies* (New York: J. D. Torrey, 1863) 523.

[92]"John Brown" (Boston: J. F. Nash, 1860). (See appendix.)

....

And ye on earth, my army! tread down God's grapes till blood
Unto your horses' bridles hath out His wine-press flowed!
The day of vengeance dawns,—the day of wrath of God—His
  soul is marching on![93]

This version uses the winepress imagery from Revelation that also appears in Dred's speech to Edward Clayton in *Dred of the Dismal Swamp*, Gilbert Haven's Sumner sermon, and the "Battle Hymn of the Republic," a reminder of the pervasiveness and cultural currency of images from the book of Revelation.

During the war some writers tried to make the song more literary. This did not necessarily make it more popular, but it did signal the attempt to make the song function on an aesthetic level rather than a purely propagandistic one. "If people WILL sing about Old John Brown," sighed Henry Howard Brownell, a Northern poet, "there is no reason why they shouldn't have words with a little meaning and rhythm in them," and he wrote his own set of words. The imagery in his version, produced in 1862, is explicitly apocalyptic:

He has gone to be a soldier in the army of the Lord,
He is sworn as a private in the ranks of the Lord—
He shall stand at Armageddon with his brave old sword—
When Heaven is marching on
Glory, glory, hallelujah, &c.
For heaven is marching on.[94]

By the time the Civil War was winding down, the Brown myth evolving in the songs had refocused on his efforts to liberate the slaves. According to one contemporary account, the Union troops who entered Charleston Harbor were greeted by blacks crying, "Glory Hallelujah! dis is de army ob de Lord! we watched for you dis four long year, we's happy

---

[93]L. Holbrook, "The Massachusetts John Brown Song," *Songs of the Soldiers*, ed. Frank Moore (New York: G. P. Putnam, 1864) 125–27. (See appendix.)

[94]Henry Howard Brownell, "Words That Can be Sung to the 'Hallelujah Chorus'" *Songs*, ed. Moore, 168–69. The date accompanying these words is 17 April 1862. (See appendix.)

now!"[95] As the Union officers marched through the streets of Charleston, they sang the John Brown song and were soon joined by tearful blacks. By this time, Brown is not just the righteous soldier or the Christian martyr or the apocalyptic hero. He has become the savior of the slaves:

> John Brown was John the Baptist, of Christ we are to see,
> Christ who of the bondmen shall the Liberator be,
> And soon throughout the sunny South the slaves shall all be free,
> For his soul is marching on. [Glory, &c.]
> ....
> Ye soldiers of Freedom, then strike, while strike ye may,
> The Death-stroke of oppression, in a better time and way,
> For the dawn of old John Brown, has brightened into day,
> And his soul is marching on. [Glory, &c.][96]

Brown's heroic stature increased during the war despite the emerging reports of the conspiracy, the revisionist descriptions of his raid, and documentation of the extent of his mental instability. In 1870 Thomas Keely of New York published a print celebrating the ratification of the Fifteenth Amendment (Figure 3).[97] The central illustration depicts the 19 May celebration, and it is surrounded by scenes of hardworking, prosperous black citizens and heroes of abolitionism and the Civil War. At the lower corners of the large central illustration reside portraits of two martyred heroes of the cause: Abraham Lincoln and John Brown. And in 1877 a tribute to the fifteenth amendment and to Brown, Lincoln, and Sumner included verses describing both his martyrdom and his prophecy of the coming war:

> Fourteenth of October, fifty-nine
> John Brown said to his comrades, "We'll arrive
> At Harper's Ferry at the hour p. m. nine,
> Though on that wicked ground we be crucified."

---

[95]John Smith Dye, *History of the Plots and Crimes of the Great Conspiracy to Overthrow Liberty in America* (New York: Published by author, 1866; reprint, Freeport NY: Books for Libraries Press, 1969) 244.

[96]Ibid., 245.

[97]"The Fifteenth Amendment, Celebrated May 19, 1870," color print, #678:49. This item is reproduced by permission of The Huntington Library, San Marino, California.

....
When Mason and others, with Governor Wise,
Asked him why he was guilty of this great crime,
He astonished them in his deep replies–
"The root I strike will cost money; lives in time."
....
"By inspiration from God I am sent
To strike a blow at the root of sin's cursed cause;
With force of arms—intellect that Jehovah sent.
Ah! For this same reason there will be war."[98]

The John Brown phenomenon marked the most militant episode in the events leading to the Civil War. As warfare became inevitable tolerance eroded, and the two sides polarized into equally firm predictions of victory. The results of the opening battles of the war would lend credence to the Southern version of apocalyptic self-assurance.

---

[98]"Equality for All Men Before the law," music given for "Windham," by Daniel Read, words by Wh. H. Curd (Chicago: W. H. Curd, 1877) print #671 (40). This item is reproduced by permission of the Huntington Library, San Marino, California (see appendix).

3

SOUTHERN RIGHTEOUSNESS
AND THE FIRST MANASSAS

Adalbert Volck, a German immigrant dentist living in Baltimore, became the best-known iconographer of the Confederate cause. Technically a Copperhead, Volck aimed intense visual vitriol at the North.[1] His print "Worship of the North" responded to events in 1860 and 1861 (Figure 4).[2] The theme of the print is human sacrifice committed by a primitive pagan culture. The altar's base is "Puritanism," the foundation for what the South regarded as unique Northern sins and signs of fanaticism: "atheism," "rationalism" (referring to the inspiration of the Declaration of Independence and the Red Republicanism of Jacobin France); "witchburning," "socialism," "free love," and "spirit rapping" (all signs of Northern infidelity that horrified Southern evangelical Christians); and the topmost stone, "Negro Worship," the explanation for the primitive savagery displayed by the North.

Inspiration for this grisly sacrifice comes from the platform of the Chicago Republican convention of 1860, with Lincoln as its hero and a black man as its idol. Its motto, presumably referring to the war, is "The end sanctifies the means." A statue of John Brown, another individual who could lay claim to the Chicago motto, is labeled with his nickname, "Ossawatomie." The high priest who has just committed the murder is

---

[1]Mark E. Neely, Jr., et al., point out that Volck's drawings were printed and circulated in the North. See Mark E. Neely, Jr., et al., *The Confederate Image: Prints of the Lost Cause* (Chapel Hill: University of North Carolina Press, 1987) 44. See also Frederick S. Voss, "Adalbert Volck: The South's Answer to Thomas Nast," *Smithsonian Studies in American Art* 2/3 (1988): 67–87; Harold Holzer, "Confederate Caricature of Abraham Lincoln," *Illinois Historical Journal* 80/1 (Spring 1987): 23–36; Bruce W. Chambers, "The Southern Artist and the Civil War," *Southern Quarterly* 24/1-2 (1985) 71–94; Bruce Catton, "A Southern Artist on the Civil War," *American Heritage* 9/6 (1958): 117–20.

[2]Courtesy of the Library of Congress.

the Rev. Henry Ward Beecher, assisted at the left of the print by Charles Sumner. Generals Benjamin Butler and John C. Fremont (in pioneer garb) worship at the altar, while General Henry Halleck brandishes shattered slave shackles. These figures were included because they emancipated slaves or otherwise harassed slaveholders in Missouri and Louisiana in late 1861 and early 1862. Other supporters of abolitionism look on with approval, and Harriet Beecher Stowe kneels on a copy of *Uncle Tom's Cabin* at the right of the picture. A ludicrously festive Winfield Scott lends his blessing, as do the war profiteers in the background behind him. Serpents and skulls are scattered around the periphery of the scene. The cloud of smoke from the censer at the left rises to the sky as if pointing to a grotesque witch figure riding a skeletal beast. Surmounting the scene is the label, inscribed not once but twice: Ego (read "egotism"). The entire scene strives to represent everything that is not righteous, not Christian.

These references to savagery and diabolism allude to the greed Southerners were always willing to ascribe to the North, but the print's primary focus is the antislavery movement. Although its choice of images is extreme, this print contains an intriguing, comprehensive description of Southern attitudes toward the North that appeared repeatedly in sermons, poetry, and art throughout the Confederacy.

Before the Civil War, the predominant strain of antislavery apocalypticism in the North was premillennial, long on imminent doom and short on hope. According to this view, anyone who supported slavery, South or North, hastened the approaching End, and the entire nation would suffer punishment. Southerners initially concurred. Eugene Genovese has noted that eighteenth-century figures such as George Whitefield and Samuel Davies saw the inconclusive stretches of the Revolution as signs of God's disapproval of the treatment of slaves, if not the institution itself.[3] In the eighteenth and early nineteenth centuries it was possible for Southerners to be self-critical about both the practice and the actual institution of slavery.

This line of thinking in the South, however, was gradually subducted underneath a more positive view, a determined response to the attacks of the abolitionists. Southerners, particularly members of the clergy, rose to defend slavery as a social institution, a divinely mandated white

---

[3]Eugene Genovese, *A Consuming Fire: The Fall of the Confederacy in the Mind of the White Christian South* (Athens: University of Georgia Press, 1998) 126.

responsibility, a positive good, and a reinforcement of Scripture. This view tended to favor a postmillennial approach, where warnings were confined to lapses from ideal slaveholding and were tempered by hope.[4] James Moorhead has noted that the leading proslavery voices James Henley Thornwell, Robert Dabney, John Giradeau, and John Adger were all postmillennialists who thought slavery would be purged of its abuses in the millennium.[5] Like their antebellum Northern counterparts, Southern clergymen also believed they lived in the Redeemer Nation.[6] James O. Farmer, Jr. has noted that Thornwell, a leading advocate of Old School Presbyterianism, was able to explain the slavery issue within the context of conservative religious and political thought.[7]

Northern clergy, anticipating the Redeemer Nation's triumph, tended to employ jeremiad rhetoric to purge their nation's sins and elicit repentance and reform. Simultaneously, many Southern ministers became fearful that the national government was becoming hopelessly secular, even atheistic. The tendency of abolitionists to reject biblical literalism if it seemed to sanction slavery reinforced those fears. Mitchell Snay has pointed out that "throughout the antebellum era, slavery remained at the center of Southern clerical thought on the sectional controversy."[8] As secession talk increased, Southern churchgoers were increasingly likely to hear the national government associated with the Babylon of Jeremiah and Revelation and to hear the admonition, "Come out of her, my people" (Rev 18:4). Before a new (Confederate) Redeemer Nation could arise, the wickedness of the Northern Babylon had to be dealt with. This setting encouraged an intensely apocalyptic interpretation of events. Instead of directing prophetic doom at the entire country, as antislavery Northerners did in their jeremiads, proslavery

---

[4]Genovese has pointed out that as Southern clergy "rallied their people to secession and war," they understood the gap between ideal slaveholding and actual practice, and "called for repentance and reform." *Consuming Fire*, 5. This took place in a hopeful postmillennial context.

[5]Moorhead, "Mainstream Protestantism," *Encyclopedia of Apocalypticism*, 3:84–85.

[6]Mitchell Snay, *Gospel of Disunion: Religion and Separatism in the Antebellum South* (Chapel Hill: University of North Carolina Press, 1993) 186.

[7]James O. Farmer, Jr., *The Metaphysical Confederacy: James Henley Thornwell and the Synthesis of Southern Values* (Macon GA: Mercer University Press, 1986). See especially Farmer's discussion of Thornwell's dedication sermon for Zion Church (built by whites for a black congregation) in Charleston, 26 May 1850, 220–26.

[8]*Gospel of Disunion*, 215.

doomsayers targeted infidel abolitionists, greedy free-labor capitalists, and grasping, ungenerous Yankees.

At the onset of the Civil War, many Southerners were confident their cause would prevail because it was right in the sight of God. With a clarity honed by decades of defense against abolitionist charges, they saw their struggle as a revolution rivaling the one in1776. In fact, it might be even purer since it was solidly based on Christian principles, whereas the Founding Fathers had allowed secularism to creep into their declarations and documents. Many Southerners also compared themselves favorably against philanthropic New Englanders who claimed to serve the slaves' best interests by trying to free them. Only a benevolent, Christian slaveholder, these Southerners maintained, could truly care for the slave, who had been placed under the care of the white race in order to acquire Christianity, and, perhaps, return to Africa to convert his brethren.[9]

Furthermore, slavery was only one of several issues upon which Southerners built their sense of righteous confidence. The slavery sentiment had developed largely in response to abolitionist charges, but an even earlier point of conflict was states' rights, dating back to the Revolutionary period and the Articles of Confederation. The first working arrangement of the United States continued to appeal to some Southerners, who were dismayed to see the strengthening of power in the central government that accompanied the Constitution. The federal government's encroachment on their economy led to the first whispers of secession during the Jacksonian era and in response to the tariff issue. The slavery controversy only refined and intensified existing conflicts. When Southern leaders looked back on their record of stressing the individual rights of freemen and their pious reliance on the literal Word of God, they found plenty of assurances that they were working out a divine plan for the world. If battles lay in the future, they would represent more than earthly interests. Because the Southern case for divine approval was so clear-cut, its opponents must be aiding the devil. This

---

[9]This opinion prevailed among the Southern clergy, even those who readily admitted that slavery, while not a sin, was a great evil; for example, see the Rev. Samuel B. How, *Slaveholding not Sinful: an Argument before the General Synod of the Reformed Protestant Dutch Church* (New York: John A. Gray, 1855) 6. At the same time, however, there was also a thread of dissent from the prevailing view, as described by David B. Chesebrough, *Clergy Dissent in the Old South, 1830–1865* (Carbondale: Southern Illinois University Press, 1996).

conflict between absolute good and absolute evil seemed to signal Armageddon.[10]

Charles Colcock Jones, Jr., the mayor of Savannah in 1861, expressed his region's confidence in a letter to his clergyman father during the opening days of the Civil War. Southern virtue, he declared, would ensure the favor of the "God of Battles." A just deity would not allow "a blinded, fanatical people," who had set aside equality, right, honor, and the writ of habeas corpus, "to triumph in this unholy war." Without being Pharisaical, the South could "honestly thank God that we are not as they are."[11]

Certain their cause was righteous and believing the affairs of nations were important enough to invite the participation of God, many Southerners found reassurance in their initial military maneuvers. The Reverend Charles Colcock Jones, Sr., expressed this assurance in a letter to his son: "A kind Providence seems to watch over our Confederacy."[12] Even more evidence to support this belief became available during the

---

[10]For detailed studies of these aspects of southern life, see Jeanette Reid Tandy, "Pro-Slavery Propaganda in American Fiction in the 1850s," *South Atlantic Quarterly* 20 (January–March 1922): 41–50; and Donald G. Matthews, *Religion in the Old South* (Chicago: University of Chicago Press, 1977). Southern defenses of slavery against abolitionist attacks include Leander Ker, *Slavery Consistent with Christianity* (Jefferson City MO: W. Lusk, 1842); Holland Nimmons McTyeire, *Duties of Christian Masters* (Nashville: Southern Methodist Publishing House, 1859); Frederick Augustus Ross, *Slavery Ordained of God* (Philadelphia: J. B. Lippincott, 1867; reprint Miami FL: Mnemosyne Publishing CO., 1969); William Carpenter Wisner, *The Biblical Argument on Slavery* (New York: Leavitt, Trow & Co., 1844); Henry Clarke Wright, *Self-Convicted Violators of Principle* (n. p., 184?); E. N. Elliott, ed., *Cotton is King and Proslavery Arguments* (n. p.: Pritchard, Abbott & Loomis, 1860; reprint New York: Negro Universities Press, 1969); and J. C. Mitchell, *A Bible Defense of Slavery and the Unity of Mankind* (Mobile: J. Y. Thompson, 1861). For Southern predictions of the outcome of the war, see James Warley Miles, *God in History* (Charleston: Evans & Cogswell, 1863). James Williams, *The South Vindicated* (London: Longman, Green, Longman, Roberts & Green, 1862) declared that the Civil War was a second War of Independence in America. John B. Thrasher, *Slavery a Divine Institution* (Port Gibson MS: Southern Reveille Book & Job Office, 1861) said that abolitionism originated with Red Republicanism in Jacobin France.

[11]Charles Colcock Jones, Jr., to the Rev. and Mrs. C. C. Jones, 30 May 1861, *The Children of Pride: A True Story of Georgia and the Civil War, Selected Letters of the Family of the Rev. Dr. Charles Colcock Jones*, ed. Robert Manson Myers (New Haven: Yale University Press, 1984) 71–72.

[12]The Rev. Charles Colcock Jones, Sr. to C. C. Jones Jr., 20 April 1861, *Children of Pride*, 52.

first major meeting of the armies, at Manassas Junction on 21 July 1861. This battle matched equally raw troops who fought inconclusively until the Union forces were suddenly put to rout. Their panic produced a disgraceful retreat all the way back to Washington, DC and led Northerners to the sober conclusion that God must not be on their side, at least not yet.[13]

Not just Confederate outrage at the violation of their border brought the victory, Southerners pointed out. Certainly exploits such as the fortitude of the First Virginia (Stonewall) Brigade had contributed to the success of the battle, but the victory was God's. For many Southern Christians, their experience paralleled God's involvement with the Children of Israel. The Reverend Stephen Elliott, Episcopal Bishop of Georgia, compared the South's victory to the Israelite escape from Pharoah at the Red Sea. It was an "answer to prayer" and proof of "the presence of God."[14] God did not merely give his passive approval to the conflict; he involved himself directly in its outcome just as he had aided Elisha against the Syrians: "Could the eyes of our fainting, dying children have been opened that day to see spiritual things, I feel sure that they would have seen horses and chariots of fire riding upon the storm of battle, and making those that were for them, more than those that were against them."[15]

C. C. Jones, Jr., proclaimed the victory was "without parallel in the history of this western world."[16] To the wife of Colonel Clarke of the Fourteenth North Carolina Regiment, it may have been slightly less significant, but it did provide an opportunity to give the South a victory anthem. Ironically, she adopted the same meter Julia Ward Howe would use a few months later for the verses of "The Battle Hymn." Mrs. Clarke's song, titled "The Battle of Manassas," acknowledged God's hand in the conflict, vindicating the South and humiliating the North:

---

[13]An example of the Northern response to this battle may be found in a sermon by the Rev. Horace Bushnell, *Reverses Needed: A Discourse Delivered on the Saturday after the Disaster of Bull Run* (Hartford: L. E. Hunt, 1861). Bushnell maintained that God allowed the North to experience adversity during the early days of the war in order to remind them of the war's purpose and to strengthen their resolve.

[14]Stephen Elliott, *God's Presence with Our Army at Manassas!* (Savannah: W. Thorne Williams, 1861) 20.

[15]Ibid., 13–14.

[16]Charles Colcock Jones, Jr., to the Rev. C. C. Jones, 24 July 1861, *Children of Pride*, 98.

"Now glory to the Lord of Hosts!" oh, bless and praise His
    name,
That He hath battled in our cause and brought our foes to
    shame,
And honor to our Beauregard, who conquered in His might,
And for our children's children won, Manassas' bloody fight.
Oh, let our thankful prayers ascend, our joyous praise resound,
For God—the God of victory, our untried flag hath crowned!

The following stanza identifies one of the chief sins of the
North–pride–and equates it with presumption. This vice was rewarded
with a deadly and bloody reversal of Union expectations:

They brought a mighty army, to crush us with a blow,
And in their pride they laughed to scorn the men they did not
    know,
Fair women came to triumph, with the heroes of the day,
When "the boasting Southern rebels" should be scattered in
    dismay.
And for their conquering Generals, a lordly feast they spread.
But the wine in which we pledged them, was all of ruby red!

Northern pride was accompanied by a decadence that could only
invite divine retribution:

The feast was like Belshazzar's—in terror and dismay,
Before our conquering heroes, their armies fled away.
God had weighed them in the balance, and His hand Upon the
    wall,
At the taking of Fort Sumter, had fore-doomed them to their
    fall.
But they would not heed the warning, and scoffed in unbelief,
Till their scorn was changed to wailing, and their laughter into
    grief![17]

---

[17]Mrs. Clarke, "The Battle of Manassas," *The Southern Poems of the War*, comp.
Emily Virginia Mason (Baltimore: J. Murphy & Co., 1867) 55–58. (See appendix.)

This song uses a favorite image of both Southern and Northern writers: that of Belshazzar, the Old Testament king of Babylon who read his kingdom's demise in mysterious fiery letters on the wall of his palace, as described in Daniel 5. Since Belshazzar's experience revolved around the concept of judgment and since "Babylon" is used in the book of Revelation to symbolize the enemies of God at the end of the world, this experience became important for apocalyptic literature. The proud, presumptuous Belshazzar's death at the hands of invading troops shortly after he saw the writing reassured anyone able to identify him with the enemy. Clarke interpreted the fall of Fort Sumter as the handwriting on the wall, and Manassas was the military defeat signaling the fall of the corrupt Northern empire.

An 1863 broadside celebrating Southern victories made a more explicit connection between the First Manassas and the Last Judgment. It included a poem written to celebrate "Bull's Run" (actually Blackburn's Ford) on 18 July and "Manasseh" on 21 July. This first provides reassurance for the South, whose martyred inhabitants will be raised up at the Last Judgment:

> When the Great Judge, Supreme and Just
> Shall once inquire for blood;
> The humble soul, who mourns in dust,
> Shall find a faithful God.
>
> He from the dreadful gates of death,
> Does his own children raise;
> In "Southern States," where with cheerful breath,
> They sing their Father's praise.

While the South receives these tokens of divine favor, the North reaps the results of its sins: "Our foes shall fall with heedless feet, / Into the Pit, they made And Fanatics perish in the act, / Which their *own* hands had spread." The fanaticism of the wicked is related to the concept of pride in Mrs. Clarke's poem. The North's error lies in its reliance on personal views rather than God's: "Thus by Thy judgements, mighty God, / Are Thy deep Counsels known; / When men of mischief are destroyed, / The *snare* must be their own." Another reason for the demise of the North is its willful disdain for the laws of God. Disobedience makes

Northerners the actual rebels in this war: "The wicked shall sink down to hell; / Thy wrath devour the lands, / That dare forget Thee, or rebel, / Against Thy known commands."[18]

The "known commands" most flagrantly ignored by the North, in the Southern view, were those biblical passages describing the slaves' subordinate, even cursed role in society. In this poem, the Southern sympathizer assumes a superior tone. The North has been defeated because of its disobedience, a form of arrogance that, in the Southern view, had led to ill-considered aggression.

The South, according to the Reverend C. C. Jones, Sr., was able to claim that "we have not sinned against [the North]."[19] This feeling of blamelessness encouraged a condescending attitude toward the opposition. Jones's fellow Presbyterian minister, Reverend James Henley Thornwell, advised "pity" and "commiseration" for the North shortly before formal secession took place. The United States, by falling prey to degeneracy and corruption, was ruining the legacy of the founding fathers and receiving just punishment: "The sin must be enormous where the punishment is so fearful."[20]

Apocalyptic upheaval could be expected to accompany these intimations of judgment. The corruption of the North had, according to the Methodist writer W. H. Seat, led the new World into a "time of trouble" that would continue "until the rising despotism of the North shall be broken in pieces."[21] While the depraved North constituted the final threat to the world, the South, according to Seat, was the "final antitype" of Old Testament Israel, the reality that ancient Zion had merely symbolized. Furthermore, God's direct involvement could be seen in the outcomes of Civil War battles: "There are comparatively few intelligent and thoughtful men in the Confederate States, who do not

---

[18]Charles Caylat, "Of 'Bull's Run,' the 18th; and Manasseh, the 21st July, 1861," in *The Glorious Southern Victories!*, broadside, Confederate States of America, 25 February 1863. See appendix.

[19]Rev. Charles Colcock Jones, Sr., to Charles Jr., 30 May 1861, *Children of Pride*, 67.

[20]The Rev. James Henley Thornwell, "Our National Sins," *Fast Day Sermons: or, the Pulpit on the State of the Country* (New York: Rudd & Carleton, 1861) 27–28.

[21]W. H. Seat, *The Confederate States of America in Prophecy* (Nashville TN: Methodist Publishing House, 1861) 134.

acknowledge the hand of God in the battles that have been fought, and especially in that of Manassas Plains."[22]

Although the Battle of Manassas would remain the primary example of God's favor in Southern eyes, the outcomes of subsequent clashes continued to meet expectations, at least through the summer of 1862. Religious revivals among Southern troops ensured God's continued protection and became another reason, in the eyes of one clergyman, for Confederate success in the Peninsula campaign: "Christ was on the battle-field as well as 'in the camp,' and...He manifested His saving power...during that bloody campaign in 1862."[23]

This optimistic attitude toward the role of the Confederacy in God's plan continued until the battle of Antietam in late September of 1862, but it appeared only sporadically thereafter.[24] C. C. Jones, Jr. was certain that "if God still favors our cause and inspires our armies and leaders as He has done...for some time past, the enemy will be forced to keep his troops for home defense." In addition, Jones noted, Generals Jackson, Lee, and Stuart were "pious men all" who had been "specially blessed in all of their enterprises."[25] When the South began to feel the pressure of superior Northern supply lines and manpower, it found a rallying point in biblical sources. When defeat finally became a reality, the South's certainty about its opponents' diabolism only increased.[26]

---

[22]Ibid., 141–42. Seat believed that the war would continue to progress swiftly, that the blockade would be broken by a "power from the east," and that the war would end "without the sorrows of a terrible political redemption." This would deepen the impression that a divine interpretation of the war was correct (142).

[23]John William Jones, *Christ in the Camp, Or, Religion in Lee's Army* (Richmond: B. F. Johnson & Co., 1888) 282.

[24]Even as late as the summer of 1864, the Confederate government exuded confidence that God was administering military defeats to the North. The repeated failures of the huge Union army to enter Richmond led the Confederacy to claim that their own peace overtures were being conducted from a position of strength rather than weakness. "The repeated and disastrous checks, foreshadowing ultimate discomfiture," went this rationale, "are but a continuation of the same Providential successes for us." See the manifesto of the Congress of CSA, by Hon. William C. Rives, Richmond *Sentinel,* 18 June 1864, as quoted in John Minor Botts, *The Great Rebellion: Its Secret History* (New York: Harper and Brothers, 1866) 48.

[25]C. C. Jones, Jr., to Rev. C. C. Jones, Sr., 10 September 1862, *Children of Pride,* 291–92.

[26]In a bitter footnote to the war, Col. Angus W. McDonald, CSA, accused the North of being in league with the devil because only the devil could be so successful in warfare.

Although Southern attitudes toward the North had developed long before the war, they were adjusted readily to the belief that the conflict was a battle for independence, an American Revolution more glorious than the first because it was led by devout Christians. In this view, the North had begun to veer from orthodoxy soon after the Revolution, unduly influenced by the Red Republicanism of the godless French Revolution and the excesses of Robespierre. The battle against secularism still continued, according to the Reverend C. C. Jones, Sr., who wrote to his daughter that "the Revolutionary struggle was not more important than the one in which we are now engaged," and pointed out that so far in the war the Lord had been on their side.[27] Bishop Elliott maintained that "we are fighting to prevent ourselves from being transferred from American republicanism to French democracy," and to drive away "the infidel and rationalistic principles which are sweeping over the land."[28]

Although antebellum abolitionists were derided in the South for repudiating the US Constitution's protection of slavery, once the Confederacy was formed Southerners were quick to point out the flaws in that document. C. C. Jones, Jr., objected strenuously to the possibility that his state might be overrun by "inhuman and infidel hordes who threaten us with invasion, dishonor, and subjugation." He noted that the Confederate Constitution had been "born of prayer," whereas "the old Federal Constitution was a godless instrument." Jones believed that the United States was being punished "for this practical atheism and national neglect in not...acknowledging His supremacy."[29] The Confederacy, however, would not make a similar mistake. When the permanent Confederate government was established in February 1862, C. C. Jones, Sr., commented on the relationship between the Federal and Confederate constitutions. The United States constitution did not acknowledge God, he reminded his son, and no U. S. president had ever "openly expressed

---

Abolitionism, he maintained, was the unnatural offspring of Puritanism and radicalism, products of the North. Greeley was a "falsifier of truth," George Barrell Cheever a "wretch, most blasphemous," and Sumner "the most brazen pimp to a depraved public taste." *The Two Rebellions, or, A Treason Unmasked* (Richmond: Smith, Bailey, & Co., 1865) 16, 67–68.

[27]The Rev. C. C. Jones, Sr., to Mary Mallard, 26 October 1861, *Children of Pride*, 141.

[28]Elliott, *God's Presence*, 21.

[29]C. C. Jones, Jr., to the Reverend and Mrs. C. C. Jones, Sr., 29 July 1861, *Children of Pride*, 102–103.

the orthodox faith of the gospel." The Confederate constitution, on the other hand, was ushered in with fasting, humiliation, and prayer, and the first Confederate president was "accredited a *Christian man*."[30]

The high level of piety so many Southerners detected in their cause coincided with the belief that the Confederacy was the antitype of biblical Israel, destined to play a significant prophetic role in the history of the world. It had been created during the last hours of earth's history in order to represent genuine, orthodox Christianity in a final struggle with the forces of fanaticism and evil.

One Confederate author saw the Confederate government as God's representative that would reign through the millennium until the Second Coming. He described his government as "the millennial confederate, states-rights republican royalty, with God in Christ as its acknowledged head and author," which had been transformed from promise into reality. Following the peace of Armageddon, Christ would reign by these representatives until his visible return.[31]

Southern fiction aided in shaping Southern attitudes toward the North and assigning apocalyptic meaning to contemporary events. An improbable Confederate literary hero of the Civil War era was the Virginia writer Nathaniel Beverly Tucker, who had died in 1851. He had written a novel in 1836, *The Partisan Leader*, which addressed the nullification crisis.[32] In 1850 he participated in a Southern convention formed to discuss the possibility of secession if the compromise bill then before Congress passed with any amendments unfavorable to the South.[33] Both the novel and his speech at the 1850 convention were republished in the Confederacy in 1862. The speech received a new title, *Prescience*, and proclaimed the Southern ideal of "equality or independence."

---

[30]The Reverend C. C. Jones, Sr., to C. C. Jones, Jr., 3 March 1862, *Children of Pride*, 207.

[31]J. P. Philpott, *The Kingdom of Israel from its Inception Under Joshua...to the Second Advent of Christ.... The Confederate States shown to be the Grand Antitype...* (Fairfield TX: Pioneer Office Print, 1864) 43.

[32]Nathaniel Beverly Tucker, *The Partisan Leader: A Novel, and an Apocalypse of the Origin and the Struggles of the Southern Confederacy* (n. p., 1836; reprint, Richmond: West & Johnston, 1862).

[33]Nathaniel Beverly Tucker, *Prescience: A Speech Delivered by the Honorable Beverly Tucker of Virginia* (Richmond: West & Johnston, 1862). This speech was delivered in Nashville, Tennessee, on 13 April 1850.

The novel also dwelt on the idea of Southern independence, and in fact it predicted Southern secession. President Martin Van Buren would be called Martin the First, according to Tucker, and the North would keep him in office for the twelve years preceding the beginning of the story. The fictitious title page of the novel gives its publication date as 1856 and describes a war that had supposedly taken place in 1848 and 1849, after the South had seceded. Virginia is a staging ground for Federal troops, and one of the groups opposing them is a guerrilla unit led by Douglas Trevor. This intrepid soldier is dedicated to harassing the Federals out of Virginia, even though his own brother is a US Army colonel. Tucker assumes this prophesied battle will occur as a result of the nullification controversy, but he also introduces frequent digressions on other controversial issues: states' rights, free trade, and proslavery paternalism.[34] He invokes the racial issue by giving an example of Southern reaction to the abolitionist assaults of the North. A plantation owner, Mr. B., explains the truth of Southern black/white relations to Douglas Trevor. In this speech Tucker also summarizes the primary grievances of the South against the North, which include the selfish grasping of the skinflint Yankee, the artificiality of philanthropic motives, and the North's Puritan antipathy toward Southern Cavaliers:

> They [our Northern brethren] have not the qualities which would enable them to comprehend the negro character. Their calculating selfishness can never understand his disinterested devotion. Their artificial benevolence is no interpreter of the affections of the unsophisticated heart. They think our friend Jack [a slave] here to be even such as themselves, and cannot, therefore, conceive that he is not ready to cut his master's throat, if there is anything to be got by it. They know no more of the feelings of our slaves, than their fathers could comprehend of the loyalty of the gallant cavaliers from whom we spring; and for the same reason.[35]

Clearly, according to this passage, the slaveowner's understanding of the Negro, as well as his treatment of the slave, is superior to a

---

[34] See Robert J. Brugger, *Beverly Tucker: Heart Over Head in the Old South* (Baltimore: Johns Hopkins University Press, 1978) 122.

[35] Tucker, *Partisan Leader*, 122.

Northerner's. Tucker's confidence in the fidelity of the Negro is remarkable considering that his book was published just five years after the Nat Turner rebellion had thrown his home state into panic.

Tucker took great pains to give his prophecy literary power. Since the late 1820s he had sensed a crisis looming over the United States, and he invoked sublime imagery to represent that crisis. His novel is filled with references to the sublime, and it transforms the slopes of the Blue Ridge Mountains into craggy, awe-inspiring peaks reminiscent of the Alps. This aesthetic concept directly shaped his worldview and enabled Tucker to invoke sublime imagery as the official language of revolution. In his interpretation of Burke's doctrine of the sublime and the beautiful, Tucker sees order as beautiful and chaos as sublime. Part of that vision, according to a biographer, was "a cataclysm that would be more than a metaphor, of a social-political cloudburst that would wash away evil as it cleansed and reinvigorated."[36] Even after the nullification controversy that had inspired the novel died away, Tucker refused to abandon the issue, insisting the Union would be destroyed.

Although Tucker was somewhat of an eccentric, many of his opinions were echoed by a member of the literary mainstream, the South Carolinian William Gilmore Simms. In 1829 Simms supported the Union to such an extent he had taken an unpopular stand against nullification. His concern, however, that the North would destroy slavery and thereby eliminate slaveholders, chief benefactors of the American Negro, led him to become an apologist for the institution and eventually to lose his unionist sentiments.[37]

Simms became disillusioned with President Zachary Taylor for not demonstrating goodwill toward the South, and when South Carolina erupted into a controversy in 1850 between secessionists and cooperationists, he felt a need to clarify his political philosophy. A result of that shift was his work of fiction *Southward Ho!*, published in 1854.[38] Although this book was not one of Simms's most successful pieces of

---

[36]Brugger, *Tucker*, 66.

[37]Simms eventually defended slavery in two books: *Slavery in America* (Richmond: T. W. White, 1838) and *The Morals of Slavery* (Charleston, 1852; reprint, New York: Negro Universities Press, 1968).

[38]William Gilmore Simms, *Southward Ho! A Spell of Sunshine* (Chicago: Donohue, Henneberry & Co., 1890). William P. Trent, in *William Gilmore Simms*, American Men of Letters Series (Boston: Houghton Mifflin, 1892; reprint, New York: Greenwood Press, 1969) 209, describes the book as a "dull southern *Decameron.*"

fiction, it is an important document of Southern attitudes just before the war. It consists of a series of tales told by travelers on a ship sailing from New York to South Carolina. The uniting thread of these tales is their criticism of the North. According to one biographer, Simms's motivation for including storytellers from many parts of the South was to promote a spirit of cooperation among the Southern states that would eventually lead to secession.[39]

One of the most intriguing passengers on the ship is a mysterious man whom the passengers eventually discover is an Alabamian. He is "a little shrivelled-up person in striped breeches, with a mouldy yellow visage and green spectacles."[40] Because he always has something witty and cynical to say, his shipmates choose him to be their official orator on the Fourth of July. In a speech equaling William Lloyd Garrison's 1831 oration in the ferocity of its jeremiad rhetoric, the Alabamian points out that Southerners are too prosperous and content to notice the storm breaking around them. He blames extremists in Massachusetts for creating the storm, but he criticizes Southerners for ignoring it. The beasts of Babylon, he says, represent "us poor boobies of America."[41] The South must acknowledge that "There is no peace, no harmony, no union among us.... As a people, we are already sundered.... Until we come back to justice...the breach will widen and widen, until a great gulf shall spread between us, above which Death will hang ever with his black hammer; and across which terror, and strife, and vengeance, shall send their unremitting bolts of alarm and fire!"[42] Before millennial peace can be achieved and the nation can once again be founded on just principles, according to Simms and his narrators, the nation must experience a wide range of apocalyptic horrors.

This passage from Simms illustrates the tendency of Southern writers to identify their opponents with the devil and invoke supernatural aid in overcoming them. Once the association had been made, it was easy to believe the final battle between good and evil was indeed being fought. In the words of the poet St. George Tucker, the Confederacy was battling the "guile of the Puritan demon," and Southerners were encouraged to

---

[39]Jon L. Wakelyn, *The Politics of a Literary Man: William Gilmore Simms*, Contributions in American Studies, No. 5 (Westport CT: Greenwood Press, 1973) 175.

[40]Simms, *Southward Ho!*, 219.

[41]Ibid., 249.

[42]Ibid., 251–52.

join ranks under the "cross of the South" in order to "crush the foul viper neath Liberty's heel."[43] A basic Southern dislike of the Puritan temperament made it easy to believe that this powerful force in the North was associated with the devil. Southern writers did not hesitate to associate their Puritan enemies with Cromwell. Puritans had, according to one writer, been "the pest of all the world, / Since Cromwell's bloody days."[44] Disdain for Puritanism shaped the content of Adalbert Volck's print, "Worship of the North," discussed at the beginning of this chapter.

The connection of the North with Cromwell and the Puritans became virtually an ethnic issue in the South. A poet warned that "the saints of Cromwell rise again, / In sanctimonious hordes," to do battle against "Danish pluck," "Huguenotic will," "Norman grace and chivalry," and "the fiery Celt's impassioned thought." Yankee presumption claimed even the proud South as part of its manifest destiny: "TO SAINTS OF HEAVEN WAS EMPIRE GIVEN, / AND WE, ALONE, ARE SAINTS!" Whereas the South kept most of its blacks enslaved in order to protect and nurture them, the North was forcing Americans to "kneel as slaves, / Till Africans are free!" This behavior cried out for divine retribution, and its arrival was imminent: "Look North—look West—the ominous sky / Is starless, moonless, black, / And from the East comes hurrying up / A sweeping thunder-rack!"[45]

Southerners developed an explanation of the alliance they saw between Puritan fanatics and abolitionist infidels; they were both in league with the devil. The abolitionists, according to this interpretation, were either meddling Puritans or philanthropic freethinkers who imposed their opinions on sovereign states. The Puritans had cultivated their hypocrisy to such an extent, according to Angus McDonald, that they dwelt upon the evils of their enemies—whether the Antichrist, the woman of Babylon, or the "Amalekitish people of Old England." Puritan hearts needed someone to hate, and the generous, large-hearted Southern people had become their target.[46]

---

[43]St. George Tucker, "The Southern Cross," *The Southern Poems of the War*, ed. Mason, 13. (See appendix.)

[44]"Yankee-Doodle-Doo!" *The Southern Soldier's Prize Songster, Containing Martial and Patriotic Pieces* (Mobile AL: W. F. Wisely, 1864) 19. (See appendix.)

[45]Joseph Brennan, "A Ballad for the Young South," *South Songs: from the Lays of Later Days*, ed. Thomas Cooper De Leon (New York: Blalock & Co., 1866) 51–55.

[46]McDonald, *The Two Rebellions*, 25.

The excesses of the abolitionists perfectly suited Puritan fanaticism, according to the rebels. Furthermore, the tendency of the abolitionist movement to reject any Scripture that might be interpreted to support slavery was seized upon as a sign of infidelity. According to the Confederate historian James Williams, abolitionists became infidels by saying that absolute democracy is divinely ordained even though the Bible did not support this concept.[47] Southerners believed they saw a dangerous tendency among fanatical Northerners to rely so much on their individual beliefs that they no longer needed God or the benevolent, hierarchical society he had ordained.

Once their opponents were identified with diabolism, some Southerners proceeded to assign them satanic traits. In this view, because the end of the world was near, Satan was enlarging his forces for the final battle, and he found plenty of recruits in the North and among Southern advocates of compromise. The reason the South was forced to experience the difficulties of war, C. C. Jones, Jr. told his father, was because its inhabitants had diluted their principles years before when Henry Clay led them to two compromises. If the South had "manfully resisted the first aggression," Jones declared, "we might have stifled the serpent in its den."[48]

The combination of the portentous events of the war and the intransigence of the opponent encouraged Confederates to assign apocalyptic significance to their foes. The author of a book purportedly written by a semi-literate ex-slave identified abolitionism as the seven-headed, ten-horned beast of Revelation 13.[49] Thus supporters of slavery and the Southern lifestyle were able to label their opponents as blasphemers while they equated themselves with the persecuted saints at the end of the world.

Southern assurance of the accuracy of such a vision of the future owed much to the region's confidence in biblical literalism. The clouds on the horizon spied by Simms's Fourth of July orator were stirred up by religious renegades in the North who were forsaking Scripture. Since the Old Testament made it clear that slavery existed in Hebrew society and

---

[47]James Williams, *South Vindicated*, 236.

[48]C. C. Jones, Jr. to C. C. Jones, Sr., 28 January 1861, *Children of Pride*, 42.

[49]Harrison Berry, *Slavery and Abolitionism as Viewed by a Georgia Slave* (Atlanta: Franklin Printing House, 1861) 9. This pamphlet was written in response to the Harpers Ferry raid and appeared just before the Southern states seceded.

since the New Testament was ambiguous on the subject, supporters of slavery claimed their reading of Scripture was more reliable than abolitionist hermeneutics. Furthermore, they maintained, abolitionism tended to create agnostics or even atheists who were willing to exalt their radical principles of freedom and equality above Holy Writ.

According to one clergyman, the country was divided into two theories of right and wrong, and the antislavery battle merely represented a larger conflict, which pitted "the liberty of the individual man, of atheism, of Red Republicanism, of the devil" (in the North) against "the liberty of man, in the family, in the State, the liberty from God" (in the South).[50] Southern virtue could be preserved most readily by separation from the North. The decision of Southern states to secede would be defended even in the twentieth century as the only morally responsible choice when the United States became increasingly atheistic and rationalistic. The historian William Sumner Jenkins has pointed out that the biblical defense of slavery was the earliest proslavery argument, giving the South "high ground" upon which to build a moral defense of the institution.[51]

The South reached this plateau because of the intensity of Northern attacks on Southern morals. As Martin Marty has noted, "When people experience moral stigmatizing, they need strong justification for their actions."[52] Much of the Southern literature on slavery is a defensive reaction against Northern attacks. Southern apocalyptic urgency was as great as the Northern abolitionist version, but the Southern form demanded separation from the corrupt North before God's righteous wrath descended on the guilty nation.

Southern defensive anger was directed both at the Northern clergy and at writers such as Harriet Beecher Stowe. In 1861 John B. Thrasher identified envy and hatred against the South as the reasons that "fanatical

---

[50]Ross, *Slavery Ordained of God*, 52.

[51]William Sumner Jenkins, *Pro-Slavery Thought in the Old South* (Chapel Hill: University of North Carolina Press, 1935; reprint, Gloucester MA: Peter Smith, 1960) 206–207. Mark A. Noll has pointed out that although many evangelical Protestants in other countries had rigorous standards of biblical interpretation equal to those practiced by their Southern coreligionists, they had "only contempt for efforts to defend southern slavery on the basis of the Bible." "The Bible and Slavery," *Religion and the American Civil War*, ed. Miller, et al., 52.

[52]Martin Marty, *Righteous Empire: The Protestant Experience in America* (New York: The Dial Press, 1970) 63.

writers in the North" had chosen to "repudiate God's sanction of slavery."[53] James Williams, writing in reaction to the John Brown affair, singled out Harriet Beecher Stowe and Charles Dickens as "professional horror mongers"; they had created "slanders and libels and caricatures" of slavery, incidents that had "no existence, except in the pernicious books referred to."[54] A long narrative poem, titled "The Hireling and the Slave," sought to depict the reality of Southern slavery while it defended the South against the accusations of Harriet Beecher Stowe. The poem reveals the depth of Southern bitterness:

> There Stowe, with prostituted pen, assails
> One half her country in malignant tales;
> Careless, like Trollope, whether truth she tells,
> And anxious only how the libel sells,
> To slander's mart she furnishes supplies
> And feeds its morbid appetite for lies
> On fictions fashioned with malicious art,
> The venal pencil, and malignant heart,
> With fact distorted, inference unsound,
> Creatures in fancy, not in nature found—
> ....
> [Stowe is] a moral scavenger, with greedy eye,
> In social ills her coarser labors lie;
> On fields where vice eludes the light of day,
> She hunts up crimes as beagles hunt their prey.[55]

Harriet Beecher Stowe is portrayed as a typical Yankee whose main concern is making a dollar. She is the antithesis of the ideal woman, and her malice is sufficient to make her a valuable assistant to the diabolical forces in the North.

---

[53]Thrasher, *Slavery a Divine Institution,* 20–21. Thrasher included a number of prominent Northern clergymen, namely "Wayland, Channing, and Barnes, with whom we will connect the name of Dr. Paley," and calls them "either infidels or wilful perverters of holy writ" (21).

[54]James Williams, *Letters on Slavery from the Old World: Written During the Canvass for the Presidency in 1860* (Nashville TN: Southern Methodist Publishing House, 1861) 197.

[55]William John Grayson, *The Hireling and the Slave, Chicora, and Other poems* (Charleston SC: McCarter, 1856) 40–42.

The South was able to develop an offense as well as a defense, however. Because the North had ignored Scripture, went this rationale, the war came down to "a direct antagonism with the authority of Divine Revelation."[56] This topic eventually became the subject for a work of fiction. Ebenezer Warren wrote a novel, *Nellie Warren*, which pits a Northern girl, Nellie, and a Northern pastor, Dr. Daniel Pratt, against Nellie's Southern uncle, Mr. Thompson, in a controversy over the slavery issue. The uncle wins the argument, Dr. Pratt becomes a cowardly chaplain who participates in the debacle at First Manassas, and Nellie accepts the superiority of her uncle's point of view and marries a Southerner. In the process, Warren gives Mr. Thompson an opportunity to explain how the South developed its biblical arguments supporting slavery. It has, Thompson explains, the abolitionists to thank. Many Southerners had believed slavery was wrong until the institution was attacked by abolitionists on moral grounds. "Knowing that the Bible alone was infallible on moral subjects," Thompson explains, Southerners began to search the Scriptures. This process led them to the conviction that slavery is right.[57]

Besides discovering that slavery is scripturally correct, Warren's Southerners also learned something about their opposition. The abolitionists had made antislavery their religion. They preached more sermons against slavery than against "drunkenness, theft, debauchery, or any other sin."[58] Since this religion was antichristian in its treatment of Scripture, says Warren, Southerners easily associated it with the great beast of Revelation.

Slavery also became an explanation of how the horrors of the war would eventually lead to the millennium. According to James Williams, the unity of Southern freemen ensured that the storm clouds would dissipate into millennial peace: "The clouds are over our heads,...and the storm is still raging around us,...but behind the clouds we can...see the dawning of the bright and glorious sunlight."[59] The new world that was to follow the war was one in which racial relationships in the South would

---

[56]David Seth Doggett, *The War and Its Close (On the Occasion of the National Fast)* (Richmond: Enquirer Book and Job Press, 1864) 8.

[57]Ebenezer W. Warren, *Nellie Norton: or Southern Slavery and the Bible* (Macon GA: Burke, Boykin & Co., 1864) 46.

[58]Warren, *Nellie Norton*, 46–47.

[59]James Williams, *The South Vindicated*, 444.

not change. According to E. N. Elliott, the president of a college in Mississippi, the "conflict of civilization with barbarism" warranted the exploitation of inferior races. "Not to go back to former times, it is this precept which has converted the former howling wilderness of this Western World, into an earthly paradise." The natural progress of civilization would roll back and blot out the "mongrel races...to make room for the onward march of a higher civilization."[60] In this view, it was the duty of the superior races to use inferior groups to subdue the earth.

The prospect of millennial bliss enabled Southerners to pursue their positive explanation of slavery. In this line of reasoning, the notion that all men were created equal was unbiblical because true Christian benevolence required an unequal society. Inferiority made possible "the exercise of benevolence and beneficence," and superiority was necessary "for the exercise of love, and the obedience that follows love."[61] Some Southern writers were willing to concede that slavery was an evil, a result of sin, but they maintained that the institution of slavery itself was not a sin. It was, according to William Sumner Jenkins, "the most perfect relation of the races in the South."[62] American slavery was a missionary institution that enabled Africans to learn a better way of life. It also encouraged white masters to increase their unselfishness by looking after their slaves. The Reverend James Henley Thornwell explained the extent of the master's duty: "The souls of our slaves are a solemn trust and we shall strive to present them faultless and complete before the presence of God."[63]

The sense of positive obligation on the part of the white Southerner was providential, according to the Reverend George D. Armstrong, pastor of the Presbyterian church in Norfolk, Virginia. He tied the Southern victory at the first battle of Manassas directly to the slavery issue. Southerners had to fight, he said, because the safety, as well as the "very existence" of the "dependent race" required the protection of its masters. He had begun warning his parishioners of the issues at stake even before the war began. "I did not see," he said, "how we, as honest,

---

[60]E. N. Elliott, "Slavery in the Light of International Law," *Cotton is King*, 732.

[61]*Introduction to a History of the Second American War for Independence or the Civil War in the United States* (Confederate States of America: n. p., June 1863) 25.

[62]Jenkins, *Old South*, 215.

[63]James Henley Thornwell, *The Rights and Duties of Masters* (Charleston: Walker & James, 1850) 541, as quoted in Jenkins, *Old South*, 215.

Christian men, could answer to God for our act, did we surrender one iota of this control [over our slaves]."[64]

Protecting and evangelizing the slaves both signaled the end of the world and hastened its approach. According to Bishop Stephen Elliott, the evangelization of the slaves marked one effort by the Almighty to accomplish "the regeneration of a fallen world." When the gospel was preached to every creature on every continent, "as a witness to all the world, then will the end come, and Christ shall be set upon his Holy Hill of Zion."[65] The best divine instruments to evangelize the untouched corners of Africa were the Christianized slaves from the American South. Defending this purpose against the aggressions of an ungodly North was holy war.

Masters felt confident they understood what their slaves thought of this arrangement. They could point out that the slaves remained relatively docile during the war, failing to foment the mass revolts some had predicted. The slaves, "heretofore supposed to be the most dangerous part of society," have remained calm and hardworking, "laboring for the sustenance of those whom they hear denounced as their enemies, contented, cheerful, docile and affectionate."[66] Bishop Elliott echoed this conviction by pointing to the slave as the assurance that the South would ultimately succeed in the war: "God will not permit his purposes to be overthrown.... He has caused the African race to be planted here under our political protection and under our Christian nurture."[67] Perhaps, Elliott suggested in an allusion with perhaps inadvertent irony, God had even loftier plans for the slaves. His chosen people, the Hebrews, had after all been slaves for four hundred years, "until they were disciplined to go forth and become a nation among nations."[68]

William Gilmore Simms maintained that slavery rescued Negroes from cannibalism and gave them "fecundity," increased "health and

---

[64]George D. Armstrong, *The Good Hand of Our God Upon Us: A Thanksgiving Sermon, Preached on Occasion of the Victory of Manassas, July 21st, 1861* (Norfolk: J. D. Gillselin, Jr., 1861) 10.

[65]Stephen Elliott, *Our Cause in Harmony with the Purposes of God in Christ Jesus* (Savannah: John M. Cooper, 1862) 8.

[66]Rev. C. H. Wiley, *Scriptural Views of National Trials: or the True Road to the Independence and Peace of the CSA* (Greensboro NC: Sterling, Campbell & Albright, 1863) 199.

[67]Elliott, *Our Cause*, 10.

[68]Ibid., 10.

strength," improved "physical symmetry and animal organization," elevated morality, and extended the life span. These points demonstrated the morality of the institution of slavery, according to Simms. They also proved that the Negro was placed in Southern white hands by Providence, for his good. The whites' reward: Providence "has paid us from his labor for our guardianship."[69]

Supernatural wisdom also explained the difference between the red man and the black man. Bishop Elliott explained that African slavery in America "had its origin in an act of mercy." Negro slavery was undertaken "to save the Indian from a toil which was destroying him." Invoking a metaphor of Christ almost reminiscent of Uncle Tom, Elliott pointed out that "while the Indian has perished, the substitute who was brought to die in his place, has lived, prospered and multiplied."[70] In the opinion of another Southern writer, that fact spoke well of Christian slaveowners, who acknowledged their "solemn duty" to consider themselves missionaries to their slaves.[71]

The duty of bringing Christianity to the slaves weighed heavily on the minds of many Southern Christians, who recognized that slaveowners were perhaps the only avenue of bringing the gospel to their slaves. The Reverend Charles Colcock Jones, Sr. had devoted much of his ministry to evangelizing slaves, and after the war began he reminded the Confederacy of its responsibility: "None can come in from abroad to relieve us. The negroes of the Confederate States are thrown entirely upon the care of the churches...within those States."[72] If the North prevailed and the slaves were freed, their souls would be in danger. James Williams maintained that the brand of racism practiced by a victorious North would be crueler to Negroes than the benevolent Southern system had been. While neither the independence of the South nor its subjugation would put an end to slavery, Williams maintained that the latter would enslave the white race and leave the condition of the black race unchanged—except, indeed, that the Negro would pass from the dominion of those who treat him kindly to the dominion of those who would, but for his labor value, deny

---

[69]Simms, *Slavery in America*, 83.

[70]Elliott, *Our Cause*, 12. This was a sermon given on Thursday, 18 September 1862, the day after Lee's defeat at Antietam.

[71]Wiley, *Scriptural Views*, 196.

[72]Charles Colcock Jones, Sr., *Religious Instruction of the Negroes* (Richmond: Presbyterian Committee of Publication, [1862?]), 25.

him a home and a country; who mock him with the name of brother and treat him as a reptile.[73] Such stereotyping was one way of pointing out an uncomfortable reality about the North. Within their own literature, Northerners struggled with the discrepancy between the idealistic impulse to achieve racial justice and the realities of Northern racism.

Because prewar verbal attacks on Southern institutions had been extremely condemnatory, the South countered with an equally strong defensive reaction that left little room for self-criticism. The South had to assure itself first that its beliefs were correct, and therefore it developed an extraordinarily literal interpretation of the Bible. Ironclad exegesis quickly led to a polarization of the United States that pitted absolute good against absolute evil and made it possible for the South to identify its conflict with Armageddon. Southern writers used the devices of creative writing to transform abstractions into immediate realities, thereby increasing enthusiasm for the war's early battles. Much of this literature predicts a rapid progression of wartime events to a satisfactory resolution in the millennium.

---

[73]Williams, *South Vindicated*, xviii.

4

HOLY WAR–ANTIETAM AND THE EMANCIPATION PROCLAMATION

On 15 April 1861, the day after Major Robert Anderson surrendered Fort Sumter to the Confederates, President Lincoln called up 75,000 state militia for ninety days and took steps to defend Washington, DC. The Confederates interpreted Lincoln's move as an act of aggression. Most Northerners saw it as an occasion for patriotism, whatever they thought of abolition, slavery in the territories, or the other prewar strains between North and South. A typical response to Lincoln's call for troops was a print published by Kimmel and Forster in New York, titled "The Outbreak of the Rebellion in the United States 1861" (Figure 5).[1] The print documents two Southern sins, secession, and slavery. Two allegorical figures, Justice and Liberty, stand at the center underneath the American eagle. Liberty steps forward onto a set of broken shackles and a cat o'nine tails, while Justice aims her unsheathed sword at a hissing, crowned serpent wrapped around a palmetto tree, symbol of the rebellion in South Carolina. At the feet of these two central figures is a widening crack in the earth representing secession. James Buchanan slumbers near the abyss while John Floyd, Buchanan's secretary of war and later a Confederate general, scoops government money into a bag. (Floyd's actions in late 1860 aided Confederate seizure of government fortifications.)

Underneath the hissing snake and palmetto tree stand Alexander Stephens and Jefferson Davis, who are handing a mutilated United States flag to a mob. Davis points to Fort Sumter in the background, where lines of troops have formed nearby. The left, or Southern, side of the print is all storm and chaos, filled with clamoring, desperate-looking men. The right side of the print pictures the North. Abraham Lincoln, accom-

---

[1]Courtesy of the Library of Congress.

panied by General Winfield Scott, stands next to Liberty. Men gather at their feet to give money, weapons, and military service to their country. Women and children (who are missing from the Southern side) look sorrowful but acquiescent. In the background a group of civilians is being exhorted to join the military, and behind them lies a river flanked by large buildings and factories, symbols of peaceful prosperity. On the other side of the river is a set of rugged mountains with the sun setting behind them. This part of the illustration apparently bestows the concept of "westward the course of empire takes its way" on the North. It may also be referring to the expectation that the western states and territories would remain loyal to the North.

Combatants on both sides during the Civil War tended to polarize the situation into a conflict between absolute good and absolute evil, a trait very apparent in this print. It creates a sense of unity and harmony on the right side, while discord, strife, and incompetence rule the left, due to the inspiration of the Prince of Darkness. Supernatural involvement is apparent on both sides, since Liberty points to heaven and Justice deals with the devil or his representative. In this view, mortal armies will not be the only combatants in the upcoming war.

While not explicitly biblical, the allegorical figures in this print share the mixture of foreboding and hope that permeated conventional apocalyptic references. During the war a significant group of writers, theologians, and politicians in the North employed apocalyptic imagery in their responses to the war. Although there were numerous totally secular interpretations of the conflict, the strife invited the creation of a religious myth to support the war effort. The predominant religious interpretation in the North linked the military affairs of the war with the status of slavery. When the Lincoln administration timed the announcement of the Emancipation Proclamation to coincide with military success at Antietam in September 1862, it became easier than ever to believe that the war's outcome depended on the slavery issue. This belief pervades poetry and sermon literature of the period, and it was a popular theme of prints and political cartoons.

In a sense, the Civil War for the North was a holy war like every holy war any country has ever fought. A religious nation faced a great crisis, its citizens read in Scripture that holy nations would face great crises, and they invested the issues of the war with eternal significance. The Civil War, however, held additional meaning for the North. As Ernest Lee

Tuveson has pointed out, its events supported a long-established pattern of belief indicating that the United States would play a central role in the apocalypse.[2] The English-speaking people of North America saw themselves as the spiritual antitype of biblical Israel even before they became a nation. Since the United States was populated by a diverse group of immigrants, it was a microcosm of the globe and a logical location for events of worldwide significance.

The extent of this belief is illustrated in the work of Henry Howard Brownell, a Northern journalist and poet. Focusing on the crucial months after Abraham Lincoln's election, Brownell wrote a poem, "Annus Memorabilis," describing the US Congress in 1860 and 1861. He predicts the coming conflict will be fought on the familiar battleground between Right and Wrong, in the midst of a "tempest that shall try if we are of God or no." Its purposes will reach far beyond temporal politics, and it will be "not a war of men, but of Angels Good and Ill." He compares the American conflict to the meeting of Michael and the Dragon described in Revelation: "But we all have read, (in that Legend grand and dread,) / How Michael and his host met the Serpent and his crew." The nature of the struggle has been left to the imagination in the biblical account "(Calm as dew the Apocalyptic Pen)," but the nation can look forward to a destruction of evil as complete as that described by Revelation.[3]

The divinely sanctioned role of the United States in its battles was unquestioned by many Northerners. This assurance explained both victories and defeats; victories indicated that God had enabled His side to win, and defeats meant that God needed to teach his people a lesson. Since God's battles were fought on the moral level, he could not allow his people to win while they harbored sin. They must be purged of their evil in order to achieve military success. Such reasoning led Northerners to hold that their national sins were responsible for early defeats. The fact that slavery continued unmolested during the first part of the war produced great moral uneasiness in the North. This most obvious of sins was one cause of their setbacks, many reasoned. Temporary defeat would compel the North to identify and overcome its sins, which would then

---

[2]Tuveson, *Redeemer Nation,* 195–96.

[3]Henry Howard Brownell, "Annus Memorabilis," *Lines of Battle* (Boston: Houghton Mifflin, 1912) 56–58. (See appendix.)

enable it to win the war, destroy the forces of evil forever, and usher the rest of the world into the millennium.

Religious thinkers in the North identified the conflict with apocalyptic events even before the beginning of hostilities. On 4 January 1861, as Southern states discussed following South Carolina out of the Union, the nation's churches observed a day of fasting and prayer. A Lutheran pastor in Philadelphia, Joseph Seiss, commented on the revolutionary implications of these events. A new order was developing, and both governments and other institutions would be "shaken and greatly changed, if not wholly dissolved."[4] Spiritual Babylon, which Seiss associated with hierarchies throughout the world, must collapse because it had mistreated God's people. According to Seiss, the disruption was a result of general corruption rather than specific sins. Such extensive evil could only mean that prophecies predicting the end of the world were being fulfilled.

The Babylon metaphor also appeared in visual responses to events. A Currier and Ives print, probably produced in 1862 at the outset of the Peninsula Campaign, shows an alarmed Jefferson Davis reading a warning message on the wall, while startled legislators in the background prepare to flee (Figure 6).[5] Distressed by the prophecy of imminent Northern victory, Davis blurts out a threat to perceived enemies, including John Minor Botts.[6] The artist creates the impression that Southerners were driven to desperate measures because their defeat was imminent. The act of identifying Davis with Belshazzar and the South with Babylon also indicates Northern confidence in the significance of its battles.

Some Northern Christians were already practiced at seeing such events as clear signals that biblical apocalyptic prophecy was being fulfilled to the letter. George Barrell Cheever had foreseen these results in 1841 when he noted that the "lines of prophecy" were converging, indicating "some mighty consummation."[7] One wartime commentator, C. Bowen, was able to ascribe contemporary meaning to virtually every

---

[4]Joseph Augustus Seiss, *The Threatening Ruin: or, Our Times* (Philadelphia: Lutheran Publishing House, 1861) 31.

[5]Used by permission of the Henry E. Huntington Library, San Marino, CA.

[6]Botts, an avowed neutral, was arrested in Richmond for treason against the Confederacy on 1 March 1862. See Botts, *The Great Rebellion: Its Secret History* (New York: Harper and Brothers, 1866).

[7]George Barrell Cheever, *God's Hand in America* (New York: M. W. Dodd, 1841) 129.

apocalyptic passage in the Bible. To Bowen, Daniel and Revelation were direct predictions of the activities of the United States and its "counterfeit presentiment, the slave power of the Southern Confederacy."[8] Bowen referred to the "fervent heat," "great noise," and melting elements of the apocalypse as "sublime events" performed in the theaters of battle in the United States. The American government would become the "foundation of Christ's kingdom of heaven."[9] It earned this distinction by being located at the literal end of the earth, the final stop in the westward spread of Christianity. All nations, as represented by the immigrant population of the United States, had gathered in one location to be judged on their fitness for Christ's kingdom.[10] Bowen was able to compare prominent individuals and events of his day with horned beasts, time prophecies, and even characters in the book of Job. His explanation that the revolting horrors of the war signaled sublime events was calculated to elicit a response of fascinated terror from his audience. Similar rhetoric also provided energy for sustaining the war through months of Northern defeat.

The North could find reassurance in the conflagration of civil war because of its knowledge that the conflict was "to purify our country as if by fire," as Massachusetts minister George Ellis informed his congregation when the war broke out.[11] Just after the war ended, a former chaplain of the Second Massachusetts Infantry, the Reverend Alonzo Quint, looked back to the initial months of the war. It was still possible for him to describe that period in sublime terms: "There brooded over our country clouds of divine wrath. The air grew heavy. It seemed hard to breathe. The blackness grew fearfully. Then the heavy roll of the thunder crashed. Then the forked lightning played. Tempests howled, and fire struck, and the track of the fierce storm ploughed furrows of wrath."[12] Quint's sermon illustrates the tendency of clergymen to resort to the use of sublime imagery, which provided an appropriate vocabulary for explaining the upheavals of the war. (See chapter 1.) The Reverend

---

[8]Bowen, *Bible*, title page.

[9]Ibid., 65.

[10]Ibid., 6.

[11]George Edward Ellis, "Our Civil War: A Discourse Delivered in Harvard Church April 28, 1861," *Bunker Hill Aurora*, 11 May 1864, 1.

[12]Alonzo Hall Quint, *National Sin Must Be Expiated by National Calamity* (New Bedford: Mercury Press, 1865) 10.

Herrick Johnson associated these events with the shaking of nations that the Old Testament prophet Haggai predicted would take place just before the advent of the Messiah.[13] The North's struggles are great, according to Johnson, because its real foe, the devil, requires "signal and mighty powers" to dispossess him of "his kingdom and sovereignty."[14] The Civil War, then, was not just a conflict between two quarreling groups of people; it was a battleground for the legions of God and the devil in the struggle for control of the world and ultimately the universe.

Although Northern writers sometimes wrote about the approaching war in tones of triumph similar to those that pervaded so much Southern literature, they were more likely to predict that doom, God's wrath, and divine judgment would temporarily overwhelm them before their cause eventually triumphed. The military reverses experienced by the North during the early part of the war supplied at least a partial explanation of this rhetoric. Another possible cause for the pessimism is the strength of the jeremiad tradition in the North: The expectation that God's people must experience a time of testing and tribulation before they were ready to assume their leading role in the millennium had been preached from Puritan pulpits for two hundred years. Now that the war had come it was inevitably invested with significance. As the Reverend George Ellis told his congregation, "each war is for a higher and nobler stake."[15]

Occasionally a Northern writer would point to the enemy as the supreme villain and target of God's wrath. Frederick Henry Hedge, for example, told a Congregational audience that the North must "either kill the serpent Secession, or disfang and disable it for future harms."[16] More frequently, however, Northern writers tended to be preoccupied with the enemy within. Even after some military successes, Nathan Sydney Smith Beman told his congregation during a Thanksgiving day sermon, the brilliant light that had once settled over America had been replaced by "a preternatural midnight, in the early evening."[17] The reason for the sense of gloom perceived by so many, James Freeman Clarke explained, was

---

[13]See Haggai 2:6, 7. Nineteenth-century commentators readily applied passages such as this one to the Second Coming.

[14]Herrick Johnson, *The Shaking of the Nations* (Pittsburgh: W. S. Haven, 1864) 10.

[15]Ellis, "Our Civil War," 1.

[16]Frederick Henry Hedge, *The National Entail* (Boston: Wright & Potter, 1864) 17.

[17]Nathan Sydney Smith Beman, *Our Civil War: The Principles Involved, Its Cause and Cure* (Troy NY: W. W. Scribner, 1863) 9.

that the war was a "judgment" and was "full of God's judgments."[18] Clarke believed it was appropriate to assume divine involvement in a war when a law of God was clearly at stake. Frederick Henry Hedge invested governments with the same accountability experienced by individuals; he declared that "a people can no more escape retribution in their national destiny than an individual can escape it in his individual destiny."[19]

Although the jeremiads of the opening days of the war frequently cited selfishness or avarice as punishable sins, slavery eventually emerged as the primary offense. George B. Cheever identified it as the most significant crime of the nation shortly before the war began. He said that "the deep damnation of our guilt" lay in stealing slave children from their parents and from God. The country was "a nation of menstealers" masquerading as missionaries.[20] John Smith Dye, a hyperbolic historian, believed that slavery was an "unpardonable sin against human nature [and] our great national sin against the Holy Ghost."[21] Dye's comment was directed against the South, but many Northerners were willing to assign part of the guilt of slavery to their own region, since it had allowed the institution to exist. Cheever saw a parallel between the United States in the mid-nineteenth century and the Hebrews during the time of Jeremiah, whose deliberate establishment of slavery resulted in "the wrath of God coming down upon the whole land and people without remedy."[22] Even after several defeats and the victory at Antietam, Nathan Beman told his congregation that "we have not been sufficiently chastized as a nation." The North was accessory to the "great sin of the republic—oppression" and must expect to be scourged by God out of many sins, including slavery.[23] These views were not restricted to orthodox Protestant faiths. Shortly after the first battle of Manassas, Emma Hardinge, a spiritualist speaker, told her audience that America would not achieve its goals "so long as broken hearts and clanking chains, whether of gold or

---

[18]James Freeman Clarke, *Discourse on the Aspects of the War* (Boston: Walker, Wise, & Co., 1863) 12.

[19]Hedge, *National Entail,* 13.

[20]George B. Cheever, *The Sin of Slavery, the Guilt of the Church, and the Duty of the Ministry* (Boston: John P. Jewett & Co., 1858) 8.

[21]John Smith Dye, *The Great Conspiracy,* 11.

[22]George Barrell Cheever, *God Against Slavery: and the Freedom and Duty of the Pulpit to Rebuke It, as a Sin Against God* (Cincinnati: Am. Reform Tract and Book Society, [1857]) 36.

[23]Beman, *Our Civil War,* 34.

iron, drag her down. If you Americans have not within yourselves the principle of courage to break down those fetters, thank your God—his own right hand has done it for you, even with the dreadful sword of civil war."[24]

This preoccupation from a varied host of preachers and writers explains both the motivation that produced "The Battle Hymn of the Republic" and the enthusiastic popular response to the song.[25] When Julia Ward Howe accompanied her husband, Sanitary Commission member Dr. Samuel Gridley Howe, to a grand review of McClellan's troops on 18 November 1861, the ceremonies were interrupted by a Confederate skirmish. Soldiers and civilians alike were forced to beat a hasty and somewhat ignominious retreat from Munson's Hill, Virginia, to the capital in what must have been reminiscent of the retreat from the Manassas battlefield a few months earlier. This trip, however, was more tedious than frightening, and the Howes, their minister, James Freeman Clarke, and Massachusetts governor John Andrew and his wife passed the carriage ride singing marching songs, concluding with "John Brown's Body." As Julia Ward Howe later described the event, "The soldiers seemed to like this, and answered back, "good for you!" Mr. Clarke said, "Mrs. Howe, why do you not write some good words for that stirring tune?" I replied that I had often wished to do this, but had not as yet found in my mind any leading toward it."[26] By the wee hours of the next morning, Howe's mind must have been working on the poem on both conscious and subconscious levels, because she found herself awake early in the morning, and "as I lay waiting for the dawn, the long lines of the desired poem began to twine themselves in my mind. Having thought out all the stanzas, I said to myself, 'I must get up and write these verses down, lest I fall asleep again and forget them.' So, with a sudden effort, I sprang out of bed, and found in the dimness an old stump of a pen which

---

[24]Emma Hardinge, *America and Her Destiny: Inspirational Discourse Through E. M., by the Spirits*, August 25, 1861 (New York: Robert M. DeWitt, 1863) 14–15.

[25]Detailed explications of the "Battle Hymn" may be found in Wilson, *Patriotic Gore*, 91–98; Tuveson, *Redeemer Nation*, 197–202; Deborah Pickman Clifford, *Mine Eyes Have Seen the Glory* (Boston: Little Brown, 1979) 138–47; Mary H. Grant, *Private Woman, Public Person: An Account of the Life of Julia Ward Howe from 1819 to 1868* (New York: Carlson Publishing, 1994) 139–211; and Edward D. Snyder, "The Biblical Background of the 'Battle Hymn of the Republic,'" *New England Quarterly* 24/2 (1951): 231–38.

[26]Julia Ward Howe, *Reminiscences 1819–1899* (Boston: Houghton Mifflin, 1900) 274–75.

I remembered to have used the day before."[27] What Howe did was borrow the tune of a popular marching song, which had been lifted in turn from a revivalist hymn, and replace its popular but undistinguished lyrics with a powerful poem about The Day of Jehovah, as described in the prophetic books of the Old Testament and in Revelation.[28]

Howe transformed the massive military buildup she had witnessed around Washington, DC into a description of the holy war that was to precede the millennium. The images were obviously familiar to her and to her audience, and the majority of them are taken from Scripture. Howe was intimately acquainted with traditional interpretations of the Apocalypse. She refers to the Second Coming in her first line: "Mine eyes have seen the glory of the coming of the Lord."[29] The consciously archaic "mine" recalls King James English and provides an emphatic entrance to the writer's eyewitness viewpoint. The coming of the Lord is not an event in the distant future; it is being reported by an eyewitness. This line sets the tone of emphatic certainty that gives the poem its power. "He is trampling out the vintage where the grapes of wrath are stored; / He hath loosed the fateful lightning of His terrible swift sword." The harvest imagery of the wine press, drawn from Revelation 14:20, indicates a sense of completion; the foe no longer deserves mercy and is now being subjected to the wrath of God, which is being squeezed out, concentrated, and intensified, and which results in the destruction of nations by the two-edged sword (analogous to the harvester's sickle of Rev 14:14) that comes out of the mouth of God (Rev 19:15). The full fury of God expressed in these images could only descend upon a foe whose cup of iniquity was full, whose harvest of sin was ripe, and who was thoroughly evil. The implacable rhythm of the final line describes a God who will not be turned back by mercy: "His truth is marching on."

The next stanza describes the holy warriors who participate in the world's last battle, which Howe identifies with the coming of the Lord: "I have seen Him in the watch-fires of a hundred circling camps; / They

---

[27]Ibid., 274–75.

[28]Louise Hall Tharp, "The Song that Wrote Itself," *American Heritage* 8/1 (December 1956): 11. Tharp states that the music was composed by a Southerner, William Steffe, about ten years earlier. Originally, it was a camp meeting hymn entitled "Say Brothers Will We Meet You Over on the Other Shore?" Snyder, "Battle Hymn," 233.

[29]Julia Ward Howe, "The Battle Hymn of the Republic," *The Atlantic Monthly* 9 (February 1862) 1. (See appendix.) This version differs slightly from Howe's original poem. The *Atlantic* version is the one that became widely known during the war.

have builded Him an altar in the evening dews and damps; / I can read
His righteous sentence by the dim and flaring lamps: / His day is
marching on." The image of the first line reflects the scenes Howe
witnessed when her train approached Washington in the evening. It may
have also reminded her of the biblical reference to the battle against Gog
and Magog, signaling a tendency to combine Armageddon and the last
battle.[30] The righteous army has built an altar to their Lord, which implies
not only devotion and worship but sacrifice as well. The righteous soldier
must be willing to lay down his life for his country's cause.

God has given his army a righteous sentence to administer. How
they will accomplish that feat is spelled out in the following verse: "I have
read a fiery gospel writ in burnished rows of steel: / 'As ye deal with my
contemners, so with you my grace shall deal; / Let the Hero, born of
woman, crush the serpent with his heel, / Since God is marching on.'"
The "fiery gospel" of the first line is certainly not the good news of
salvation. Rather, it is the grim reality of the punishment that awaits
those who have rejected God's plan and have, apparently, committed the
unpardonable sin. The rows of gleaming bayonets and polished rifle
barrels will enforce the sentence, and the intensity with which the soldiers
wield their weapons will be rewarded with reciprocal portions of God's
grace. Although the Savior of Genesis 3:15 was to bruise the head of the
serpent, or Satan, here he will crush it. (The image of the Lord or his
representative crushing a dragon or serpent pervaded Northern drawings
during the war.)

The fourth stanza adds the element of judgment (only implied
before) to the references to ritual cleansing. "He has sounded forth the
trumpet that shall never call retreat; / He is sifting out the hearts of men
before His judgment-seat: / Oh, be swift, my soul, to answer Him! be
jubilant, my feet! / Our God is marching on." The inexorability of the
first line echoes the sentiment of the short lines that close each stanza and
reminds the audience of the terrible finality of this battle. Eternal destiny
will be decided here. Symbolic of that irreversible decision is the reference
to the judgment in the second line. The sifting or shaking process will
separate the righteous and the sinners, and the separation is eternal.

When the reader reaches the third line of the fourth stanza, the eager
response is a foregone conclusion. The punishment of God's enemies has

---

[30]Tuveson, *Redeemer Nation,* 202.

been described graphically even before the details of the judgment are spelled out. The extreme opposites of good and evil have been defined, and the righteous soldier will not hesitate to enlist. "Our God is marching on," and he will not wait for stragglers.

The final stanza may appear to signal a significant change of mood: "In the beauty of the lilies Christ was born across the sea, / With a glory in his bosom that transfigures you and me: / As he died to make men holy, let us die to make men free, / While God is marching on." This is the only reference to Christ the Savior as opposed to the judge and disciplinarian. It might be possible to create a clear division between the wrathful Old Testament deity of the first four stanzas and the gentle Jesus of the final stanza, except for the fact that the Hero, born of woman, crushed the serpent in the third stanza.[31] The reference to "glory" in line 2 provides a link with the first stanza, but whereas the initial use of the word implies the sublime, even terrible effect of the Day of Jehovah, the final "glory" seems to describe the transfiguration of the righteous army to a godlike appearance. The final stanza does refer to the crucifixion, but the interpretation is a stern, Calvinist one: Christ died to make men *holy*. He provided the transfiguring glory that creates the sharp contrast between the forces of good and evil described in the poem. The end of that third line alludes to Christ's sacrifice and also to the army's sacrifice mentioned in the second stanza. The death of Christ "to make men holy" is analogous to the death of some of the righteous army "to make men free," and here lies the key to the conflict for many Northerners by the time they read this poem in early 1862; the Civil War had become a holy battle to eliminate slavery. In their eyes, the conflict provided the final sorting, the complete delineation between good and evil, and the opportunity to make a Christlike sacrifice that would wipe out the last, largest sin and enable the millennium to begin.

A study of nineteenth-century revivalism in America explains the pervasiveness of the poem's apocalyptic imagery and demonstrates broad public familiarity with its language.[32] On this occasion, however, the

---

[31]The third stanza shows that Christ is not just the "effeminate," "remote" figure dismissed by Edmund Wilson in *Patriotic Gore*, 96.

[32]See Whitney Cross, *The Burned-Over District: the Social and Intellectual History of Enthusiastic Religion in Western New York 1800–1850* (Ithaca: Cornell University Press, 1950); Timothy Smith, *Revivalism and Social Reform in Mid-Nineteenth Century America*

darkly Calvinistic images in the "Battle Hymn" flowed from the pen of an "advanced thinker," a reformer who believed in humanistic progress, a parishioner of Theodore Parker and James Freeman Clarke, and a friend of Ralph Waldo Emerson. The fact that Julia Ward Howe turned to these "old grim ideas of a cosmic war of good and evil," says Ernest Lee Tuveson, "shows how deeply such ideas have penetrated the national mind."[33]

One critic sees a regressive tendency in this retreat to familiar old images: "Julia, like so many liberal Christians, had reverted to the stern evangelical creed of her childhood."[34] Another reason could also explain her unexpected vocabulary, however: Transcendentalist doctrine made no provision for dealing with a wrenching national calamity such as the Civil War. It was not part of the stately vision of human progress that had appealed to New England intellectuals. The war came, and the war had to be explained. Julia Ward Howe could interpret the war most readily by relying on the familiar apocalyptic imagery of her Calvinist upbringing and the references to the Day of Judgment in the Bible she read daily.[35]

The Northern public during the Civil War was not concerned with whether Julia Ward Howe's lyrics matched her ideology. They did appreciate the fact that the words read the national mood. The existing popularity of the "John Brown's Body" melody and the stirring, patriotic strains of her poetry invited mass adoption of the song as a battle anthem and eventually resulted in the sincerest form of flattery.

A song imitating the style of the "Battle Hymn" but lapsing into "sweet promises," "soft leaves," and "birds...jubilant...within their lofty

---

(New York: Abingdon Press, 1957); and Cushing Strout, *The New Heavens and the New Earth: Political Religion in America* (New York: Harper & Row, 1974).

[33]*Redeemer Nation*, 198.

[34]Clifford, *Mine Eyes Have Seen the Glory*, 146.

[35]Years later, near the end of her life, Howe reconciled her belief in the nation's material and moral progress with her religious roots. After her religious odyssey from "Puritan belief" to Swedenborg, Parker, the Boston Radical Club, Frank Abbot, Jesus, and Socrates, she confessed, "I must say that the earliest view is that which I hold to most, that, namely, of the heavenly Being whose presence was beneficence, whose word was judgment, whose brief career on earth ended in a sacrifice, whose purity and pathos have had much to do with the redemption of the human race from barbarism and the rule of the animal passions" (*Reminiscences*, 208). Provided that her use of the term "judgment" can stretch far enough to accommodate the severe imagery of the poem, her statement meshes with the "Battle Hymn" rather well. The contrast between the general belief and the actual poem, however, remains startling.

towers," managed to capture some of Howe's fervor in the title and the first stanza:

> The day our fathers waited for is dawning on us now;
> I see the mantle falling on the prophet at the plough;
> I hear the trumpet ringing where the victors strike the blow,
> Our men are marching on.
> Glory, glory, Hallelujah, glory, glory Hallelujah,
> Glory, glory, Hallelujah,
> Our men are marching on.[36]

The lyrics of both the "Battle Hymn" and "Our Men are Marching On" reveal the tension between the reality of present violence and the promise of future peace and progress. Doomsday rhetoric fit the war situation, and its urgency provided motivation to action.

Howe's song inspired Union troops, who soon devised a number of variations. Soldiers in Arkansas admired the song, and eventually they produced two military versions of their own, one for the freemen and one for the blacks. Both songs express the confidence that the combatants are fighting on God's side of the war, and the black version particularly indicates that its soldiers are holy warriors.[37]

The popularity of the "Battle Hymn" broadened the Northern audience who made a connection between the war and slavery. It became commonplace to associate the institution with the military setbacks of 1861 and early 1862. The Reverend E. Davies, a Methodist clergyman, paralleled the Civil War with the plagues of Egypt and associated it with the last plagues of Revelation. Since the world had outlived the age of miracles, he stated, God would not turn rivers into blood or cover the land with frogs, "but we have not outlived the government of a just God, who punishes nations in this world, seeing they cannot be punished in the world to come." Because the entire nation had participated in the sin of slavery, "the sum of all villainies," God had sent the "awful war," and

---

[36]"Our Men are Marching On," *Encyclopedia of Popular Songs* (New York: Dick & Fitzgerald, 1864) 68–69. (See appendix.)

[37]Lieut.-Col. A. W. Bishop, "Arkansian Battle-Hymn," *Songs of the Soldiers*, ed. Moore, 182–84; Captain Lindley Miller, "Marching Song of the First Arkansas," *Songs of the Soldiers*, ed. Moore, 206–208. (See appendix.)

"for this cause he has suffered the Union army to be repulsed again and again."[38]

Deep, intangible explanations for the conflict were the key to the identification of hidden reasons for military setbacks. Union defeats, according to Moncure Daniel Conway, were not the fault of Union generals. Rather, the American nation, a "drugged sleeper," was slumbering through the dying appeals that liberty was making "to watch with me one hour."[39] Conway even assigned specific slave-related causes to specific losses. He believed that the US had lost the first battle of Manassas "chiefly because General McDowell's colorphobia must cut off the Negro's hope, and with it his own only sources of information."[40] General McDowell, by refusing to protect runaway slaves, was also losing a prime source of military intelligence.

Northern writers who opposed slavery believed the United States would continue to suffer defeats until it recognized that sin, particularly the sin of slavery, underlay national misfortune. Repentance and reformation must then follow. Decades of compromise and conservatism needed to be overthrown, wrote the Reverend E. S. Stanley, and since a moral law had been broken, a moral adjustment must be made. He called for both "personal and national repentance" for the sin of slavery, the "cause of our sorrow," and assured that its annihilation would bring victory. Long before the federal government acknowledged that slavery was partly a military issue and therefore must be addressed, the clergy was calling for official repentance. In an 1861 sermon, the Reverend Henry D. Moore, a Congregational minister who served as a chaplain with the 13th Maine Regiment, identified slavery as the national sin and civil strife as God's dispensation of punishment.[41] Underneath the sense of outrage that a Christian nation could tolerate slavery is a layer of optimism typical of Northern antislavery commentary. It follows the pattern of jeremiad rhetoric by promising rewards for a turnaround in behavior. Moore speculates what would happen to the nation if Abraham

---

[38]E. Davies, "Watchman, What of the Night?" *Zion's Herald and Wesleyan Journal* (22 April 1863): 1.

[39]Moncure Daniel Conway, "The Golden Hour," *Addresses and Reprints*, 154.

[40]Moncure Daniel Conway, *The Rejected Stone, or Insurrection vs. Resurrection in America* (Boston: Walker, Wise & Co., 1862) 55.

[41]Henry D. Moore, *Our Country—Its Sin and Its Duty* (Portland ME: H. Packard, 1861) 18.

Lincoln would closet himself with God and spend a day fasting and praying and then lay before his cabinet a document freeing slaves. He asks, "Would not that meet with a shout coming up from the length and the breadth of the land, as the sound of many waters; and would not the great conscience of the country heave with the emotions of joy, because the danger was past, the duty done, and the glory of the nation spread to the ends of the earth without a stain upon its purity?"[42] Repentance is essential in this line of reasoning, because once national sins were renounced and forsaken, the country could expect to prosper and to win battles. Moore implies that the nation has the capacity to forsake its sins and to provide a perfect example to the rest of the world.

The idealism of emancipation activists regularly outpaced the pragmatism of the federal government. Because the nations of the world had delayed so long in addressing slavery, declared Henry Ward Beecher, "God is pouring out the vial of his wrath," and any nation that had helped to perpetuate slavery would suffer the effects.[43] Before the war began, Beecher had been optimistic about the nation's ability to see the evils of slavery and to eliminate the institution. He had seen "a nobler spirit" arising, and he fully expected the slavery issue to be resolved short of warfare.[44] Once the war was underway, however, Beecher predicted that military requirements would force emancipation, not as a political (or presumably moral) act, but as a military necessity.[45] By this time Beecher seems to have accepted the possibility that moral issues might be resolved for pragmatic reasons.

Supporters of emancipation did not expect the war to be resolved until the government decided to eliminate slavery. Efforts to destroy secession and to preserve the union at all costs would fail, said these individuals, unless the nation addressed the slavery issue as well. The nation could bury secession, said the Methodist writer E. S. Stanley, but "the abolition of wrong is immortal." In order to get at the root of the

---

[42]Moore, *Our Country*, 21.

[43]Henry Ward Beecher, "The Southern Babylon," *Freedom and War: Discourses in Topics Suggested by the Times* (Boston: Ticknor & Fields, 1863) 332.

[44]Henry Ward Beecher, "The Nation's Duty to Slavery" (October 30, 1859) in *Freedom and War*, 21.

[45]Henry Ward Beecher, *War and Emancipation* (Philadelphia: T. B. Peterson, 1861) 20. This was a Thanksgiving sermon preached at Plymouth Church, Brooklyn, on 21 November 1861.

problem, "slavery must die."[46] In the spring of 1862 the Reverend Charles Boynton stated that the carnage of the war resulted from the North's refusal to face the slavery issue. The nation could either sacrifice another hundred thousand lives or, "with manly independence and courage... utter that one word, emancipation, and thus strike the strength of our foe away...and emerge from this great battle as from a purifying furnace."[47]

As the Northern government came to understand that secession would not be eliminated in a swift military operation, the necessity to deal with slavery grew. The Confederacy dug in for a long conflict, strengthening its position with slave labor. The Lincoln administration made tentative moves in the direction of emancipation in the summer of 1862. On July 14 Abraham Lincoln asked Congress to compensate states that abolished slavery within their boundaries. For the first time in history, the government had offered to aid states that wanted to end slavery. This preliminary step received praise from William Aikman, a Presbyterian writer, who believed that slavery would not have died without the war. Aikman noted that although this action was relatively minor, it indicated a permanent trend toward emancipation. The government, which so many emancipationists had accused of being corrupt, immoral, and blasphemous, now became "a risen sun, [and] it has brought a day whose glorious light we have not yet appreciated."[48]

For those who attributed Northern defeats to the slavery issue, the initiatives of the Lincoln administration toward emancipation boded well for the military. Their assumptions seemed to be confirmed when, on 17 September 1862, the Army of the Potomac stifled Robert E. Lee's invasion of Union territory at the Battle of Antietam. Although the victory was not overwhelming, Lee's retreat to Virginia was significant for the North. The relationship of the Antietam campaign to Abraham Lincoln's plans for emancipation made the victory doubly important to many individuals.[49]

---

[46]E. S. Stanley, "National Fast Day Sermon on 'The Times,'" *Zion's Herald and Wesleyan Journal* (9 October 1861): 1.

[47]Charles Brandon Boynton, *God's Hand in the War* (Cincinnati: "Free Nation" Office, 1862) 14.

[48]William Aikman, *The Future of the Colored Race in America* (Philadelphia: William S. Young, 1862) 8.

[49]For a detailed description of the relationship of the emancipation question to Antietam, see Stephen W. Sears, *Landscape Turned Red: The Battle of Antietam* (Boston: Ticknor & Fields, 1983; reprint, New York: Warner Books, 1985) 46–49 and 350–59. The

Gilbert Haven, a Methodist clergyman and abolitionist, verbalized the opinions of supporters of emancipation in several sermons built around specific Civil War events. He describes the events of the early part of the Civil War in sublime natural imagery evocative of Milton's description of the chaotic state of Earth before creation. He points out the shift in the fortunes of the North after it decided to abolish slavery: "the government refused to speak the word of Liberty, and destruction came. That word appeared, and light broke dimly over the black and maddening waves. The waves still roared, and were troubled. The mountains shook with the swelling thereof. But a new creating spirit was brooding upon its turbulent depths."[50] To Haven, that shift came about when General McClellan, a Democrat who did not oppose slavery strongly enough to suit the abolitionists, was removed as the commander of the Army of the Potomac a few weeks after Antietam. Haven said McClellan's doom was sealed during the Peninsula campaign in the summer of 1862, when he forbade visitors to a Northern army camp to sing an abolitionist hymn that Haven termed "the grandest hymn of the war": "We wait beneath the furnace blast / The pangs of transformation; .../ What gives the wheat-fields blades of steel? / What points the rebel cannon? .../ Hark to the answer—Slavery!"[51] Haven pinpointed the event as the beginning of the disasters on the Peninsula. He also was able to explain why eastern armies prospered when General Grant eventually took command. Grant had realized the need to eliminate slavery after his defeat at Big Bethel, and from then on he acknowledged the need to destroy slavery and began winning, according to Haven.

Even after the Emancipation Proclamation took effect in 1863 and even after Grant had become general-in-chief in 1864, Haven maintained, the nation had not renounced slavery thoroughly enough to deserve victory. The nation also needed to admit that it had sinned and to express contrition for its acts. In 1864 he urged, "We almost begin to confess our sins. We have not yet done it. This [Emancipation] Proclamation comes the nearest to it."[52] For Haven, correcting the injustice was not enough. In order for the United States to win the war, in his

---

victory enabled Lincoln to produce the emancipation document he had prepared during the summer and had held until the North's military situation improved.

[50]Haven, "Why Grant Will Succeed," *National Sermons*, 401.

[51]Haven, "Why Grant Will Succeed," 399.

[52]Haven, "The Crisis Hour," *National Sermons*, 423.

view, the country must express guilt and contrition in addition to putting a halt to sin.

Noticeable among the array of responses to the Emancipation Proclamation is the sense of relief that the national sin had been expunged. Even though the proclamation was a war measure and even though it did not address the status of slaves in the loyal border states, its implications were clear enough to satisfy many abolitionists. A few days after the proclamation took effect, Henry Ward Beecher drew a parallel between the freeing of the slaves in America and the freeing of the peasants in Russia. For Beecher these two acts were sufficient to dispel the gloom of the apocalypse and to bring forth millennial light. The recognition of individual freedom would ensure God's support in the coming great battle, which would be more illustrious than any other "because never since the sun shone, never since governments were ordained, has there been an issue so absolute, so perpendicular, so crystalline, so devoid of all side issues" as this one between liberty and slavery.[53] The Emancipation Proclamation did not mean the end of the war, a Methodist editorial warned, but it did mean "the beginning of the end, as we entered the year of jubilee, Jan. 1, 1863." The document had put the nation right in the eyes of the world and before God. "May we not now look for military success?" it questioned.[54] Stephen Hodgman saw the same sublime picture described by Henry Ward Beecher. The first of January 1863, he said, would forever be celebrated "as the day when the sun of America, first shone forth with an unclouded splendor." The political heavens had threatened to pour out a storm, he explained, and at last it burst out and descended "in a flood of desolating vengeance. But...the heavens have been purified...and the sun of our freedom begins to shine forth."[55]

Individuals who had maintained belief in the importance of slavery gave the Emancipation Proclamation credit for Northern success throughout the rest of the war. George Searle Phillips, a Methodist writer who combined a strong sense of nationalism with the belief that America was the true Holy Land, saw the results of the proclamation in Union

---

[53]Henry Ward Beecher, "The Southern Babylon" *Freedom and War*, 439. This sermon was preached on 4 January 1863.

[54]"The War—When Shall it End?" *Zion's Herald and Wesleyan Journal* (18 February 1863): 1.

[55]Hodgman, *Nation's Sin*, 200.

victories at Gettysburg, Vicksburg, Chattanooga, and Knoxville.[56] The proclamation signaled a moral reformation "without parallel in the history of the world, [which] can only be accounted for by the special interposition of God."[57]

The centrality of the Emancipation Proclamation to Union military success is also apparent in drawings commemorating the event. A cartoon titled "Breaking that Backbone" (Figure 7)[58] associates the two themes of secession and slavery. Jefferson Davis holds a chained, dragon-like beast with fearsome teeth, named "Rebellion," and invites Northerners to try to break the creature's backbone. In the background, a defeated figure dejectedly holds his tiny hammer labeled "Compromise." General Halleck, General McClellan, and Secretary of War Stanton are lined up with large blunt mallets titled "Skill," "Strategy," and "Draft" that obviously will not do the job. Lincoln, dressed in his familiar rail-splitter garb, is last in line and holds the only weapon capable of beating Jefferson Davis at his game: a fearsome axe labeled "Emancipation Proclamation." The illustration does not specifically identify the beast's ancestry, but the items mentioned in the drawing are a precise echo of the widespread Northern belief that all secular, military efforts to resolve the conflict would be fruitless unless accompanied by God's weapon, the Emancipation Proclamation.

A more comprehensive portrait of the situation was created in 1865 in a four-color chromolithograph, "Proclamation of Emancipation," by L. N. Rosenthal of Philadelphia (Figure 8).[59] In the extreme foreground is a group at top center that includes the American eagle and portraits of the Founding Fathers. Their shadow lies across the top of a copy of the Emancipation Proclamation. This sheet of paper overlaps the edges of several small portraits: feminist abolitionists Lucretia Mott and Lydia Maria Child at the top, and a group of abolitionists, politicians, and clergymen at the bottom, with Abraham Lincoln at the center, directly beneath Washington.

---

[56]George Searle Phillips, *The American Republic and Human Liberty Foreshadowed in Scripture* (Cincinnati: Poe and Hitchcock for the author, 1864) 214.

[57]Phillips, *American Republic*, 216.

[58]Courtesy of the Library of Congress.

[59] This item is reproduced by permission from the Huntington Library, San Marino, California.

The Proclamation and portraits are linked to the background scenes by the allegorical figures of Liberty and Education at the lower left and right corners, whose feet press down upon a winged, three-headed serpent. They are balanced in the top corners by two additional female figures. At the left is a winged she-devil hovering over a cluster of three figures: the devil, in the center, is whispering to Jefferson Davis on the left and Alexander Stephens on the right. Below them are four scenes associated with slavery: a slave being whipped, a slave auction, a slave hanging from the ceiling of a cell by chains around his neck, and, at the bottom, a runaway slave pursued by hunters and hounds, kneeling and pleading to the allegorical figure of Liberty, who protects him with her sword and points to the proclamation. At the top right is a female angel figure blowing a trumpet and portraying beneath her the fruits of emancipation: black children in school, a united black family, a black farmer plowing in front of a tidy cottage, and finally a kneeling black figure surrounded by books and tools, watching as the allegorical figure of Education points to the world of technology and commerce now open to him.

This illustration is very specific in its emphasis on the Emancipation Proclamation as the righteous instrument that will defeat the devil and create a utopian world for the slave, which, in the context of mid-nineteenth-century American politics and religion, must be considered millennial. This new age is heralded by the trumpet-wielding angel, which would have been a familiar symbol to readers of Revelation.

The new world of hope for the slave is described in a poem said to have been dictated by an illiterate escaped slave, Thomas Peck, at the time of the Emancipation Proclamation. He refers to the occasion as the "day of Jubilee" described in the Old Testament, an occasion when Hebrew slaves were freed. The comprehensive knowledge of current events displayed in several stanzas indicates that Peck probably had some assistance in producing the poem. He praises the New York *Tribune* and its editor, Horace Greeley, who advocated "the colored man / Learning his A B C."[60] Literacy for the slave had religious, social, and economic implications. It received rhetorical emphasis in this poem because it is the key to the utopian future of the Negro, as illustrated in Rosenthal's print.

---

[60]Thomas Peck, "Day of Jubilee," *Zion's Herald and Wesleyan Journal* 34 (18 February 1863): 1. (See appendix.)

In some ways, the beliefs that tied slavery to the war seem most appropriate to theologians, politicians, and armchair soldiers. It is comparatively easy to glorify warfare and to read cosmic meaning into battles from a safe distance. The actual horrors of battle tend to obscure such idealistic concerns. A striking phenomenon about Civil War apocalypticism, however, is that the concept appears in the writing of soldiers in combat. An example is Henry Howard Brownell, who continued his work as a journalist until his war poems attracted the attention of Admiral David Farragut and resulted in an invitation to the writer in 1862 to enlist and serve as the admiral's secretary. Although his civilian poetry reflects his belief in the apocalyptic significance of the war, the imagery becomes even more explicit in the poems he wrote during battle. Brownell endangered his life many times by remaining in the midst of the fighting while taking notes, sometimes jotting them down in extemporaneous verse. He aimed to recreate the atmosphere of battle rather than to refine those experiences with rhetorical polish. He told his publisher that "many of the pieces were almost absolute improvisations, and nearly all written on the spur of some passing occasion."[61]

A civilian poem from early 1862 indicates Brownell's inclination toward apocalyptic imagery. Titled "The March of the Regiment," it describes a newly constituted regiment marching off to war. The soldiers are fighting for "God and the Right" and are willing to die, if necessary, for "the dear old Fatherland." Their enemy includes all the entities that have promoted the slave trade. Brownell follows the usual pattern of creating a visual impression by using sublime imagery to describe warfare:

> Welcome, the sulphury cloud in the sky!
> Welcome, the crimson rain!
> Act but the dream ye dared to form,
> Strike a single spark!—and the storm
> Of serried bayonets sweeping by,
> Shall swell to a hurricane!

He goes on to create a hellish picture of the "Ordeal of Fire in War," featuring the pagan Old Testament deity Moloch, who is "Throned on his

---

[61]Henry Howard Brownell to James Thomas Fields, 24 September 1865, Henry Howard Brownell collection FI 444, Henry E. Huntington Library, San Marino, CA.

Ghizeh of bones, and fed / Still with hearts of the holy dead." This
creature has also patronized the slave trade, which is the cause of the fiery
conflict. Moloch, however, is going down to defeat, and is returning to
hell. The enemy, like Belshazzar, is oblivious to the "Doom that waits the
Beast," still sharing the "Harlot's Feast" and drinking from her "blood-
grimed Cup." Brownell pursues the apocalyptic imagery by comparing
the present conflict with the destruction of Babylon:

> Mark, 'mid the Fiery Dew that drips,
> Redder, faster, through black Eclipse,
> How Sodom, to-night, shall sup!
> (Thus the Kings, in Apocalypse,
> The traders of souls and crews of ships,
> Standing afar, with pallid lips,
> While Babylon's Smoke goes up!)

The American war, however, is just a prelude to the main event,
Armageddon, which is imminent:

> Aye, 'tis at hand!—foul lips, be dumb!
> Our Armageddon is yet to come!
> But cheery bugle, and angry drum,
> With volleyed rattle and roar,
> And cannon thunder-throb, shall be drowned,
> That day, in a grander, stormier sound—
> The Land, from mountain to shore,
> Hurling shackle and scourge and stake
> Back to their Lender of pit and lake—[62]

The poet prophesies that this "Armageddon" will destroy the
weapon of the enemy, slavery, along with the enemy itself. There are
some interesting relationships between this poem and one written by
Brownell in battle conditions on an occasion when a righteous military
force fought a "dragon" in the shape of a Southern ironclad ship.
Brownell's use of imagery in this later poem indicates he may have
believed Armageddon had come at last. When Brownell joined the Navy

---

[62]Henry Howard Brownell, "The March of the Regiment," *War-Lyrics* (Boston:
Ticknor and Fields, 1866) 74–79. (See appendix.)

he accompanied Admiral Farragut on his flagship, the *Hartford*. On 5 August 1864, he participated in the naval battle at Mobile Bay, which resulted in the capture or destruction of all of the Confederate fleet at that location and in the eventual capture of Fort Gaines, Fort Powell, and Fort Morgan. Brownell stayed on the deck of the *Hartford* during the battle and saw a number of crewmembers cut down by the cross fire. He wrote his long narrative poem describing the event, titled "The Bay Fight," immediately after the battle, relying on notes he had taken during the fighting. This poem emphasizes secession as the sin of the South, but the apocalyptic imagery is similar to his earlier poem, which identified slavery as the primary sin.

After a leisurely description of the fleet's approach to Confederate shores through subtropical latitudes, Brownell describes the beginning of the long-anticipated battle with the sublime imagery he customarily used to introduce battle scenes: "The day at last, as ever, came; / And the volcano, laid so long, / Leaped forth in thunder and in flame!" The apocalyptic foe soon enters the action, in the form of the fearsome Confederate ironclad ram *Tennessee*, the "Dragon of iron shell." He personifies the ship, describing how it lay in wait for the *Hartford*: There he was, belching flame from his bow, / And the steam from his throat's abyss / Was a Dragon's maddened hiss— / In sooth a most cursed craft!"

Brownell describes the battle as a sublime firestorm ordained by God:

And lightning from every port—
Scene of glory and dread!
A storm-cloud all aglow
With flashes of fiery red—

....

Worth our watch, dull and sterile,
Worth all the weary time—
Worth the woe and the peril,
To stand in that strait sublime!
Fear? A forgotten form!
Death? A dream of the eyes!
We were atoms in God's great storm
That roared through the angry skies.

Even with that assurance, the US seamen worried that the day might be lost to the "Darker Powers," whose shots were accompanied by the "howl of hell." After describing the main action of the battle with journalistic accuracy, Brownell depicts the climactic confrontation between the *Hartford* and the *Tennessee* as a battle between God and the devil. Eventually Northern forces cornered the "hideous Thing" and pierced the spine of the "huge Sea-Hog," which "vomited flame no more."

Looking back on the battle, Brownell comments that God's kingdom must be inaugurated by the machinery of war, the only force strong enough to purge the world of evil:

> Ah, ever, when with storm sublime
> Dread Nature clears our murky air,
> Thus in the crash of falling crime
> Some lesser guilt must share.
>
> Full red the furnace fires must glow
> That melt the ore of mortal kind:
> The Mills of God are grinding slow,
> But ah, how close they grind!
> To-day, the Dahlgren and the drum
> Are dread Apostles of his Name;
> His Kingdom here can only come
> By chrism of blood and flame.

In Brownell's view, the sins being purged by this battle are God's only recourse to destroy evil; meanwhile, blood and flame function as the chrism, or sacramental anointing oil, of the righteous warriors. Brownell seems determined that every drop of violence within mankind must be squeezed out by this intense warfare, leaving not one vestige of discord to mar the millennium, which seems to be foreshadowed in a passage near the end of the poem: "Be strong: already slants the gold / Athwart these wild and stormy skies; / From out this blackened waste, behold, / What happy homes shall rise!"[63]

---

[63]Henry Howard Brownell, "The Bay Fight," *Lines of Battle*, 31–32.

Another apocalyptic battlefield poet was Obadiah Baker, who saw action at Shiloh and Corinth and wrote poems about the battles. He continued to revise his work for fifty years after the end of the war, but apparently with no goal of publication in mind. Unlike Brownell, who had been invited to participate in the fighting because of his writing ability, Baker chose to fight in the war and then decided to write about it. His views of the war's relationship to politics and theology echo the opinions of civilians who were more distant from the battlefield. Like the abolitionists, he believed that the government's indecision on the slavery issue was responsible for the inconclusive results of early battles. In a poem of over 200 lines he describes slavery as the "great National Sin." He prophesies that slavery will be eliminated, causing "joy on earth and in Heaven," and rewarding the work of Wendell Phillips and other abolitionists. "John Brown's soul it is marching on," Baker declares, "Its mission is not staid."[64]

Baker identified secession and slavery as causes that doomed the South eventually to fall, and in another poem he describes military setbacks as a strategy of God for bringing his people to accept the concept of Emancipation: "Twas thus we had our reverses / Our Eagle off was shorn / Our country was not ready for / Emancipation morn."[65]

The tendency to link the issues of secession and slavery, and then to work out a scheme of supernatural involvement in the war's events, provided a powerful incentive for continuing the war. If indeed the conflict was occurring in order to separate absolute good from absolute evil, it must be pursued to its conclusion. Any compromise developed before that point would short-circuit the process of national purification and vindication.

The Northern interpretation of the apocalyptic significance of the Civil War is marked by unshakable confidence that the war was a holy cause. This belief lent meaning to every battlefield action. The fact that the North experienced many military reverses early in the war did not dissuade Northerners from pursuing their interpretation; rather, it provided them with an opportunity to employ jeremiad rhetoric and to

---

[64]Obadiah Ethelbert Baker, "A Review of War Doings Dedicated to Lincoln," Baker collection. This item is reproduced by permission of the Huntington Library, San Marino, California.

[65]Obadiah Ethelbert Baker, "Secession and Slavery," Baker Collection. This item is reproduced by permission of the Huntington Library, San Marino, California.

purge national sins. Early defeats also helped to strengthen the conviction that the war would not go well for the North until the slavery problem had been satisfactorily addressed. The sense of jubilation and relief among many Northerners at the advent of the Emancipation Proclamation indicates that these individuals believed the holy war would come to a rapid, satisfactory conclusion. The fact that it did not was to produce fundamental changes in the way Northerners viewed the war.

THE SOUTHERN CROMWELL AND THE MOSES OF THE NORTH HEROES OF THE HOLY WAR

Although Adalbert Volck's prints were satirical, even vicious, when aimed at the North, the tone shifts drastically when Confederate heroes become the focus. His most reverential portrayal is "Scene in Stonewall Jackson's Camp," circa 1863 (Figure 9).[1] Although it is not known whether the drawing was made before or after Jackson's death on 10 May, the image began a mythologization that would continue for decades.[2] In this print Jackson leads his soldiers in a prayer service. All of the men, from the humblest privates to the officers, look devout, repentant, and thoughtful. Volck's decision to depict this aspect of the camp life of the Confederacy's most feared warrior suggests a link between Jackson's prayers and his military success. A similar theme also appears in a newspaper reporter's account of a worship service at Jackson's camp. The reporter described how Jackson led his troops in prayer before battle and then depicted what occurred when the fighting was over:

> After a battle has been fought, the same rigid remembrance of Divine Power is observed. The army is drawn up in line, the general dismounts from his horse, and there in the presence of his rough, bronzed-face troops, with heads uncovered and bent awe-stricken to the ground, the voice of the good man, which but a few hours before was ringing out in quick and fiery intonations is now heard, subdued and calm, as if overcome by the presence

---

[1]Courtesy of the Library of Congress.

[2]Mark E. Neely, Jr., et al., *The Confederate Image*, 123 have traced the adaptation of Volck's drawing by John Chester Buttre and Peter Kramer. The ensuing print was offered for sale for nearly thirty years after the war.

of the Supreme Being in holy appeal to "the Sapphire throne."...Are you surprised, after this recital, that "Stonewall" Jackson is invincible, and that he can lead his army to certain victory whenever God's blessing precedes the act?[3]

The tendency of many individuals in both the South and the North to interpret the Civil War in apocalyptic terms affected the way they perceived and described their leaders. Because biblical prophecies of the end of the world did not dwell on specific personages, Christian citizens identified their apocalyptic heroes with characters from history. Two individuals whose careers lent themselves to apocalyptic mythmaking were General Thomas J. Jackson and President Abraham Lincoln.

Lincoln's role as a hero and martyr figure is familiar to students of the war. Our very familiarity with Lincoln tends to obscure Jackson's status as a crucial Southern symbol of apocalypse. Today we must look to the historical role of Oliver Cromwell to explain what American Civil War troops well understood. By transforming military conflict into holy warfare, Cromwell had enabled many Roundhead supporters to interpret their strife in apocalyptic terms. Civil strife, holy warfare, and apocalyptic purpose led some Americans, particularly the Scotch-Irish Presbyterians of the Shenandoah Valley and southwestern Pennsylvania, to similar conclusions about their own civil war. The Pennsylvanians, determined to duplicate Cromwell's feats, formed the 100th ("Round Head") Pennsylvania Regiment.[4] By their own account, their military success was due to their sobriety and their Sabbathkeeping.[5] The Round Head Regiment's Southern counterpart, the First Virginia Brigade, found Cromwellian inspiration in their commander. Stonewall Jackson was a devout Presbyterian who transmitted his religious intensity to his "foot-cavalry" in pre-battle prayer sessions. The religious atmosphere of his army camp and his battle victories reinforced the impression of many Southerners that Jackson's military efforts had been blessed by God.

---

[3]Dispatch from Richmond, August 10, 1862, to *Charleston Courier*, quoted by John W. Jones, *Christ in the Camp, Or, Religion in Lee's Army* (Richmond: B. F. Johnson & Co., 1888) 277–78.

[4]See Samuel Penniman Bates, *History of Pennsylvania Volunteers 1861–1865*, 4 vols. (Harrisburg: B. Singerly, 1870) vol. 3.

[5]Editorial, *The Camp Kettle* (Round Head newspaper) 21 September 1861, 2.

Abraham Lincoln's religious orientation was very different from Jackson's. He did not belong to any Christian denomination—indeed, his closest associates later whispered that he was an infidel—but his sense of destiny and his apocalyptic rhetoric developed into a mythology more powerful than varieties originating within narrow sectarian boundaries. These two individuals were probably the most singular and unorthodox heroes of the conflict even before they were elevated to martyrdom; the fact that they both died as a result of the war made them even more appealing as national heroes. Each came to symbolize apocalyptic issues in human form, and an analysis of this phenomenon helps to explain how America's sectional conflict became a holy war.

According to Stonewall Jackson's widow, who published a biography of her late husband in 1892, he did not grow up in a strongly religious environment. Orphaned while a young child, he lived with relatives until he enrolled at West Point. It was not until he went to Texas to fight in the Mexican War that he became actively interested in religion. In 1849, when he was twenty-four years old, he was baptized into the Episcopal church. After he moved to Lexington, Virginia, to teach at the Virginia Military Institute, he acquired an interest in Presbyterianism and joined that denomination in 1851.[6] Jackson embraced his religious faith with a martial earnestness that soon immersed him in the activities of his local church, and he even testified publicly in spite of his innate shyness. Not long after he joined the church he wrote to a relative that "The subject of becoming a herald of the cross has often seriously engaged my attention…. It was the profession of our divine Redeemer, and I should not be surprised were I to die upon a foreign field, clad in ministerial armor, fighting under the banner of Jesus."[7] Although Jackson's aspirations to the ministry were not literally realized, he did emphasize religious piety among his troops with evangelistic fervor.

Jackson, who had served in the US army during the Mexican War, found a religious explanation for joining the Confederate Army when the Civil War began. His biographer James I. Robertson, Jr. has noted that Jackson saw the birth of the Confederacy as an event ordained by God.

---

[6]Mary Anna Jackson, *Life and Letters of General Thomas J. Jackson* (New York: Harper & Brothers, 1892) 57.

[7]Thomas J. Jackson to Mrs. Neale (his aunt) *Life*, ed. Mary Jackson, 60. Mrs. Jackson does not date this letter, but it apparently was written several years before the Civil War.

Since God would certainly give the victory to the side that followed his teachings most closely, and since the Confederate Constitution repeatedly invoked the deity, Jackson felt that his duty was clear. "The Confederacy as Jackson envisioned it was the next step in the history of Christian people," Robertson noted. "He would serve it and, by doing so, glorify God. To Jackson, this war was a call to wage both a political battle and a religious crusade."[8] His original command, the First Virginia Brigade, was made up largely of soldiers of Scotch-Irish stock from the Shenandoah Valley of Virginia; they and Jackson's largely Presbyterian chaplain corps made Cromwellian comparisons easily, despite the tendency of many Southerners to equate Cromwell with despised Northern Puritanism.[9] Several of the chaplains also distinguished themselves in military roles, including Jackson's chief of staff Robert L. Dabney and "Fighting Chaplain" Abner Crump Hopkins. Hopkins was also instrumental in the religious revivals that occurred in the camps of the Army of Northern Virginia in the winters of 1862 and 1863.[10] While the chaplains led out in these revivals, Jackson himself put them in motion, worrying that the sins of the army would reduce its effectiveness.[11] Jackson himself was deeply affected by the revivals. In April 1863, a few weeks before Chancellorsville, he was finishing his official report on the Second Battle of Manassas as he observed the extent of the revivals in the camp. The results suggested to him that the army would become even more effective, given its deepened religious conviction: "For these great and signal victories our sincere and humble thanks are due unto Almighty God. We should in all things acknowledge the hand of Him who reigns in heaven and rules among the armies of men.... We can but express the grateful conviction of our mind that God was with us and gave us the victory, and unto His holy name be the praise."[12]

Jackson called his men together for prayer before going into battle and strongly urged them to attend religious services on Sunday. While

---

[8]James I. Robertson, Jr., *Stonewall Jackson: The Man, the Soldier, the Legend* (New York: MacMillan, 1997) 213.

[9] See chapter three.

[10]James I. Robertson, Jr., *The Stonewall Brigade* (Baton Rouge: Louisiana State University Press, 1963) 20. See also Robert G. Tanner, *Stonewall in the Valley: Thomas J. "Stonewall" Jackson's Shenandoah Valley Campaign, Spring 1862* (Garden City NY: Doubleday, 1976).

[11]Robertson, *Stonewall Jackson*, 683.

[12]Jackson manuscript, quoted in Robertson, *Stonewall Jackson*, 697.

the reticent Jackson was unlikely to lead in prayer in a public way, as depicted by Volck, he did begin to hold a prayer meeting in his mess every morning following the religious revivals in the winter and spring of 1862 and 1863.[13] If he was forced to fight on Sunday, the army worshiped on the following day. Jackson's intense religious fervor appealed to a pious strain of Southern religion, which explains why he was sometimes compared with irascible Old Testament prophets or with Cromwell.[14]

Although some of Jackson's men scoffed at his devout behavior at the beginning of the war, their admiration of his toughness and his victories eventually led to their acceptance and even adoption of his religion. When they made camp after a march, chapel tents were among the first to be pitched.[15]

The victories of Christian commanders indicated to some Southerners that God was firmly on their side. Reid Mitchell has noted that the belief that the Confederate army was more pious than its Northern counterpart "became one way of claiming moral superiority for the Confederacy itself."[16] C. C. Jones, Sr. noted that God had given great

---

[13]Byron Farwell, *Stonewall: A Biography of General Thomas J. Jackson* (New York: W. W. Norton, 1992) 488. An analogous experience for Northern troops took place on the Gettysburg battlefield on 2 July 1863. Just before one of General Winfield Scott Hancock's brigades, the Irish, entered combat to support the Third Corps, its Catholic chaplain, Rev. William Corby, requested an opportunity to give a general absolution to all the men, Catholic and Protestant. The scene was later depicted in a painting, *Absolution Under Fire*, by a nineteen-year-old artist Paul Henry Wood in 1891. See William Corby, C. S. C., *Memoirs of Chaplain Life: Three Years with the Irish Brigade in the Army of the Potomac* (New York: Fordham University Press, 1992) 181–86. The Wood painting tended to be seen in the context of sacrifice, not heroism; many of its soldiers were dead within minutes of Father Corby's prayer.

[14]An indication of the type of appreciation Southerners had for Cromwell may be found in a sermon by Reverend John W. Jones, *The Southern Soldier's Duty: A Discourse Delivered to the Rome Light Guards and Miller Rifles, May 26, 1861* (Rome GA: D. H. Mason, 1861) 13. Jones told his audience that an army of pious men would be invincible, and that "this was true of Cromwell's army,…[especially] that wonderful regiment led by himself, and known as the Ironsides." Note that the context for this praise of Cromwell is very different from passages where Southern critics associated Cromwell with Puritan fanaticism and antagonism to the South's Cavalier heritage. Presbyterians who revered Stonewall Jackson deeply appreciated Oliver Cromwell's piety–and his military success.

[15]Robertson, *Stonewall Brigade*, 25.

[16]Reid Mitchell, "Christian Soldiers? Perfecting the Confederacy," *Religion and the American Civil War*, ed. Miller, et al., 301.

blessings to Jackson.[17] Another writer, a Confederate soldier, makes an explicit comparison between Jackson and Cromwell: "It was the religious fanaticism of Cromwell's puritanic army which made it invincible. It is the genuine religious tone of Jackson's which, under a pious commander, has thus far rendered it unconquerable."[18] Jackson's affinity with the prophets of the Old Testament, particularly Moses, is spelled out in popular songs written in response to his victories. In "Stonewall Jackson's Way" he appeals to God to "'stretch forth thy rod'" against the North,[19] and "The Stonewall Banner" compares Jackson's battle flag to the Children of Israel's pillar of fire.[20]

As one biographer has described it, Jackson had no doubt "that prayer and his Christian beliefs made him a better general, calming his perplexities and anxieties, steadying his judgment and preventing him from leaping to rash conclusions."[21] Two days after Jackson was wounded at the battle of Chancellorsville, he revealed his own thoughts about the relationship between his religion and his military life when he confided to his chief chaplain, Rev. B. Tucker Lacy, that he believed God still had a place for him in his country's military work. While Jackson still saw unfinished work for him to do a few days before he died, throughout his Civil War career he stated repeatedly that he was ready to die at any time. His religious certainty made him utterly unafraid in battle, which contributed to his effectiveness as a leader. It also gave his utterances a tone of fatalism similar to that of Herman Melville and Abraham Lincoln, who were not conventional Protestants, as Jackson was, but who were undeniably influenced by the Calvinist God Jackson worshiped.

Jackson's death on 10 May 1863, after being wounded at Chancellorsville, having his arm amputated, and contracting pneumonia, was a powerful psychological blow to the South. His apparent invulnerability had been an important element of Southern optimism.

---

[17]C. C. Jones, Sr. to C. C. Jones, Jr., 2 June 1862, *Children of Pride*, 252.

[18]Anonymous Confederate soldier in a letter to the *Southern Lutheran* in the fall of 1862, as quoted in William W. Bennett, *A Narrative of the Great Revival…in the Southern Armies* (Philadelphia: Claxten, 1877) 212.

[19]"Stonewall Jackson's Way!" (Richmond: J. W. Randolph, 1863). (See appendix.)

[20]"The Stonewall Banner!" (Richmond: J. W. Randolph, n.d.). (See appendix.) This song claims that Jackson's banner is a more sure guide than the pillar of flame, a significant statement since the pillar of flame was supposed to have been provided by God.

[21]Farwell, *Stonewall*, 520.

When Mrs. C. C. Jones, Sr. heard of Jackson's death she recorded her hope that God would "raise up friends and helpers to our bleeding country!"[22] Jackson was accorded a hero's funeral in Richmond,[23] and writers strove to express his significance in poems and songs. One songwriter acknowledged Jackson's affinity with Moses in death, just as others had noted a correlation in the two men's lives: "He entered not the nation's Promised Land, / At the red belching of the cannon's mouth; / But broke the House of Bondage with his hand— / The Moses of the South!"[24] Herman Melville wrote poems less partisan than might be expected coming from an author who had seen several close relatives and friends march off to war. He wrote a poetic tribute to Jackson, who was, according to Melville, "True as John Brown or steel."[25] While Jackson himself would have seen such a phrase as a backhanded compliment at best, Melville correctly notes a certain implacable focus that the two shared despite their opposite records of military success. While the war continued, Jackson could remain a symbol of the Exodus, a leader who had sacrificed his own life while leading his people to the Promised Land.

Even after the Civil War, when the South had many additional fallen heroes to memorialize, Jackson remained as, Charles Reagan Wilson has noted, "the quintessential Confederate martyr-hero" in the thinking of the Southern clergy.[26] Although the Moses metaphor no longer applied, Jackson still resembled Cromwell or a "stern Old Testament prophet-warrior."[27] The first major Southern memorial of the war was a statue of Jackson dedicated in Richmond on 26 October 1875. One reason for this continued reverence for Jackson was that at the time of his death the

---

[22]Mrs. C. C. Jones, Sr. to C. C. Jones, Jr., 19 May 1863, *Children of Pride*, 373.

[23]See Robertson, *Stonewall Brigade*, 191–92.

[24]Harry Flash, "Jackson," *South Songs*, ed, De Leon, 29. The author also makes an oblique reference to the Crucifixion: "While his country staggers with the Cross, / He [Jackson] rises with the Crown!" (29) See appendix for the complete text of this poem. For comparison of Jackson with other southern martyrs, see the following poems in the appendix: "Albert Sidney Johnston," "Zollicoffer," and "Lines to the Memory of Father Turgis."

[25]Melville, "Stonewall Jackson Mortally Wounded at Chancellorsville (May 1863)" *Collected Poems of Herman Melville*, ed. Howard P. Vincent (Chicago: Packard and Co., 1947) 52–53. (See appendix.)

[26]Charles Reagan Wilson, *Baptized in Blood: the Religion of the Lost Cause, 1865–1920* (Athens: University of Georgia Press, 1980) 20.

[27]Ibid., 51.

South was still successful on the battlefield. The Southern clergy, who were largely responsible for keeping the Confederate flame alive after the war through the religion of the Lost Cause, had other compelling reasons for emphasizing Jackson's heroism, however. He was the most devout of public men, and his religious fortitude was impressive. Wilson notes that the clergy's "underlying admiration for him was due to his unbending righteousness, the holy wrath he could unleash."[28] Thus Stonewall Jackson's deeds became the underlying text for an apocalyptic faith that refused to dissipate even in the face of military defeat.

Whereas Stonewall Jackson's actions—his worship regimen and his battlefield successes—were responsible for his stature as a latter-day Cromwell, Abraham Lincoln's heroic qualities grew out of his own verbal interpretation of the war and the status of a modern day Moses accorded him by a significant part of the slave population. His speeches transcended their expository function and became some of the greatest literature of the period. Although Lincoln came into the presidency with anything but an orthodox Christian worldview, the events of the war seemed to impose upon him the conviction that the conflict was unfolding according to a divine plan.[29] In his public pronouncements during the war Lincoln eventually came to describe it in clearly apocalyptic terms.

Probably because he did not acquire this awareness through the teachings of a particular denomination, Lincoln took a broad view of the meaning of the war's events. Unlike many other apocalyptic doomsayers, he did not allegorize contemporary individuals and events into exact equivalences with biblical beasts and time periods. Instead, he broadly

---

[28]Ibid.

[29]For a description of Lincoln's religious beliefs, see the memoir written by his former law partner, William Herndon, *Herndon's Life of Lincoln: The History and Personal Recollections of Abraham Lincoln* (New York: Albert & Charles Boni, 1936) and also Emmanuel Hertz, *The Hidden Lincoln: From the Letters and Papers of William H. Herndon* (New York: The Viking Press, 1938). These accounts describe Lincoln as a fatalist and virtual infidel, and although these characteristics may be most accurately applied to his youth, biographers and acquaintances agree that Lincoln was not an orthodox Christian. Edmund Wilson believes that although opportunism may have been part of the reason for Lincoln's grasp of apocalyptic rhetoric, he eventually came to believe the doctrine personally: "It is nevertheless quite clear that he himself came to see the conflict in a light more and more religious...under a more and more apocalyptic aspect"(*Patriotic Gore*, 106).

interpreted the evils of war as evidence of the wrath of God against the sins of men, in cadences reminiscent of the Old Testament prophets.

Lincoln held an apocalyptic view of the conflict from the beginning of his presidency. Even before he took office, he spoke of the "coming storm" that would result when God's patience ran out. He attributed the approaching conflict directly to slavery and remarked that God had tolerated the institution until clergymen began to defend it with Scripture and with claims that the institution was divinely sanctioned. This step, according to Lincoln, showed that "now the cup of iniquity is full, and the Vials of Wrath will be poured out."[30] During his First Inaugural Address, Lincoln recognized the factor of divine intervention in the affairs of men but left open the question of where God's allegiance lay: The side that could demonstrate the presence of "the Almighty Ruler of nations, with his eternal truth and justice," would see "that truth, and that justice" prevail.[31] The subsequent events of the summer of 1861 compelled Lincoln to declare that the United States, although formerly blessed by God, was now being punished for its sins, and he proclaimed a national fast day on the last day of September, 1861. Lincoln remarked that the change in national fortunes forced the country "to recognize the hand of God in this terrible visitation, and in sorrowful remembrance of our own faults and crimes as a nation and as individuals, to humble ourselves before Him." Once this was done, the United States must "pray that we may be spared further punishment, though most justly deserved."[32] In this jeremiad Lincoln insists that the country must accept responsibility for misfortune brought about by national sins. Like other jeremiads, this passage implies that a change of behavior will win divine favor.

The belief that the battle was actually God's dominated Lincoln's thinking during the autumn of 1862, while his administration wrestled with the issue of emancipation. Many of his statements regarding the influence of God on human events were written during this time. Again

---

[30]Isaac Newton Arnold, *The History of Abraham Lincoln and the Overthrow of Slavery* (Chicago: Clarke & Co., 1866) 688–89. In this passage Arnold is quoting a discussion Lincoln had in the autumn of 1860 with a Mr. Bateman, Superintendent of Public Instruction for Illinois.

[31]Abraham Lincoln, "First Inaugural Address, March 4, 1861," in *The Collected Works of Abraham Lincoln,* ed. Roy P. Basler (New Brunswick NJ: Rutgers University Press, 1953) 4:270.

[32]Lincoln, "Proclamation of a National Fast Day, August 12, 1861," in *Works,* 4:482.

and again he mused that both antagonists were praying to God and claiming his patronage while in reality God was on neither side. On 13 September 1862, an interdenominational Christian delegation presented an emancipation memorial to Lincoln, instructing him that it was God's will for the slaves to be freed. On 21 September (Antietam had occurred in the intervening days), Lincoln replied wearily that he had been approached with "the most opposite opinions" by religious individuals "who are equally certain that they represent the divine will." He pointed out that "the rebel soldiers are praying with a great deal more earnestness, I fear, than our own troops." Lincoln said he sincerely desired to know the will of God, but since the age of miracles had passed he must arrive at the answer through the painful processes of logic. "Whatever shall appear to be God's will," he assured the delegation, "I will do."[33] Another individual who visited Lincoln at that time recalled that the president pointed out the irony and inconsistency of the situation: "Now, I believe we are all agents and instruments of Divine Providence.... Yet...here is one half of the nation prostrated in prayer that God will help to destroy the Union and build up a government upon the corner-stone of human bondage. And here is the other half, equally earnest in their prayers and efforts to defeat a purpose...repugnant to their ideas of human nature and the rights of society, as well as liberty and independence."[34] Since both sides claimed to be Christian while fighting for opposite results, Lincoln saw only one explanation: self-deception. "Somewhere there is a fearful heresy in our religion," he said, again adopting the jeremiad tone. Regardless of individual human convictions of right, God controlled events in ways inscrutable to man. "I am no fatalist," Lincoln maintained, but "God alone knows the issue of this business. He has destroyed nations from the map of history for their sins."[35] Lincoln saw hope even in this dark picture, but the source of hope lay in God, not man.[36]

---

[33]Lincoln, "Reply to Emancipation Memorial Presented by Chicago Christians of All Denominations, September 21, 1862," in *Works*, 5:420.

[34]The Reverend Byron Sutherland to the Reverend J. A. Reed, Nov. 15, 1872, as quoted in Francis Grierson, *Abraham Lincoln, the Practical Mystic* (New York: John Lane Company, 1918) 10–11. Sutherland had visited Lincoln in 1862 and in this letter is quoting Lincoln's comments.

[35]Grierson, *Lincoln*, 11–12.

[36]See Lincoln's "Meditation on the Divine Will, Sept. [30?], 1862," in which he wrote a private note in response to the pressure he had been receiving from the public: "The will of God prevails. In great contests each party claims to act in accordance with the

Lincoln's belief that God controlled the events of the Civil War and that the war signaled punishment for national sins finds its fullest expression in his Second Inaugural Address, his most universal, non-particular statement on the holy war. In this document Lincoln assumes that the war is "one of those offences" sent by God to chasten the earth. Both sides of the conflict were imploring the same God to aid them against the other, so it was obvious that both sets of prayers could not be answered. Instead, they have both been given "this terrible war, as the woe due to those by whom the offence [American Slavery] came." Although each side could hope fervently for an end to the war, citizens must remember that such a resolution would result entirely because of God's grace, not from any human merit. God could conceivably will the war to continue "until all the wealth piled by the bond-man's two hundred and fifty years of unrequited toil...and until every drop of blood drawn with the lash, shall be paid by another drawn with the sword."[37]

The assumptions of Lincoln's statements in this document about the role of God in human events are much more sweeping than those he made in the early part of the war. The series of ideas that developed throughout three years of fighting coalesces here into a concise and powerful statement that the war was actually God's war and an apocalyptic battle as well. Virtually alone among observers of that period, Lincoln did not strongly identify his own point of view with God's. His logical honesty would not allow that interpretation in the light of events. If God had been wholeheartedly on the side of the North, he would have ended the conflict long before the spring of 1865, even if his followers had required some punishment for their sins. Lincoln was not willing to admit that God supported the South, but his ambivalence dictated generalizations that transcended partisan politics and contentious

---

will of God. Both may be, and one must be, wrong. God cannot be for and against the same thing at the same time. In the present civil war it is quite possible that God's purpose is something different from the purpose of either party; and yet the human instrumentalities, working just as they do, are of the best adaptation to effect his purpose. I am almost ready to say that this is probably true; that God wills this contest, and wills that it shall not yet end. By his mere great power on the minds of the now contestants, he could have either saved or destroyed the Union without a human contest. Yet the contest began. And, having begun, he could give the final victory to either side any day. Yet the contest proceeds." Quoted in *The Literary Works of Abraham Lincoln*, ed. Carl Van Doren (New York: Readers Club, 1942) 221.

[37]Lincoln, "Second Inaugural Address, March 4, 1865," in *Works*, 8:333.

exegesis of Scripture. In fact, this timeless quality of Lincoln's interpretation of the war probably aided the popular view of Lincoln among both his friends and enemies as a larger than life historical figure.

Lincoln's stature as an apocalyptic hero is evident in Francis Grierson's memoir, *The Valley of Shadows*, an account of life on the plains just before the war. Although it was written many years after Appomattox, the book reconstructs the lives of prairie preachers and politicians as Grierson remembered them from his boyhood. He admits some retrospective interpretation in the preface when he remarks that "in looking back I have come to the conclusion that the power displayed...[in] the *ante-bellum* days in Illinois was a power emanating from the spiritual side of life."[38] In general, however, Grierson's book seems to recreate faithfully the spirit of those earlier times. According to Grierson, many of the people who watched Lincoln debate Douglas concluded that he was "the prophetic man of the present and the political saviour of the future."[39] Grierson notes the identification of Lincoln as apocalyptic prophet, savior or Christ figure, and a modernday Moses who would lead the slaves to freedom. In the book a backwoods preacher tells his congregation that "thar ain't but one human creatur' ekil to [freeing the slaves], en that air Abraham Lincoln. The Lord hez called him!"[40]

Lincoln's status as an apocalyptic warrior was portrayed by David Gilmour Blythe in the 1862 painting "Lincoln Crushing the Dragon of Rebellion" (Figure 10).[41] In this detailed painted cartoon, Lincoln attacks a fire-breathing dragon that is destroying buildings, music, and art, presumably pulling down the nation. The creature brings with it an apocalyptic firestorm. Lincoln cannot hope for help from Tammany Hall in the background, which represents quibbling over slavery provisions in the Constitution, and he is shackled by that document. He is a lonely warrior fighting against great odds.

Lincoln understandably elicited equally powerful negative responses from the South. Southerners feared that his presidency would

---

[38]Francis Grierson, *The Valley of Shadows: The Coming of the Civil War to Lincoln's Midwest, A Contemporary Account*, ed. Bernard DeVoto (Boston: Houghton Mifflin, 1909; reprint, New York: Harper and Row, 1966) vii.

[39]Grierson, *Valley*, 198.

[40]Ibid., 17.

[41]Courtesy, Museum of Fine Arts, Boston. M. and M. Karolik Collection.

permanently alter their social system, and his election precipitated the secession of several states. Although Lincoln took a cautious public stance on the subject of slavery as he assumed the presidency, many Southerners equated him with the abolitionists. One Southern narrator attributed Lincoln's election to the growing spirit of fanaticism in the North, which eventually led "the abolition Party" to elect Lincoln to the presidency in a "strictly sectional vote." To this writer, "Lincoln's election was the signal for patriotic and thinking men of the South to prepare for severing finally and forever our connection with the North."[42]

During the early years of the war Southerners preferred not to credit Lincoln with extraordinary abilities except perhaps the capacity to ingratiate himself with fanatical politicians more clever than he. It was convenient for them to view him as a grotesque, provincial politician whose physical appearance led to endless gibes about his relationship to apes. Because he came from the frontier, his manners were presumably not much better. The cultured wives of Southern politicians were pleased to hear that their departure had left a social vacuum in Washington, now presided over by the gauche Midwestern housewife Mary Todd Lincoln.[43] Later in the war, however, Lincoln became a more menacing figure to Southerners. Eventually, because it had failed to defeat Lincoln's armies, the South could no longer dismiss him as a buffoon. He became the instigator of the war and therefore a candidate for divine retribution.

C. C. Jones, Jr. formed this opinion as early as the summer of 1862. While McClellan's Peninsula Campaign got underway, Jones confided to his parents that the Lincoln government was squandering its enormous resources and setting itself up for the collapse of "the wretched policy which gave rise to this unholy and most unjust war." Lincoln would receive the proper reward for his chicanery: "The day of retribution, though deferred, must come; and when it does arrive it will be terrible in the extreme."[44] For many Southerners, this retribution was meted out at Lincoln's assassination.

---

[42]W. L. Gammage, *The Camp, the Bivouac, and the Battle Field* (Selma AL: Cooper & Kimball, 1864) 8. Gammage was a brigade surgeon in the Fourth Arkansas Regiment.

[43]See *Mary Chesnut's Civil War*, ed. C. Vann Woodward (New Haven: Yale University Press, 1981) 21 for Mrs. Chesnut's description of the bleakness of Washington social life at the time of Lincoln's first inauguration.

[44]C. C. Jones, Jr. to Rev. and Mrs. C. C. Jones, Sr., 16 June 1862, *Children of Pride*, 261.

One of the most profound reactions to the apocalyptic character of Abraham Lincoln came from the slaves. Although they were ambivalent, at best, toward Yankees, there was a widespread recognition by the slaves of a special relationship between themselves and Lincoln.[45] Ex-slave interviews indicate that the realities of American political life filtered down to the slaves in unusual ways.

One Georgia slave who was an adult during the war said that the fighting commenced when Jefferson Davis and Lincoln met in a room, whereupon Davis chose a gun as his weapon and Lincoln chose a Bible; "Thus Davis *began* the war but Lincoln had God on his side and so he *ended* it."[46] Another slave also mentioned the conflict between Davis and Lincoln and reported that it was resolved "when Mr. Abraham Lincoln come to dis passage in de Bible: 'My son, therefore shall ye be free

---

[45]Primary sources for this section include ex-slave narratives and interviews and slave songs recorded by researchers. An important source of material on slave life, including slave perceptions of Abraham Lincoln, is the collection of ex-slave interviews conducted by the WPA in the 1930s: George P. Rawick, ed. *The American Slave: A Composite Autobiography*, 42 vols. (Westport CT: Greenwood Press, 1972, 1979). Methodological suggestions on using these interviews may be found in: John W. Blassingame, "Using the Testimony of Ex-Slaves: Approaches and Problems," *The Journal of Southern History* 41/4 (November 1975): 473–92; Raymond Hedin, "The American Slave Narrative: The Justification of the Picaro," *American Literature* 53/1 (January 1982): 630–45; Raymond Hedin, "Muffled Voices: The American Slave Narrative," *Clio* 10/2 (Winter 1981): 129–42, and Norman R. Yetman, "Ex-Slave Interviews and the Historiography of Slavery," *American Quarterly* 36/2 (Summer 1984): 181–210. In addition to the slave songs collected by Thomas Wentworth Higginson in *Slave Life in a Black Regiment*, other important collections include Miles Mark Fisher, ed., *Negro Slave Songs in the United States* (Ithaca NY: Cornell University Press, 1953) and William Francis Allen, ed., *Slave Songs of the United States* (New York: A. Simpson, 1867). Analyses of slave songs may be found in Eugene Genovese, *Roll, Jordan, Roll: The World the Slaves Made* (New York: Pantheon, 1974); Lawrence W. Levine, "Slave Songs and Slave Consciousness: An Exploration in Neglected Sources," *Anonymous Americans*, ed. Hareven 99–130; Lawrence Levine, *Black Culture and Black Consciousness: Afro-American Folk Thought from Slavery to Freedom* (New York: Oxford Univ. Press, 1977); Albert J. Raboteau, *Slave Religion: The "Invisible Institution" in the Antebellum South* (New York: Oxford Univ. Press, 1978); Lucile Price Turner, "Negro Spirituals in the Making," *Musical Quarterly* 17/4 (1931): 480–85; and Clifton Joseph Furness, "Communal Music Among Arabians and Negroes," *Musical Quarterly* 16/1 (1930): 38–51.

[46]Rawick, ed., *American Slave*, 13:45. This is a report of an interview with Phil Towns, born in 1824 and age 113 at the time of the interview.

indeed,' he went to work to sot us free."[47] A number of slaves mentioned that there was a supernatural explanation for Lincoln's decision; he was acting as an instrument of God.[48] Such beliefs indicate that to these slaves, release from their bondage was a religious issue rather than a social or secular revolution. Said another ex-slave, "Abraham Lincoln was an instrument of God sent to set us free, for it was God's will that we should be freed."[49]

Along with their tendency to tie the war directly to religious issues, the slaves readily compared Lincoln to Moses. Their songs are filled with references to such Old Testament events as the year of jubilee, when slaves were freed.[50] As far as the slaves were concerned, the war freed them because God had heard their prayers and sent them a new Moses: "When de war was over de people jus' shouted for joy. 'Twas only because of de prayers of de cullud people dey was freed, and de Lawd worked through Lincoln."[51] When Lincoln visited Richmond after it fell to Union troops and just a few days before his assassination, there indeed seemed to be a bond between him and the slaves who flocked into the streets to see or even touch their savior. Lincoln's assassination completed the transition for them from a Moses figure to a redemptive Christ figure, and both of these images were intermingled with the concept that the Civil War was an apocalyptic conflict, ushering in a better age.

Civil War apocalyptic thought was characterized by its tendency to incorporate imagery from the Exodus and the Crucifixion in its picture of the end of the world. In a general sense, the war itself was the nation's

---

[47]Rawick, ed., *American Slave*, 12:8. Transcript of an interview with Elisha Doc Garey, ex-slave from Georgia.

[48]See comments by Georgia ex-slaves Jefferson Franklin Henry ("I thinks it was by God's own plan that President Abraham Lincoln sot us free") and Charlie Hudson ("It was a God-sent method Mr. Lincoln used to give us our freedom") in Rawick, ed., *American Slave*, 12:192, 231.

[49]Mary Colbert, Georgia ex-slave, in Rawick, ed., *American Slave*, 12:92.

[50]Slaves also used Old Testament imagery to echo the apocalyptic predictions of Isaiah and Jeremiah. One Georgia ex-slave, Reverend Washington Allen, stated that although he personally had no use for Yankees, "God was using [them] to scourge the slave-holders just as He had, centuries before used heathens and outcasts to chastise His chosen people—the Children of Israel," in Rawick, ed., *American Slave*, 12:13.

[51]Transcript of an interview with Arkansas ex-slave O. W. Green in Rawick, ed., *American Slave*, 4:92.

crucifixion—an expiation for national sins.[52] Lincoln reinforced such interpretations in the Gettysburg Address, where he implies that the act of dying on that particular battlefield was a deed too sacred to be properly commemorated by nonparticipants. The Northern soldiers who had perished there performed a redeemer function; they "gave their lives that that nation might live." With a proper response from the American people, the nation would have "a new birth of freedom."[53] In making these statements Lincoln was verbalizing a common generalization used by Americans to give significance to the war.

When Lincoln himself died, Northerners readily applied this already powerful concept to their fallen president. It would have occurred even if he had been gunned down on a day other than Good Friday, but the Easter connection provided a yet more powerful symbol of his death's significance.[54] Because Good Friday in 1865 was not followed by an Easter resurrection, the Reverend Matthew Simpson noted at Lincoln's funeral in Springfield that "even all the joyous thought of Easter Sunday failed to remove the crushing sorrow under which the true worshiper bowed in the house of God." Simpson attempted to measure the public's response to Lincoln's life: "I believe the conviction has been growing on the nation's mind,…especially in the last years of his administration, that by the hand of God he was especially singled out to guide our government in these troublesome times."[55] Henry Howard Brownell saw the optimistic

---

[52]This interpretation was evident even at the beginning of the war. In a diary entry for Thursday, 18 April 1861, Levi Grabill, who had just enlisted in the Ohio Volunteers, reported that at a patriotic meeting, one participant declared that "if the South whip the North they will be compelled to wade through better blood than has been spilt since Jesus Christ was crucified." Manuscript Collection, Henry E. Huntington Library, San Marino, CA. Reproduced by permission of the Huntington Library.

[53]Lincoln, *Works*, 8:23. Garry Wills, commenting on this passage, says that "Lincoln did not join a separate religion to politics; he made his politics religious. And that is why his politics has survived the attack on less totally fused forms of 'civil religion.'" See *Inventing America: Jefferson's Declaration of Independence* (Garden City NJ: Doubleday, 1978) xix. This explanation accounts for the power of Lincoln's rhetoric and demonstrates why Lincoln's statements became timeless when other similar but more sectarian views remained strictly topical.

[54]James Moorhead, *American Apocalypse*, 175 notes that the Good Friday coincidence "was widely interpreted as the final blood sacrifice by which the nation was purified and reborn to its high mission."

[55]Matthew Simpson, *Funeral Address Delivered at the Burial of President Lincoln* (New York: Carlton and Porter, 1865, 9. Another reference to Lincoln as savior may be

point of view when he described the reunion in heaven of the souls of all the Union dead with Lincoln, the "Father." According to Brownell, the third of a million men were marching in a grand review to join Christ in welcoming Lincoln to heaven: "Our Father is not alone! / For the Holy right ye died / And Christ, the Crucified, / Waits to welcome his own."[56]

The combination of Moses figure and Redeemer figure is evident in the public response to Lincoln as an apocalyptic hero. Lincoln as Moses led either the slaves out of bondage or the United States out of failure and disaster. Henry Ward Beecher drew a parallel between Lincoln and Moses in his memorial address: "Again a great leader of the people has passed through toil, sorrow, battle, and war, and come near to the promised land of peace, into which he might not pass over."[57] In an apostrophe to Lincoln, Beecher made the comparison with Moses even more explicit: "Thou hast beheld Him who invisibly led thee in this great wilderness. Thou standest among the elect."[58]

In his poem about Lincoln titled "The Martyr," Herman Melville explicitly associates Lincoln with Christ by referring to Good Friday in the opening line. The main energy of the poem, however, is directed at pointing out the fury that will arise from the sorrow at Lincoln's death. Melville twice uses the incantatory refrain, "Beware the people weeping / When they bare the iron hand." Lincoln has been replaced by an "Avenger" who will execute heaven's penalty against "parricides."[59] Henry Ward Beecher echoed this steely response when he remarked: "it was fit that [the Confederacy's] expiring blow should be such as to take away from men the last forbearance, the last pity, and fire the soul with an invincible determination that the breeding-ground of such mischiefs

---

found in Walt Whitman's poem, "This Dust Was Once the Man," which states that by Lincoln's hand "was saved the Union of these States." See *Leaves of Grass*, ed. Sculley Bradley and Harold W. Blodgett (New York: W. W. Norton, 1973) 339. In this poem Whitman makes an implicit comparison between the assassination and the Crucifixion.

[56]Brownell, "Abraham Lincoln," *War-Lyrics*, 142.

[57]Henry Ward Beecher, "Abraham Lincoln," *Lectures and Orations*, ed. Newell Dwight Hills (New York: Fleming H. Revell, 1913) 265. This address was given at Plymouth Church, Brooklyn, on Sunday, 23 April 1865. In the same sermon Beecher also notes Lincoln's redemptive function in an apocalyptic situation: "He wrestled ceaselessly, through four black and dreadful purgatorial years, wherein God was cleansing the sins of His people as by fire" (266).

[58]Ibid., 267.

[59]Melville, "The Martyr," *Battle-Pieces*, 141–42 (see appendix).

and monsters shall be utterly and forever destroyed."[60] Christopher
Cranch, in his poem, "The Martyr," also called for retribution. The foe is
not human but diabolical, and the devils of the South have committed
"the most impious murder done / Since Calvary."[61] The mercy toward the
South that Lincoln had recommended was rejected in favor of stern
retribution. The imagery of destruction that had so often been associated
with the war appeared again even after the official hostilities had ceased.

Of all the occasions that encouraged Northerners to identify their
circumstances with the apocalypse, the death of Lincoln was the most
direct and powerful. The fact that it marked the first successful attempt
on a president's life, coupled with the burden of meaning already given to
the war, produced an unparalleled religious response. Henry Ward
Beecher created an analogy between citizen reaction to the assassination
and the anticipated sensations that the end of the world would produce:

> The blow brought not a sharp pang. It was so terrible that at
> first it stunned sensibility. Citizens were like men awakened at
> midnight by an earthquake, and bewildered to find everything
> that they were accustomed to trust wavering and falling. The very
> earth was no longer solid. The first feeling was the least. Men
> waited to get straight to feel. They wandered in the streets as if
> groping after some impending dread, or undeveloped sorrow, or
> some one to tell them what ailed them.[62]

Although Beecher engages in his customary hyperbole here, this
statement seems less theatrical and more forthright than many of his
apocalyptic pronouncements. Unlike his earlier prophecies of apocalyptic
doom that never materialized, here he refers to an actual but horribly
unimaginable event. He speaks with the accuracy of someone too
stunned by reality to draw fanciful conclusions.

Southerners also saw significance in Lincoln's assassination, and
although their reaction could not equal the shock felt by the North, some
did not hesitate to express their elation at Lincoln's death. Of all the
surprising events that affected the South in the spring of 1865, this was

---

[60]Beecher, "Lincoln" *Lectures*, 276.
[61]Christopher Cranch, "The Martyr," *The Bird and the Bell* (Boston: James D.
Osgood, 1875) n. p. (See appendix.)
[62]Beecher, "Lincoln," *Lectures*, 269.

the only good news to one woman. In Georgia, Caroline Jones wrote to her mother-in-law, Mrs. C. C. Jones, Sr. about her reactions of shock at Lee's defeat, despair at peace without victory, and grim satisfaction at "the righteous retribution upon Lincoln. One sweet drop among so much that is painful is that he at least cannot raise his howl of diabolical triumph over us."[63] Diarist Cornelia McDonald of Virginia expressed more reserve at the event, although her initial reaction had been elation. "A little reflection," she concluded, "made me see that it was worse for us than if he had been suffered to live, for his satisfaction had been great when we were disarmed, and he was disposed to be merciful." She also accurately predicted retribution: "Now no mercy was to be expected from a nation of infuriated fanatics whose idol of clay had been cast down."[64]

The tendency to create larger-than-life heroes of the Civil War paralleled the tendency to give prophetic significance to the war itself. In addition to identifying with biblical prophecies that had not yet been fulfilled, nineteenth-century Americans also saw reflections of themselves in past prophecies that they believed had already come true. Biblical typology created the basis for these comparisons between past and present heroes, and it explains why Americans freely wove Old Testament and New Testament figures such as Moses and Christ into their depiction of the imminent end of the world. Such a significant event called for the greatest leaders in the history of the earth, and Americans firmly expected the war to produce them. Predictably enough, both sides created their heroes in the war's image. The South had been most insistent on the purity and righteousness of its cause, and it had to look no further than the English Civil War for a model holy hero. The slaves fully expected a modern Moses to lead them to an eternal Promised Land, and Abraham Lincoln began to fulfill that purpose when he issued the Emancipation Proclamation. Because Christ's death had been accompanied by cataclysmic events, it was not difficult for Northerners to see Lincoln's death in parallel terms as a harbinger of the Second Coming.

---

[63]Caroline Jones to Mrs. C. C. Jones, Sr., 30 April 1965, *Children of Pride*, 547.

[64]Cornelia McDonald, *A Diary with Reminiscences of the War and Refugee Life in the Shenandoah Valley 1860–1865* (Nashville TN: Hunter McDonald, 1934) 260.

6

THE END OF THE APOCALYPSE
SHADES OF DESPAIR, SIGNS OF HOPE

The grim realities of the waning months of the Civil War become tangible in an 1864 painting by the Pittsburgh artist David Gilmour Blythe, *Old Virginia Home* (Figure 11).[1] Clouds of lightning-laced smoke billow up behind a ramshackle house, evoking images of the Shenandoah Valley after Sheridan's troops had laid it waste in September and October. More explicitly, Blythe lays the credit for the debacle at the feet of Henry A. Wise, governor of the state from 1856 to 1860, whose name appears on the end of the shattered barrel in the right foreground. While serving as governor Wise rejected pleas for clemency for John Brown and permitted his hanging in 1859; later he became a Confederate general. The only human form discernible in the painting is a slave, who sidles through a pool of light, his bonds sundered not by a daring abolitionist raid but by the noise and confusion of war. The slave does not appear to be anticipating a glorious Day of Jubilee; the wasted landscape holds no suggestion of millennial promise. The chaos of the scene is not random but orchestrated by the apocalyptic figures sweeping across the sky in the background, identified by Bruce W. Chambers as the marshal of War and the raven of Famine.[2] Blythe's interpretation of just who was to blame for the devastation of the South provides a counterargument to the South's version, a view that appeared in Adalbert Volck's 1863 print, *Tracks of the Armies* (Figure 12).[3] In Volck's print a weary Confederate soldier staggers at the sight of his ruined home, where vultures hover over the ravaged, nude corpse of his wife, her assailant's hair still gripped in her dead fingers. Southern outrage at Northern depravity only increased as

---

[1] The Art Institute of Chicago, all rights reserved.

[2] Bruce Chambers, *The World of David Gilmore Blythe: 1815–1865* (Washington DC: Smithsonian Institution, 1981) 96.

[3] Courtesy of the Library of Congress.

Sherman's armies approached the sea in late 1864. The Yankees were responsible for the devastation, in their view.

In the last months of the war, apocalyptic interpretations of events reflect increasing despair on both sides. Grand, glorious, and satisfyingly terrifying references to the sublime battle of battles were not durable enough to persist throughout the long, wearing years of the war, when absolute right and wrong were dulled by a numbing stream of stalemate and senseless carnage. Instead of decisively redressing clearly defined evil and obvious wrongdoing, the war became a grim waiting game to see which side could survive the onset of the Apocalypse. Even with victory in sight, Northerners did not express the delight they had been waiting so long to celebrate. The sense of an approaching literal end of the world remained until the close of the war, but it became muted and bitter. All participants agreed that war was a judgment from God; therefore, the events occurred either to eliminate sin or to bring humility and dependence to God's chosen people. As despair about the ultimate meaning of the war deepened, individuals looked for signs of hope with increasing impatience, and they welcomed any promising portent.

By 1865 it became apparent that apocalyptic language could be applied to almost any situation, from enormous victory to overwhelming defeat. The Confederacy sustained apocalyptic optimism even when it was at the brink of extinction. The dragon of the North, Southerners were told, would be loosed only for a short time, and then God would lead his chosen people to victory. The close of the war also saw a shift in the use of apocalyptic imagery by the North. Whereas rhetoric describing the end of the world during the early part of the war urged revolutionary changes in the social structure of the United States, that aim virtually disappeared in the North by the end of the war. Union military success became a defense of its existence, a vindication of the status quo. It seemed as if emancipation had cleared an enormous moral burden off the Northern conscience while actually creating little change in social practices.

Although Northerners were still capable of placing blame on the South, their primary activity was an introspective scrutiny for secret sins that could explain the prolongation of the war. In the early years of the conflict, the language of the Apocalypse had been a primary energizing factor in the war effort. The unexpectedly long duration of the war produced a general sense of exhaustion that affected apocalyptic language. Jeremiad rhetoric in the North became more intense as in-habitants of that region looked more and more closely for harbored sins. The depth of this anguish was expressed in a Methodist hymn printed in the autumn of 1864. Although it makes a typically condescending remark about the opposition, "Forgive our foes, restore to them their sight," it seems to wish more for an end to the fighting than for an ideological victory. The hymn's main concern is directed inward: "Cleanse us from guilt; allay our many fears." The atoning sacrifice predicted years earlier by Julia Ward Howe has been accomplished: "See our altars wet / With blood of sacrifice!" Another image shared with the "Battle Hymn" is the wine press. "How long, O Lord! from out the press must flow / The nation's blood-red wine?" implores the poet.[4] The bloodshed can only be stopped by the coming of the Lord.

This poem provides a striking contrast to "The Battle Hymn." God is still a "God of Battles," but his people are flawed. If they were not harboring a secret sin, the war would be over. Furthermore, in the later song the writer is uncertain about why the war is being fought. Whereas Howe's hymn stated that all of this sacrifice was done in order "to make men free," the strongest justification for the war in "Hymn for Northern People" is its ability to identify and purge sin.

In spite of the despair resulting from the prolongation of the war, it became evident that many Northerners still saw the conflict in terms of a cosmic battle. The North did not have the degree of certainty about their cause that the South had, and it spent more time reassuring itself that it indeed must be fighting on the right side. Its jeremiad rhetoric constantly probed for weaknesses and sources of guilt. The North seemed to be the most concerned about the prolongation of the war since it was overwhelmingly superior in manpower and supplies.

Northerners were willing to place significance on any event that might be interpreted as a hopeful sign that their cause would finally prevail. This attitude is summed up in an 1864 sermon by the Reverend Herrick Johnson, titled "The Shaking of the Nations." Written in response to Lincoln's declaration of a day of thanksgiving after the Northern victory at Mobile Bay and the capture of Atlanta, this sermon is designed to remind Northern Christians that the battle is indeed the Lord's. Johnson ties together texts from Haggai and Hebrews that

---

[4]"A Hymn for Northern People," *Zion's Herald and Wesleyan Journal* 35 (5 October 1864): 1. (See appendix.).

describe the shaking of the nations that will take place at the end of the world. This shaking, says Johnson, refers to "the wonderful changes and revolutions that would occur in morals and religion," resulting in the establishment of a kingdom that cannot be moved. In this passage Johnson captures the significance of the war both as an event marking the end of the world and also as a tremendous social upheaval signaled by "revolution upon revolution, moral earthquakes, changes in principalities and powers, the sweeping away of things that are made, the whole universe moved by new convulsions and upheavings, and all the nations and kingdoms of the earth trembling and shaken in the mighty birth-throes of a kingdom whose foundations will never be shaken."[5]

Johnson describes the earthquakes at the crucifixion and resurrection of Christ as the initial upheavals in a period of shaking that would continue until all evil, corrupt practices and institutions had been shaken out of the earth, leaving only solid, eternal religious truths. Here is another reason to be encouraged by disaster and tragedy. Rather than a process directed at God's people in order to purify them, the events are part of the process of isolating God's church as the only eternal reality on earth. Even as Christ brought to the world not peace, but a sword, Christianity by its very nature "*is a declaration of war to the world.*"[6] Furthermore, the Civil War, since it is fought on the behalf of liberty and equality, is much more significant than a conflict between two disagreeing political parties: "It is a war of principalities and powers, and the rulers of the darkness of this world, and spiritual wickedness in high places, no less than a war of flesh and blood."[7] It would be unreasonable to hope that the transition from Satan's kingdom to God's kingdom would take place calmly. The very intensity of the battle signals its significance.

In this sermon Johnson is developing an interpretation of the war more powerful than the mere idea that even good people needed some chastening. Much of the fascination about the war, and much of the reason for describing it in sublime imagery, is identified by Johnson in his identification of divine involvement. It is a privilege, not a burden, to live during such a period of history: "Such a view of the subject makes it

---

[5]Johnson, *The Shaking of the Nations*, 6. This is a thanksgiving sermon preached at the Third Presbyterian Church, Pittsburgh, PA, on Sunday, 11 September 1864.

[6]Ibid., 13.

[7]Ibid., 17.

glorious to live in the midst of these shakings. It is cause for thankfulness that we are permitted to see God's ways thus impressively vindicated: that to our very sight the demonstration is being made to-day: that ours is the baptism of cloud, whose night is to be followed by new sunrises of light and liberty."[8] Only severe sacrifice will be sufficient to defeat Satan forever. The darker the night of the conflict, the more glorious will be the sunrise that follows. This sunrise of course represents the dawn of the millennium, when evil will have been eliminated forever.

Another Northern clergyman reassured Union troops that this period of upheaval preceded "a period of the overthrow of despotism, and the downfall of Anti-Christ."[9] The Civil War is part of the process of making the United States a prominent power in the eyes of the rest of the world. Northern military technology, developed as a result of the war, will serve a divine purpose. God "has been for centuries preparing this nation for a vastness of military power without a parallel in the annals of mankind." The United States are God's "great military and naval depot, for raising and training the legions He has called for the last great conflict of earth."[10]

In a further search for reassurance of divine favor, Northerners literally looked to the sky. Any unusual display in the heavens was a signal that God recognized what was transpiring on the earth, and people in the North were eager to interpret these displays as tokens of divine approval for the United States. Strategically placed rainbows provided one such reassurance. An example from early in the war demonstrates how people were able to interpret these events favorably. One observer referred to a *Louisville Journal* account of an occasion when Union troops were marching through a town in Kentucky, their regimental and national flags waving. At that moment a rainbow appeared in the sky, and "a little boy, seeing it, ran to his mother, exclaiming, 'Mother, God is a Union man! he has just hung out in the sky the red, white and blue.'" The author uses this incident to point out that "there is no courage like that which springs from the consciousness that God is on our side." This confidence "gives heart to every blow of the Union forces; while the

---

[8]Ibid., 18.

[9]Robert Patterson, "The Moral Results of This War," *Christ in the Army: A Selection of the Work of the U. S. Christian Commission* (Philadelphia: Ladies Christian Commission, 1865) 139.

[10]Ibid., 137.

suspicion that they are fighting against the course of Providence...sends weakness into the rebel ranks." If the free institutions of the United States were to fail, God would have to throw out three hundred years of providential guidance in American history. Therefore, "*in the moral heavens, too, God hangs out his unmistakable sign.*"[11]

The association of the flag with a rainbow appears in a poem by E. P. Worth and published in 1864.[12] According to the line of reasoning in this poem, the design of the US flag was divinely ordained to correspond with objects in the heavens, in order to make clear the symbolism of the relationship between God and his chosen nation. This "rainbow flag" is a "celestial sign" that the "eternal word / By all shall yet be heard." Its message is peace and universal harmony. Walt Whitman, in "Song of the Banner at Daybreak," sees similar significance for the flag, although he associates it with the sunrise rather than with a rainbow. The flag and its pennant symbolize the nation and its armies, and they represent war as well as peace. The flag is a banner that leads "the day with stars brought from the night."[13] It is raised so high that it seems a part of the early morning sky, a symbol of hope during war and prosperity in times of peace.

Frederic Church portrayed a similar interpretation of the flag in his painting, "Our Banner in the Sky." Into a pattern of light and clouds at sunset, Church wove the blue field, white stars, and red and white stripes of the US flag as if this were a natural evening phenomenon. This imaginary event symbolized hope for the North. David Huntington states that the message of this painting is that "Union victory was ordained by natural history." In this view, the North is explicitly predestined for military success.[14]

In May of 1865 an unusual aurora borealis display caught the attention of Northerners and inspired a poem by Herman Melville. The poem associates the fading of the display with the disbanding of armies after hostilities had ceased. Melville's poem reflects the ambivalence of Northern uncertainty, the "dallyings of doom," the "transitions and enhancings," the "Splendor and Terror" that marked either "portent or

---

[11]Edmund H. Sears, "Signs in the Sky–Beautiful Incident," *The Monthly Religious Magazine* 27 (April 1862): 267. Emphasis original.

[12]E. P. Worth, "The Banner of the Sky," *Songs of the Soldiers*, ed. Moore, 205–206.

[13]Walt Whitman, "Song of the Banner at Daybreak," *Leaves of Grass*, 290.

[14]Huntington, *The Landscapes of Frederic Edwin Church*, 61.

promise." Both the coming and the departure of this phenomenon represent God in Melville's mind. Like God, they decreed both the coming ("the million blades that glowed") and the departure of the conflict, which came at midnight and left at the morning. The daylight that follows the aurora borealis display may not be as dramatic as the millennial dawn—it is "pale, meek Dawn"—but it provides a sign of hope that God approved of the end of the war as clearly as he had supported its beginning.[15]

The Northern artist Frederic Church was also moved to respond to a display of the aurora borealis. He witnessed a dramatic display on 23 December 1864 and produced the painting "Aurora Borealis," in 1865 (Figure 13).[16] Based on the 1864 display as well as another one he had sketched in the Arctic in 1860 and set in an Arctic landscape beyond the range of Church's own northern voyages, the painting is actually about the fate of the United States in 1865.[17] The almost monochromatic night time scene is eerily lit by the green and red glow of the luminous figures shimmering in the sky. In the visual language of 1865, the image suggests gloom and despair mitigated by the cold comfort of the uncanny, otherworldly glowing forms. The divine presence implied here is more cryptic than the explicit forms of David Gilmour Blythe's *Old Virginia Home*, but it suggests a hopeful, if inscrutable, future.

By the end of the war, the sense of apocalyptic triumph expressed in earlier works such as "The Battle Hymn of the Republic" had been replaced by a much more somber tone. Christopher Cranch celebrates the end of the war in his poem "The Dawn of Peace," but the victory has become the aftermath of demon possession: "The demon, shrieking, tears us as he flies / Exorcised from our wrenched and bleeding frame."[18] The willingness at the beginning of the war to leap into battle and spill noble Northern blood on the altars of sacrifice has been replaced by the sentiment that the end of the war is a "release too long delayed." The fierceness needed to win the war "never triumphed in a juster cause," and never was "bloody war...so justly waged." Still, the United States flag now

---

[15]Herman Melville, "Aurora-Borealis," in *Battle-Pieces*, 148–49.(See appendix).

[16]Courtesy of the National Museum of American Art, Smithsonian Institution.

[17]Franklin Kelly, *Frederic Edwin Church* (Washington DC: The National Gallery of Art, 1989) 62–63. See also William H. Treuttner, "The Genesis of Frederic Edwin Church's 'Aurora Borealis,'" *Art Quarterly* 81 (Autumn 1968): 267–83.

[18]Christopher Cranch, "The Dawn of Peace," from *The Bird and the Bell*, n.p.

"greets a cloudless morn," since peace has finally dawned. "The nation is re-born!" proclaims Cranch, but he leaves the impression that the marks of its agony are still fresh on its form.

Instead of relying on bombast or heated topical rhetoric, this poem by Cranch and Melville's "Aurora-Borealis" are relatively subdued attempts to describe attitudes in the North at the end of the war. The nation was weakened, as if by a long illness, but it had recovered and could anticipate a future free of the major sins it had fought the war to erase: slavery and the disease of secession. Along with this certainty comes an awareness that the nation does not now know God as well as it thought it did when the war began. To Herman Melville, the ways of God are inscrutable. He started the war, and he ended it in his own time. His purposes for prolonging the conflict were not entirely clear.

As Southerners attempted to find meaning in the events of the war, they energized their apocalyptic certainty in two ways: either their setbacks were sent to them in order to identify and purge sins, or they were administered in order to build the character of a righteous nation preparing for its leading role in the Apocalypse. Regardless of the explanation of their woes, Southerners projected much more confidence in the basic rightness of their cause than their Northern counterparts did. Jeremiad rhetoric was uncommon in the South during the Civil War. Even when a Southern minister attempted to preach a jeremiad, his underlying certainty in the Southern cause usually prevailed. Numerous examples of this tendency may be found in the rhetoric of Stephen Elliott, Episcopal Bishop of Georgia. Early in the conflict he had told his parishioners that although war might be sent to punish a nation, it could also arise for a helpful reason: to "purge out our old dross." The errors of the North would become more apparent, according to Elliott, thereby enabling the new Southern nation to avoid them.[19] National trials, he maintained, were a sign of God's favor. Just after the disastrous summer of 1863, he declared that "those of whom God is intending to make a nation to do his work upon earth, are precisely those whom he tries most severely." It is God's purpose to give not "merely victory, but character,"

---

[19]Stephen Elliott, Bishop of Georgia, *New Wine Not to Be Put into Old Bottles* (Savannah: John M. Cooper, 1862) 17. This sermon was preached on Friday, 2 February 1862, on a day of national humiliation, fasting, and prayer.

and "not only independence, but righteousness."[20] Not until the autumn of 1864 did Elliott's rhetoric take a more somber turn. At that time he attempted to explain why neither side was able to take advantage of its victories: "We reaped a harvest of death and nothing else. And so will it continue until God's wrath is satisfied, and therefore have I not been disturbed by our recent reverses." Still, however, Elliott maintained his righteous certainty. It is impossible for these reverses to mean more than temporary suffering and punishment, he declared, because subjugation of the South would interfere with God's purpose.[21]

Just a few days before this sermon by Elliott, on the same day that churches in the North were celebrating a national thanksgiving for military victories, the Rev. J. L. Barrows, a Baptist clergyman in Georgia, preached a sermon that was perhaps the most classic example of the jeremiad form to appear in Southern literature during the Civil War. He admits that woes result from sins, but the tone quickly reveals underlying confidence. The sins of nations are directly punishable by divine judgments, and the national sins of the South are pride, dissipation, amusements, greed (profiting from the war), blasphemy, sensuality, Sabbath profanation, and drunkenness. If, however, the people of the South should turn away from their sins, and "if they were to devote themselves to a pure life of obedience to God's known laws, all doubts as to the results of this war would be over."[22]

When Southern sermons adopted a darker jeremiad tone, the primary sinner was nearly always the external participant: the North. According to one CSA chaplain, this certainty existed because of the "high religious character of the majority of those who composed the Confederate government and its army." The firm belief that the Confederacy was upholding the correct side in a war of conscience was

---

[20]Stephen Elliott, Bishop of Georgia, *Ezra's Dilemma* (Savannah: George N. Nichols, 1863) 17. This is a sermon preached on Friday, 21 August 1863, a day of national humiliation, fasting, and prayer.

[21]Stephen Elliott, Bishop of Georgia, *Vain is the Help of Man* (Macon GA: Burke, Boykin & Co., 1864) 10. This sermon was preached on Thursday, 15 September 1864, a day of national fasting, humiliation, and prayer.

[22]J. L Barrows, *Nationality Insured!* (Augusta GA: Jas. Nathan Ells, 1864) 6–7. This is a sermon delivered at the First Baptist Church, Augusta GA, on 11 September 1864.

present not only among the military but also among "the people of the South [who] looked upon their cause as a holy one."[23]

Given the relish with which the slaves described their cause in the predictive terms of the Apocalypse and the retrospective terms of the Exodus, the tendency of their masters to make the same connection for themselves is remarkable. For example, Dr. Smyth wrote in the *Southern Presbyterian Review* in 1863 that slavery was a gift of God to help the righteous South make well-deserved profits. Abraham Lincoln, by hampering the South from fulfilling this divine design, was playing the same role Pharoah had to the Israelites of the Exodus. Again intertwining the Pentateuch and the Apocalypse, Smyth echoes Rev. 18:4 when he tells his fellow Southerners that God is speaking to them "*as with a voice from heaven*, saying, 'COME OUT OF THE UNION, MY PEOPLE.'" In the next breath, apparently oblivious to the irony of his language, Smyth asserts that "ABRAHAM LINCOLN *neither heard nor heeded this voice that spake so audibly from heaven, in the otherwise inexplicable events that were occurring around him. He hardened his heart, and stiffened his neck, and would not let the people go.*"[24]

In a related use of rhetoric, the Reverend C. H. Wiley told his countrymen that their trials were preparing them for a great role, perhaps the greatest since the Exodus. "It was not necessary for God to place a wilderness between Egypt and Canaan," he assured them, "but when individuals and nations are called to higher destinies, their way is laid through trials in order to prove their dispositions, to learn them their errors and weakness, to purge out of them follies inconsistent with the more elevated position which they would occupy, to expose the rottenness of their moral state, and to lead them to the source of health."[25] Here Wiley articulates the essence of the meaning of the Civil War for many Southerners. Their certainty was older than the war, so the explanation of the events of the war had to be shaped to fit that certainty. The departure from the Union was a foregone conclusion, and the trials that accompanied the process were going to strengthen the new Confederate nation.

---

[23]Charles Todd Quintard, *Doctor Quintard, Chaplain CSA and Second Bishop of Tennessee, Being his Story of the War* (Sewanee TN: The University Press, 1905) 1.

[24]Dr. Smyth, *Southern Presbyterian Review*, as quoted in R. L. Stanton, *The Church and the Rebellion* (New York: Derby & Miller, 1864) 294. Emphasis original.

[25]Wiley, *Scriptural Views*, 115–16.

The exodus was irreversible, as far as Southern citizens were concerned; there would be no turning back for the South. Mrs. C. C. Jones, Sr. wrote to her son Charles, Jr. that not only was the South "contending in a just and righteous cause," but it was also preferable that "WE ALL perish in its defense before we submit to the infamy and utter ruin and misery involved in any connection whatever with the vilest and most degraded nation on the face of the earth." Mrs. Jones believed that in some ways, the South deserved to suffer: "It may be our sins will be scourged to the severest extremity—and we deserve it all." The South, however, would fare much better than the North, whose punishment will be meted out directly from the book of Revelation: "when that wicked people have filled up the cup of their iniquity, God will...reward them according to their transgressions."[26]

A more wistful note appears in an 1864 poem by George Sass, "A Prayer for Peace." The author uses the standard vocabulary of the sublime to describe the perception of God's ire: "Closer the shadows crouch around our path— / The billowy storm-clouds of impending wrath." The poet speaks with the exhaustion of a people who fear that they may have been deserted by God. He invokes the wine-press imagery used by many writers early in the war to signal its importance. Now, however, it is a symbol of sin: "For two long years the wine-press we have trodden, / Sure Thou wilt hearken as we turn to Thee, / Lifting our bridal-robes, all stained and sodden / With the red tears of wounded Purity!"[27]

Any faltering of Southern resolve was stifled when the wholesale invasion of Southern territory began. The fighting around Atlanta in September of 1864 provoked intensely bitter reactions from Southern civilians. They were appalled when General William Tecumseh Sherman declared his intention to depopulate Atlanta, and they were insulted at his reply when the mayor of that city asked him to reconsider: "You might as well appeal against the thunder-storm as against these terrible hardships of war...the only way the people of Atlanta can hope once more to live in peace and quiet at home, is to stop the war, which can only be done by admitting that it began in error and is perpetuated in

---

[26]Mrs. C. C. Jones, Sr. to Charles C. Jones, Jr., 18 September 1863, *Children of Pride*, 402.

[27]George Herbert Sass, "A Prayer for Peace," *The Living Writers of the South*, ed. James Wood Davidson (New York: Carleton, 1869) 496. (See appendix.)

pride."[28] Sherman's army became the diabolical force that seemed to be overwhelming God's righteous nation. In a poem about the sacking of Atlanta, Virginia French invokes sublime imagery in her opening lines to introduce the "spectre" that will forever after be associated with "the fierce Destroyer," "Destruction," "Desolation," and occasions "where with iron-sceptre crushes every right we prized." At these times the people of the south will "groan in anguish—"GOD! THE RIGHT, IS SHERMANIZED!" Sherman has transformed Southern paradise into an outpost of hell, complete with "bale-fires of destruction, lurid on the solemn night." The fiendish Sherman: "may sacrifice the aged, and exult when woman stands / 'Mid the sunken, sodden ashes of her home, with palsied hands / Dropping over hungered children—man may thus immortalize / His name with haggard infamy—his watchword— 'SHERMANIZE!'" In this poem the writer paradoxically uses the fear and anger stirred up by this Yankee angel of destruction to encourage her countrymen. Sherman was the devil incarnate, and certainly God would not allow him to oppress the South much longer. The poet exhorts her readers to redouble their efforts to continue "working on for Southern freedom" in order to achieve the day when "the 'solitary place again shall blossom as the rose.'"[29]

Another infuriated poetic response greeted Sherman's dealing with the city of Charleston, South Carolina. William Gilmore Simms was outraged at the treatment of his hometown, and his political attitudes had become increasingly harsh. He and other Charleston poets expressed increasingly violent reactions to the presence of Northern troops. Simms's poem "The Fiend Unbound" depicts life in Charleston during the Christmas season of 1864, when its doom was imminent. Savannah had fallen to Sherman a few days before Christmas, and Charleston, the seat of the rebellion in the eyes of Union troops, was the next eagerly awaited prey. The poem mourns that a Christmas celebration is impossible, with the church deserted like a bride at the altar and the buildings adorned with blood instead of Christmas decorations. The spirit of Christmas has been replaced by "THE FIEND," who "hurls

---

[28]Letter from General William Sherman to James M. Calhoun, mayor of Atlanta, 12 September 1864, as quoted by William T. Sherman, *Memoirs of General William T. Sherman* (New York: D. Appleton, 1875) 2:126.

[29]L. Virginia French, "Shermanized," *The Southern Poems of the War*, ed. Virginia Emily Mason (Baltimore: J. Murphy & Co., 1867) 361–63. (See appendix.)

around Satanic flame." The evil spirit is the devil himself, who has been loosed after his thousand years of captivity. As if making up for lost time, he commits one outrage after another:

In hate,—evoked by kindred lands,
But late beslavering with caress,
Lo, Moloch, dripping crimson, stands,
And curses where he cannot bless.
He wings the blot and hurls the spear,
A *demon loosed*, that rends in rage,
Sends havoc through the homes most dear,
And butchers youth and tramples age!

Moloch is aided by his kindred demon, Mammon, and a host of lesser demons in a destructive rampage. The poem refers explicitly to the loosing of Satan described in Revelation 20 and then reminds the reader that the dragon will soon be eliminated:

The Dragon, chain'd for thousand years,
Hath burst his bonds and rages free;—
Yet, patience, brethren, stay your fears;—
Loosed for "a little season," he
Will soon, beneath th' Ithuriel sword,
Of heavenly judgment, crush'd and driven,
Yield to the vengeance of the Lord,
And crouch beneath the wrath of Heaven![30]

After just "a few more hours of mortal strife," the poem promises, the righteous victims of the fiend will triumph.

Another poem mentions the Anaconda plan of the North that called for slow strangulation of Southern ports with a naval blockade. This reptilian image fit in with numerous comparisons between the enemy and biblical dragons. Charleston residents were infuriated when they learned that naval gunners were shelling the city by taking aim at the spire of St. Michael's Church. Here was final proof that a righteous nation was being assailed by the wicked one. In "The Angel of the

---

[30]"The Fiend Unbound," from the *Charleston Mercury*, reprinted in Simms, ed., *War Poetry of the South*, 247–50. (See appendix.)

Church," William Gilmore Simms refers to this situation and addresses his poem to the North. He calls on "the avenging God" to vent his wrath; any delay on God's part will merely make the final punishment more severe. The South has the confidence of supernatural assistance: "And he who smote the dragon down, / And chained him thousand years of time, / Need never fear the boa's frown / Though loathsome in his spite and slime."[31] The poem closes with an appeal to stronger faith on the part of the residents of Charleston. Even at this late date, Southern hope is not destroyed.

Simms made a desperate rallying cry to his fellow South Carolinians even as the Confederacy was collapsing around them. In "Ode," he exhorts them to put aside cowardice and, now that "your cities [are] all reeking in flame," to protect their women from what will happen next. He then writes a passage that refers to the exploits of General Butler's troops in New Orleans in April 1862:

> Your virgins, defiled at the altar,—
> In the loathsome embrace of the felon and slave,
> Touch loathsomer far than the worm of the grave!
> Ah! God! if you fail in this moment of gloom!
> How base were the weakness, how horrid the doom!
> With the fiends in your streets howling paeans,
> And the Beast o'er another Orleans!

A last burst of courage is necessary, the poet exhorts his readers, in order to "smite" the enemy: "Then fail not, and quail not; the foe shall prevail not: / With the faith and the will, ye shall conquer him still."[32]

One Southern poem reveals the extent to which both sides were conscious of the manipulation of apocalyptic rhetoric for military purposes. "The War-Christian's Thanksgiving" is dedicated to the "War-Clergy" of the United States. The poet is referring not necessarily to military chaplains but to the clergymen who inspired and prolonged the war with their inflammatory rhetoric. A bitterly satiric quote from Jeremiah serves as a headnote to the poem: "Cursed be he that doeth the work of the Lord negligently, and cursed be he that keepeth back his

---

[31]William Gilmore Simms, "The Angel of the Church," *War Poetry of the South*, 294. (See appendix.)

[32]Simms, "Ode–'Do Ye Quail?'" *War Poetry*, 253–55. (See appendix.)

sword from blood." The poem depicts a group of militaristic clergy, not yet sated with blood, praying to their God: "O God of Battles! once again, / With banner, trump, and drum, / And garments in Thy wine-press dyed, / To give Thee thanks, we come!" Although wine-press imagery pervaded language on both sides of the conflict, the reference here may be to the "Battle Hymn of the Republic"; both are written in the same meter. This passage emphasizes the pomp and pageantry enjoyed by Christians who believe that their military cause is also a holy one. The poem goes on, in the bitter humorlessness characteristic of Juvenalian satire, to thank God for all of the atrocities and miseries of war. It expresses the certainty that the North is on the side of "wisdom, truth, and right" and that God "hast clothed us with the wrath / To do the work of Heaven." The narrator requests that "while the press hath wine to bleed, / Oh! tread it with us still!" The God being appealed to here is a merciless tyrant very different from Christ, who appealed only to "fond fools." The bloodthirsty persona concludes by saying "And when the last red drop is shed, / We'll kneel again—and pray!"[33]

The writer of this song struggles with the same problem that faced Abraham Lincoln in the autumn of 1862. Christians on both sides claimed the exclusive favor of God. For Lincoln, the answer was that God existed above and beyond the myopic concerns of any political power. For the writer of "War-Christian's Thanksgiving," the Northern God was an anthropomorphic monster invoked by a group of Christians who confined their Bible reading to the most bloodthirsty passages of the Old Testament. A similar point of view is expressed by Bishop Stephen Elliott in his funeral address for General Leonidas Polk in the summer of 1864. Polk had been a bishop in the Protestant Episcopal church until the war, when he was appointed as a major general by Jefferson Davis. His death gave fellow bishop Stephen Elliott the opportunity to lash out at the North, specifically the Northern clergy, as the primary instigators of the war. He summons the priests and bishops of the North to the judgment-seat of Christ, where he launches into a flight of passionate rhetoric:

> I summon you to that bar in the name of that sacred liberty which you have trampled under foot; in the name of the glorious constitution which you have destroyed; in the name of our holy

---

[33]S. Teackle Wallis, "The War-Christian's Thanksgiving," *South Songs*, ed. De Leon, 75–77. (See appendix.)

religion which you have profaned; in the name of the temples of
God which you have desecrated; in the name of a thousand
martyred saints whose blood you have wantonly spilled; in the
name of our Christian women whom you have violated; in the
name of our slaves whom you have seduced and then consigned
to misery; and there I leave justice and vengeance to God.[34]

Elliott tells the North that God will avenge his righteous dead and
closes with the hope that God will find mercy on them in the midst of his
retribution.

One Confederate artist saw signs of hope in images of Fort Sumter.
Stationed in Charleston in 1863 and early 1864 as an Army mapmaker,
Conrad Wise Chapman made many sketches of the Fort. While visiting
his ailing mother in Italy, Chapman produced thirty-one painted views of
the fort. One of the series was reproduced by the artist's father, John
Gadsby Chapman, and titled Evening Gun, For Sumter (Figure 14). It
provides a visual counterpart to aspects of Frederic Church's *Cotopaxi*
and *Our Banner in the Sky*. From Chapman's low visual angle, the
silhouetted gun provides visual weight in the dark, shadowy side of the
composition. The gun's muzzle is brightly lit, evoking suggestions of the
flames that had once burst from it. The dark, gloomy foreground con-
trasts with the brilliant luminous background that includes the Charleston skyline. Equally brilliant is the tattered Confederate flag. Certainly, a
Southern view of this scene could suggest hope shining through the
storm clouds of the war.[35]

By 1865 Southerners were confronting the reality that their
righteous nation was going to lose the war. In the Shenandoah Valley of
Virginia, Cornelia McDonald reflected in her diary about her feelings
during February 1865. In the midst of her discouragement, she wrote,
"Though I did not permit myself for a single moment to apprehend a
total defeat, I could not see or imagine how we were ever to hold out."[36]
She could not begin to comprehend that the bloodshed suffered by her
countrymen could have been for nothing or that the South's political

---

[34]Stephen Elliott, *Funeral Services at the Burial of the Right Reverend Leonidas Polk,
D. D., together with the Sermon Delivered in St. Paul's Church, Augusta, Georgia, on June
29, 1864* (Columbia SC: Evans & Cogswell, 1864) 26.

[35]Reproduction courtesy of the Museum of the Confederacy, Richmond, Virginia.

[36]McDonald, *Diary*, 247.

leaders faced imprisonment and possible execution. "The prolonged struggle, dreadful as it was, was better than defeat, and the scorn of our insolent enemies.... How furious have I grown at hearing the word 'rebel' applied to our great and good leaders."[37] Defeat tasted particularly bitter to the South because it had expected so much, both on a literal political and also on a religious level, believing that it could lead the world into the millennium. The height of its expectations was to be followed by a corresponding surge of despair and disillusionment that could be masked only partially by the rhetoric of the Lost Cause.

The cool, apparently objective, eye of the camera recorded the state of the South at the end of the war. In 1862 and 1863 Matthew Brady's and Alexander Gardner's grisly photographs brought a new level of realism and revulsion to the audiences who visited their exhibitions or purchased their photographs. The photographers who followed General Sherman's army across Georgia and South Carolina, however, told a story more symbolic and less human. On 14 April 1865, as Abraham Lincoln made plans to attend Ford's Theater that evening, photographers came to Charleston to photograph the ceremonies as the US flag was raised over Fort Sumter, exactly four years after it had been replaced by the Confederate Stars and Bars. After the ceremonies photographers fanned through the streets of the city, recording the damage it had incurred during its eighteen-month siege and evacuation.

These photographs are stark, even grim. To Northern eyes they documented the retribution for secession; in the Southern view, they provided reminders of indignities and fueled pride in the Lost Cause. One view of Charleston is notable for the rare presence of human figures, "Charleston, S. C. View of Ruined Buildings Through the Porch of the Circular Church, 150 Meeting St." (Figure 15)[38] In this photograph, the camera aims across the street at the ruined buildings in the background. Framed by the foreground rubble, the monumental ruined wall of the porch, and a stately, shell-pocked column, are four Negro boys. They would not have been difficult to recruit; they probably had tagged along with the photographer out of curiosity. By placing them at the center of this dramatic composition, the photographer lends symbolic weight to the scene. The children are intact; the church and the other reminders of antebellum Southern life are shattered. Americans who had no difficulty

---

[37]Ibid., 248.
[38]Courtesy of the Library of Congress.

reading the Apocalypse in Frederic Church's *Cotopaxi* volcanic eruption could easily see the aftermath of divine judgment in this scene.

After the war ended came the delicate task of readmitting the Confederate states to the Union. This process was particularly difficult in the light of the high expectations Southerners had maintained for their country. Their reaction to the undesirable outcome of the war is evident in resolutions adopted by the Virginia Assembly in May of 1865. Virginia proclaimed itself a member of the Union and accepted the abolition of slavery. It protested, however, the requirement of giving suffrage to the Negro, and proceeded to "denounce as unjust, oppressive and subversive of public and private liberty, the measures of Congress, known as the Reconstruction acts, which as their crowning iniquity have given birth to a [state] Constitution, which besides being in conflict with the Supreme law of the land, proscribes intelligence, lifts incompetency into places of authority, and fastens the yoke of negro supremacy upon the necks of hereditary freemen."[39] This sense of righteous indignation was a primary source of the idea of the Lost Cause that persisted in the South into the twentieth century. It was a sentiment that many Southerners were not afraid to express openly.

A few years after the war, an oration for the Southern Historical Society described the conflict from the Southern point of view; it had been a battle of conscience against the North, which had perverted the US Constitution. Since the Confederate troops had given their word of honor that they would not resume hostilities against the US government, there would be no more fighting, but the speech cautioned that "it is idle to shut our eyes to the fact that this consolidated empire of States is not the Union established by our fathers." Once again the unshakable faith of the South in the rightness of its cause is revealed. In language that sounds like a parody of the Gettysburg Address, the oration goes on to say that "a nation cannot long survive when the fundamental principles which gave it life, originally, are subverted." Although such a nation can develop a sort of forced, temporary prosperity, it is one which has "absorbed and obliterated the rights of the citizen, [it is] a prosperity which was gained by the sacrifice of individual independence, a glory which was ever the precursor of inevitable anarchy, disintegration, and ultimate extinction."

---

[39]"Resolutions of the Virginia General Assembly c. May 1865," in the Brock Collection BR Box 289 Misc. This item is reproduced by permission of the Huntington Library, San Marino, California.

Once again, even after the war, the South is exhibiting two distinguishing rhetorical characteristics: God is still in control, able to punish powerful countries that abuse their might; this assurance makes possible the doom-saying of a jeremiad form that inverts itself by pointing outward. Repentance is the only escape from catastrophe, and it requires "a voluntary return to the fundamental principles upon which our republic was originally founded."[40] The speaker acknowledges that a revolution has taken place, but he also believes that it is a false one and can be reversed by a return to earlier, purer principles. The South kept its hopes alive through the belief that it was still not too late to abandon an immoral historical course and backtrack to the point in the past where the wrong direction had been taken.

A great deal of the energy of the Lost Cause went into the effort to set the historical record straight in Southern terms. The South faced the inevitable fate of defeated nations; it had to listen to the historical accounts of the winning side proclaimed as if they were disinterested fact. D. H. Pannill, a Southern historian, expressed the sentiments of many of his countrymen in an 1891 letter. He described his history of the Army of Northern Virginia as a reply to Swinton's book on the Army of the Potomac. As an introduction he had included a history of the slavery question from the constitutional convention in 1787 to the Charleston secession convention of 1860. He believed that this background was necessary in order to show what had motivated the Army of Northern Virginia during the Civil War. Furthermore, he said, it was important to set the historical record straight because "it is proper that the rising generation should fully understand the motives that prompted their fathers in the greatest civil conflict of modern times, especially as northern writers, notably the biographers of Mr. Lincoln, are still calling them traitors or conspirators."[41]

The conclusion of the Civil War left Southern attitudes toward its issues largely unchanged. Defeat had not diminished the righteousness of its cause. For a time it was still possible to believe that the outcome of the war was not God's will. Perhaps there was a plan to let the tyrant nation run its course and reap the results of its tyranny. If so, the South would keep its faith alive until it could spring out of the ashes of the self-destroyed Union. The cause of the South was still a holy one.

---

[40]"Orations," *Southern Historical Society Papers* 13 (1889): 333.

[41]D. H. Pannill to the *Richmond Dispatch*, 17 August 1891.

This certainty did affect Southern theology, however. According to Pamela Colbenson, the Civil War had a decided impact on the course of millennial thought in the South. After the conflict postmillennial optimism, so common in earlier decades, was replaced by a conviction that only the Second Coming of Christ could alleviate the conditions of Reconstruction.[42]

The North, on the other hand, achieved its victory with the knowledge that it did not know God as well as it had thought it did before the war began. God did not bring the victory in the way Northerners had expected, and their growing uncertainty about his involvement in their affairs, along with the aggressive secularism and acquisitiveness of the late nineteenth century, eroded away their confidence. They had won the war, but they were less likely to believe that God dealt out victories on their own terms.

---

[42]Pamela Colbenson, "Millennial Thought Among Southern Evangelicals, 1830–1855," (Ph. D. diss., Georgia State University, 1980) 224.

7

APOCALYPSE THEN, APOCALYPSE NOW

The Civil War chastened Americans for many things, including their tendency to assume divine endorsement of a particular ideology. Without the benefit of chronological distance, Abraham Lincoln pointed this out in his Second Inaugural Address[1]. A logical problem occurs, Lincoln noted, when two combatants in a domestic conflict both claim to be God's warriors in a Redeemer Nation: "Both read the same Bible, and pray to the same God; and each invokes His aid against the other." Lincoln's sentence encapsulates the enormous stocks of rhetorical energy expended by both sides just before and during the war. "The prayers of both could not be answered;" Lincoln went on, "that of neither has been answered fully." Lincoln had to have a certain religious and political detachment to acknowledge this fact before the war ended; this understanding came more slowly and painfully for most Americans, South and North. The realities of unspeakable bloodshed curbed prewar confidence in human ability to understand God's intentions. "The Almighty has his own purposes," Lincoln explained in his inaugural address.[2] Never again would most Americans be quite as assured of their ability to understand and claim those purposes. In fact, as Phillip Paludan has noted, the inscrutability of God at this point in American history led to an increased emphasis on the person of Jesus and a loss of thoughtful discourse about God. "As the proponents of a social gospel increasingly emphasized Jesus, and paid less attention to God the awesome father or creator of the universe," he wonders, "was that God's punishment for killing all those young men?"[3]

Of American religious responses to the Civil War, the closest approximation to prewar certainty came from the Southern clergymen

---

[1] See chapter 5.

[2] Lincoln, "Second Inaugural Address, March 4, 1865," in *Works*, 8:333.

[3] Paludan, "Religion and the American Civil War" *Religion*, ed. Miller et al., 37.

who developed and sustained Lost Cause rhetoric. The jeremiad tradition flourished in the Lost Cause postwar vocabulary, much as it had in the North following bitter Northern defeats in the early months of the war. In his study of the Lost Cause, Charles Reagan Wilson has noted the affinity between the outlook of seventeenth-century New England Puritans and late nineteenth-century Southern preachers: "Like the Puritans, Southern Christians after the Civil War thought of themselves a chosen people."[4] Southern certainty about the moral integrity of its cause never wavered; indeed, it may have been stated even more stridently after the war than before. While military defeat required an explanation, the remonstrative but ultimately hopeful strains of the jeremiad sustained the cause for many decades.[5] Acknowledging that secession and military action were no longer options in the South, its clergy developed a role as a conscience of the entire nation, emphasizing Southern values of independence and self-government. The sense of regional identity fostered by the Lost Cause eventually informed the literary approaches of William Faulkner and other twentieth-century Southern writers.

While Southern clergy fashioned a kind of moral victory from the ashes of military defeat, the Union victory shifted about uneasily in the minds of many Americans. The remarkable congruity of the apocalyptic notions of premillennialists, postmillennialists, and "advanced thinkers" during the war dissipated with the end of hostilities. Current events provided less motivation for Christian apocalyptic interpretations, and the development of higher biblical criticism allowed most Protestants to bracket biblical books like Daniel and Revelation. In the late nineteenth century, notes James Moorhead, apocalypticism turned into "an embarrassment to many Protestants."[6] In many Protestant vocabularies,

---

[4]Wilson, *Baptized in Blood*, 80.

[5]Wilson has documented the extent to which Lost Cause rhetoric was applied to the entire nation during World War I; he identifies the Southern cleric Randolph McKim, who had served as a chaplain in the Army of Northern Virginia, as the most vigorous interpreter of World War I as a holy war (*Baptized in Blood*, 164, 171). European literary impressions of the Great War, on the other hand, tended to frame it in Joachimism, based on the writings of a thirteenth-century prophet. D. H. Lawrence saw the era of the war as a time of "Tribulation and extreme decadence," according to Frank Kermode, "Waiting for the End," *Apocalypse Theory and the Ends of the World*, ed. Malcolm Bull (Oxford: Blackwell, 1995) 257. Kermode also notes that although the perception of decadence remained after the war, the sense of apocalypse disappeared.

[6]Moorhead, "Mainstream Protestantism," in *Encyclopedia of Apocalypticism*, 3:88.

the fires of hell burned cooler, if at all, and a resurgent optimism about humanity's ability to improve itself seemed to mesh with the conclusions of evolutionary biology, negating the symbiosis between Christian apocalypticism and the rhetoric of the sublime.[7] To survive as a rhetorical and aesthetic strategy, apocalypticism would undergo a profound transformation after the Civil War. While many American Protestants took a breather from apocalyptic rhetoric, writers and other artists continued to explore its relationship to the sublime and the terrible. In doing this, however, they tended to take a breather from God and to invest their catastrophes with secular interpretations.

Mark Twain had a lot on his mind in the late 1880s. Like so many Americans, his personal identity was shaped by both his Southern origins and the robust industrial postwar economy. He saw parallels between the way medievalism was portrayed by Sir Thomas Malory in the fifteenth century and Sir Walter Scott in the nineteenth; it was fascinating but backward and over-romanticized. In that context, he mapped out a burlesque skewering romantic medievalism while contrasting it with contemporary America. During the three-year process of writing the ensuing novel, *A Connecticut Yankee in King Arthur's Court*, Twain's own evolving religious and philosophical ideas produced a book vastly different from the hilarious satire he had initially envisioned. Although many contemporary readers on both sides of the Atlantic saw the novel as a fairly simple us (Americans) vs. them (the British) exercise in cultural chauvinism, it is much more complex, and it provides a sobering apocalyptic look at America in the aftermath of the Civil War.

Throughout most of the book, the displaced Connecticut protagonist, Hank Morgan, smoothly updates sixth-century Arthurian England with the latest nineteenth-century technology and infuses the medieval country with his can-do Yankee spirit. While Twain's depiction of Arthurian England owes a great deal to Malory, its allusions to slave-owning and an agricultural economy also describe the American South

---

[7]In the conclusion of his essay about nineteenth-century Protestant post-millennialism, James Moorhead suggests that it has been vitiated by this change in emphasis, especially given the tendency of many individuals to forsake it in favor of other religious and non-religious groups with more clearly developed explanations of the end of all things: "The attempt to live without a sense of the end," notes Moorhead, "may exact from the human spirit something as costly as any vision of the *Dies Irae*" ("Mainstream Protestantism," *Encyclopedia of Apocalypticism*, 3:104).

during the Civil War. "In both frameworks," observes Twain biographer Justin Kaplan, "a civil war destroys the old order, and the Yankee has as acute a sense of loss as Mark Twain did."[8] The ending of the novel, which seemed almost to be overlooked by many of Twain's contemporaries, reflects the extent of Twain's disillusionment with postwar America.

Near the end of the book, Hank Morgan returns from a domestic interlude to discover the public loyalties and civic improvements he had installed so efficiently were negated by the medieval Church. When he realizes that all of England, including 30,000 heavily armed knights, has risen to oppose him, his ally Clarence, and fifty-two young men, he uses his Yankee ingenuity to guarantee victory. As Hank and Clarence fine-tune electrical controls that will enable them to dynamite every industrial facility, blow a deep trench around their fortress, and electrocute every human who tries to breach their defenses, Hank wonders how his English followers could have deserted him so fast:

> The Church, the nobles, and the gentry then turned one grand, all-disapproving frown upon them and shriveled them into sheep! From that moment the sheep had begun to gather to the fold–that is to say, the camps–and offer their valueless lives and their valuable wool to the "righteous cause." Why, even the very men who had lately been slaves were in the "righteous cause," and glorifying it, praying for it, sentimentally slabbering over it, just like all the other commoners. Imagine such human muck as this; conceive of this folly![9]

Although it is sometimes difficult to determine where Twain's own allegiance lies as his narrative unfolds, here he resoundingly criticizes the citizens who accept the Church's amalgamation of patriotism and religion. The difference between Civil War America and medieval England, of course, is that while in the nineteenth-century secular governments were still able to employ force in the form of draft laws, American churches had to use persuasion to enlist followers in the "righteous

---

[8]Justin Kaplan, *Mr. Clemens and Mark Twain: A Biography* (New York: Simon and Schuster, 1966) 297.

[9]Mark Twain, *A Connecticut Yankee in King Arthur's Court*, ed. Allison R. Ensor (New York: W. W. Norton, 1982) 247.

cause." In either century, however, it would be possible for Twain to see a country achieve mass participation almost instantly.

Until the end of the novel, Hank Morgan consistently uses technology to achieve progress toward a utopian, even millennial future. What Twain slips into the conclusion, however, in a narrative move worthy of Jonathan Swift, is the message that technological improvement enhances humankind's destructive ability. Hank Morgan blows up and electrocutes his enemies, achieving a holocaust recalling the worst moments of the Civil War and eerily anticipating nuclear warfare. The description of the enemy's doomed initial attack echoes eyewitness accounts of Fredericksburg and Pickett's Charge at Gettysburg:

> All the front ranks, no telling how many acres deep, were horsemen–plumed knights in armor. Suddenly we heard the blare of trumpets; the slow walk burst into a gallop, and then–well, it was wonderful to see! Down swept that vast horseshoe wave–it approached the sand-belt–my breath stood still; nearer, nearer–the strip of green turf beyond the yellow belt grew narrow–narrower still–became a mere ribbon in front of the horses–then disappeared under their hoofs.[10]

In the next instant Hank Morgan blows them all skyward in "a whirling tempest of rags and fragments." Darkness falls before the enemy counterattacks, and Hank Morgan's plan continues to unfold neatly. Electricity has provided a new level of available horrors, just a few years after the Civil War had seemed the worst catastrophe imaginable. The electric fence, which instantly, soundlessly kills anyone who touches it in the pitch black night, lends a ghastly tone to the scene. As the bulk of the English army follows the initial skirmishers to their doom, Hank Morgan realizes that "our camp was enclosed with a solid wall of the dead–a bulwark, a breastwork, of corpses, you may say." Yet it gets worse. Hank touches a button and "fifty electric suns" light up the night: "Land, what a sight! We were enclosed in three walls of dead men!" he observes.[11] While the troops who are still alive freeze in horror for a moment, Hank's men unleash thirteen Gatling guns and send the enemy fleeing back into

---

[10]Ibid., 249.
[11]Ibid., 254.

the trench, now filled with water from a diverted stream, and they drown like Pharaoh's army.

A conventional, Civil War-era apocalyptic narrative might have ended here, with losers who deserved destruction and winners who deserved to succeed. Such a solution, however, would neither satisfy Mark Twain personally nor embody what he felt was the sad truth about America; instead, an even more grim fate ends the narrative, as Clarence belatedly recognizes: "We were in a trap, you see—a trap of our own making. If we stayed where we were, our dead would kill us; if we moved out of our defences, we should no longer be invincible. We had conquered; in turn we were conquered."[12] In Twain's apocalypse, there is no redemption, no gleam of millennial hope through the black clouds of war.

Twain was clearly aware of the aesthetic effectiveness of apocalyptic imagery. David Ketterer has comprehensively described the apocalyptic symbols that pervade *A Connecticut Yankee in King Arthur's Court.* Hank Morgan is involved with fire throughout the novel, from the sun's eclipse at the beginning of the tale to his electric suns at the end.[13] He is, according to Roger B. Salomon, "a Prometheus bringing to the Middle Ages the fire of the nineteenth century."[14] Although in the end Hank Morgan does not share Prometheus' kind regard for the human race, he shares the Titan's fate of interminable suffering; Merlin places him in a trance for thirteen centuries, a condition continually disturbed by nightmares. Then he dies, destined for an oblivion darker and more permanent than the eclipse that terrified the Arthurians at the beginning of the book. And, in fact, Twain allows the book to end this way because he sees no winners or losers. According to his biographer Justin Kaplan, "Mark Twain was in effect acting out his own disintegration, measuring the failure of a precarious equilibrium. In response not to a traumatic reversal but to a steady erosion of belief, his center ceased to hold, and for the rest of his life his imaginative energies would be scattered and baffled."[15] In certain ways Twain's view resembles the fatalistic outlook of

---

[12]Ibid., 256.

[13]David Ketterer, "Epoch-Eclipse and Apocalypse: Special 'Effects' in *A Connecticut Yankee*," *PMLA* 88 (1973): 1104.

[14]Roger B. Salomon, *Twain and the Image of History* (New Haven: Yale University Press, 1961) chapter 6, as noted in Ketterer, "Epoch-Eclipse," 1105.

[15]Kaplan, *Mark Twain*, 294.

Herman Melville and Abraham Lincoln during the Civil War. Melville and Lincoln, however, still shared some common ground with Calvinism, although they differed in the details of God's interest in and compassion for humanity. Melville and Lincoln had a center that did hold; they saw some kind of divine involvement in the affairs of people, and they found ultimate meaning in apocalyptic events. The end was not really the end. Twain, on the other hand, could not be convinced that a deity worth worshiping would create humans with such enlarged capacities for destruction. Human beings were capable of destroying themselves, and when they succeeded, the end would simply be the end.

In the minds of many twentieth-century writers and artists, the religious apocalypse gave way to secular catastrophe, or to what Catherine Keller has termed the "counter-apocalypse."[16] Anticipated by Hawthorne and Melville before the war, and approached by Twain in *The Mysterious Stranger* as well as *A Connecticut Yankee*, it may also be found in the work of naturalistic writers, as in Frank Norris' portrayal of American prosperity in *The Octopus*. More recently it has appeared in John Barth's *The End of the Road* and Sam Shepard's *The Curse of the Starving Class*. Sometimes it takes the comic form used by writers such as Nathaniel West, in *The Day of the Locust*, and Thomas Pynchon, in *The Crying of Lot 49*. The term "apocalypse" is applied to these works primarily because they convey a sense of an ending (or endings), but they also transform the meaning of the term. Krishan Kumar has noted that while "the apocalyptic imagination usually carried with it...a sense of hope," in recent times it has shed hope and developed a "kind of millennial belief almost entirely emptied of...conflict and dynamism...without a sense of the future."[17] In many ways this form has resonated with the intractable problems of the twentieth and twenty-first centuries.

The graphic despair of secular apocalypse helps to emphasize the distance from 1861 to 1968. The Vietnam War, especially from the Tet Offensive onward, has seemed in many ways the antithesis of the Civil War: geographically distant, domestically fragmentary, and intellectually baffling. Begun in the clear-cut atmosphere of Cold War verities, it

---

[16]Catherine Keller, *Apocalypse Now and Then: A Feminist Guide to the End of the World* (Boston: Beacon Press, 1996) 19.

[17]Krishan Kumar, "Apocalypse, Millennium and Utopia Today," *Apocalypse Theory*, 205.

became a Gordian impossibility, epitomized by Francis Ford Coppola's *Apocalypse Now* (1979) and reinforced by the Doors song, "The End," incorporated in the opening sequence. Coppola thoroughly understands the aesthetic power of the sublime (surely Mark Twain would have been delighted with the Wagner-blaring helicopters), and he grasps the mythical dimensions of apocalyptic imagery. One dark night, Captain Benjamin Willard pauses at the last American outpost on his upriver quest, a supply depot at a bridge, to collect a final set of orders and touch bases with the commanding officer (CO). Coppola includes a scene that comments on not only the moral hopelessness of the war but also the general societal malaise it cultivated. Darting through a surreal labyrinth of trenches as exploding shells fill the sky with aimless pyrotechnics, Willard asks again and again where he can find the CO. The stunned, stoned, shell-shocked soldiers give various cryptic answers, and finally Willard returns to his boat muttering that there is no CO.[18] That view may explain why the film's conclusion succumbs to its own mythic weight. Perhaps the anticlimactic demise of Twain's Hank Morgan better epitomizes the end of secular apocalypse.[19]

Apocalypse Now also serves as a reminder of the distance between religious and aesthetic versions of apocalyptic imagery in the twentieth and twenty-first centuries. No longer does American culture bring together the sermonic techniques of preachers like Gilbert Haven and James Henley Thornwell with the poetics of a Herman Melville or even a Julia Ward Howe. Apocalyptic imagery today lacks the common focus that created the remarkable convergence of Civil War images.

---

[18]*Apocalypse Now*, prod. and dir. Francis Coppola (Paramount Studios, 1979).

[19]Not all twentieth-century apocalyptic literature has taken the form of secular apocalypse. Vestiges of Christian apocalyptic faith remained in the writings of African-American novelists such as James Baldwin, Ralph Ellison, and Richard Wright. The role of religion in the lives of black Americans influenced the work of these writers, and the importance of apocalyptic religion in their fiction parallels the emphasis it received in the slave culture. *Go Tell It on the Mountain, Invisible Man,* and *Native Son* all reflect this importance. Apocalyptic religion was a significant way of dealing with the realities of American racial injustice after the Civil War. In the South, a sense that the world is out of balance and will incur some sort of divine retribution lingers in the fiction of Southern writers such as William Faulkner and Flannery O'Connor. Faulkner's *As I Lay Dying* and O'Connor's "Everything that Rises Must Converge" and "Revelation" all warn of an imminent judgment to be exacted as retribution for Southern sins. Their apocalyptic tone lacks the self-assurance of their Civil War counterparts, but the appeal of certain forms of imagery persists in these works.

Contemporary Christian apocalyptic imagery continues to manifest its adaptability and capacity for renewal, but since preachers, writers and artists no longer share the common cultural currency held during the Civil War era, the imagery tends to inhabit a polemical arena rather than an aesthetic one.

As James Moorhead has noted, after the Civil War postmillennial Protestants tended to cede apocalypticism to the premillennialists. Although a variety of premillennial strands have emerged since 1865, a recent example of the intersection of premillennial apocalypticism and the popular imagination is dispensationalism, formed in the nineteenth century and articulated in 1970 by Hal Lindsey in *Late Great Planet Earth*. This set of beliefs includes the doctrine of the Secret Rapture, a moment before the end of time when the faithful will be taken to safety in heaven before the great premillennial Tribulation and Apocalypse. Rapture doctrine provides compelling apocalyptic imagery, recently captured in the popular polemical novels of Tim LaHaye and Jerry B. Jenkins's *Left Behind* series. While their descriptions of the great Tribulation at the end of the world can be chilling, these books let readers off the hook, in a sense; those who can envision themselves worthy of rapture would escape the sublime fears that haunted good and evil alike during the Civil War era.

The twentieth century provided many events or themes of apocalyptic magnitude: the First World War, the Holocaust, the capacity for nuclear destruction, Cold War tensions, and the potential for environmental catastrophe. Twentieth-century culture did not achieve anything resembling a coherent response to these events, but as Malcolm Bull has noted, "Although the idea of a world without end or purpose is logically coherent, infinite duration is difficult to conceive, and the notion of eternal aimlessness repugnant to the moral imagination…most are inclined to attribute at least one end to the world."[20] Explanations and envisioned ends have ranged from polemical, premillennial Christian apocalyptic interpretations, which have been perhaps more prevalent than national discourse has acknowledged, to the singular views of Jim Jones, David Koresh, and the members of Heaven's Gate to the images of secular catastrophe pervading popular culture. These secular interpretations, in turn, have sparked both a new set of powerful images and a

---

[20]Malcolm Bull, "On Making Ends Meet," *Apocalypse Theory*, 1.

new way of thinking. Jacques Derrida has aligned the intellectual practices of deconstruction with the term "nuclear criticism." This association, Christopher Norris has pointed out, results from the inability of human language to describe what the nuclear capability actually means, creating "a radical instability affecting all the discourses of knowledge and power." Not just language but thought processes themselves are inadequate to the task: "to think the possibility of nuclear war...is to think beyond the limits of reason itself."[21] In such a view, the confluence of the nuclear capability and Cartesian logic make the end of reason a certainty, even if nuclear destruction remains only a possibility.

The nuclear possibility, in spite of its implications, has not entirely displaced actual events. Twenty-first-century America has witnessed terrorist attacks on the World Trade Center and the Pentagon, the most apocalyptic moments on United States soil since the Civil War. Whether these or other events yield an apocalyptic interpretation with broad cultural coherence remains to be seen. A synchronicity of imagery could recur, however. Human history has shown that while individual applications of apocalyptic explanations to historical moments become fatigued, the imagery itself persists. In this sense, the end is not really the end.

---

[21]Christopher Norris, "Versions of Apocalypse: Kant, Derrida, Foucault," *Apocalypse Theory*, 244–45. Norris particularly notes Derrida's articles "Of an Apocalyptic Tone Recently Adopted in Philosophy," trans. John P. Leavey, Jr., *Oxford Literary Review* 6/2 (1984): 3–37 and "No Apocalypse, Not Now (full speed ahead, seven missiles seven missives)" *Diacritics* 14 (Summer 1984): 20–31.

APPENDIX

(poems are listed alphabetically by title)

ADVENT OF CHRIST
BY REGINALD HEBER

The Lord will come! the earth shall quake,
The hills their fixed seat forsake;
And, withering, from the vault of night
The skies withdraw their feeble light.

The Lord will come! but not the same
As once in lowly form he came,
A silent lamb to slaughter led
The bruised, the suffering, and the dead.

The Lord will come! a dreadful form,
With wreath of flame and robe of storm.
Master and slave alike shall find
An equal judge of human kind.

Can this be he who wont to stray
A pilgrim on the world's highway;
By power oppressed, and mocked by pride?
Oh God! is this the crucified?

Go, tyrants! to the rocks complain!
Go, seek the mountain's cleft in vain:
But faith, victorious o'er the tomb,
Shall sing for joy—the Lord is come![1]

---

[1] Reginald Heber, "Advent of Christ," *Songs of the Free,* ed. Maria Chapman (Boston: I. Knapp, 1836) 9–11.

ALBERT SIDNEY JOHNSTON
BY COL. A. W. TERRELL

Hush the notes of exultation for a battle dearly won!
Low the Chief's proud form is lying—Texas weeps another son!
Hang his battle-flag above him—drape its orange cross with black—
And while our muffl'd drum is beating, bring our Chieftain's ashes back.

Shed no briny tears above him—for the gushing drops that start
From the wounds of the Invader, from each Puritanic heart.
We must make the rich libation, to be pour'd in crimson waves,
When the gather'd strength of Texas shall avenge her slaughter'd braves!

Calm in council, brave in action, was the Hero now laid low;
Dreadful as the wrath of Heavn' to his country's vandal foe!
With a mind compos'd and ready, thro' the battle's fearful shock,
And a nerve as fix'd and steady as the storm-assaulted rock.

On the field of BUENA VISTA, 'mid the dying and the slain,
On the frozen waters of UTAH, on the parch'd and arid plain,
And wherever fame and honor were the beacon-lights for man,
Flash'd his blade, the first and brightest, like a meteor in the van.

His the form in which were blended strength and grace for high
    command;
His the soul whose fires were lighted with a love for native land;
O you saw the Texian patriot in his bearing free and high,
And a noble scorn of danger in his bold imperial eye.

Are ye worth so great a victim? are ye worthy of the dead,
Whose unconquer'd heart at SHILOH for your wives and infants bled?
Then avenge him, O avenge him; let his mem'ry nerve each soul
With resolves of giant daring, such as Texians breath'd of old.
Freemen on each broad prairie, Rangers of the Southern wild,
Texians, dream no more of danger, think of all by foes defiled—
Leave to God the quiet homestead, arm, O arm, ye tardy braves,
And with sharpen'd knives we'll greet them who would make our
    children slaves.

By the hope which God hath planted in the freeman's heart,
By your women so undaunted, by this sod beneath your feet,
By this Southern sky above you, and this balmy air around,
Tread the lurid path of vengeance, while the Invader can be found.
Christ! let thy avenging angel o'er the foeman spread his wings,
'Til beneath its shade they tremble, as did Egypt's haughty King;
Let them read MENE MENE on our pestilential coast—
Let their armies sink and wither, like Assyria's stricken host.[2]

The Angel of the Church
by William Gilmore Simms

The enemy, from his camp on Morris Island, has, in frequent letters in the Northern papers, avowed the object at which they aim their shells in Charleston to be the spire of St. Michael's Church. Their *practice* shows that these avowals are true. Thus far, they have not succeeded in their aim. Angels of the Churches, is a phrase applied by St. John in reference to the Seven Churches of Asia. The Hebrews recognized an Angel of the Church, in their language, "Sheliack-Zibbor," whose office may be described as that of a watcher or guardian of the church. Daniel says, iv. 13, "Behold a watcher and a Holy one came down from Heaven." The practice of naming churches after tutelary saints, originated, no doubt, in the conviction that, where the church was pure, and the faith true, and the congregation pious, those guardian angels, so chosen, would accept the office assigned them. They were generally chosen from the Seraphim and Cherubim—those who, according to St. Paul (I Colossians xvi.), represented thrones, dominions, principalities, and powers. According to the Hebrew traditions, St. Michael was the head of the first order; Gabriel, of the second; Uriel, of the third; and Raphael, of the fourth. St. Michael is the warrior angel who led the hosts of the sky against the powers of the princes of the air; who overthrew the dragon, and trampled him under foot. The destruction of the Anaconda, in his hands, would be a smaller undertaking. Assuming for our people a hope

---

[2] A. W. Terrell, "Albert Sidney Johnston," *Allan's Lone Star Ballads,* ed. Francis D. Allan (Galveston TX: J. D. Sawyer, 1874) 110–11.

not less rational than that of the people of Ninevah, we may reasonably build upon the guardianship and protection of God, through his angels, "a great city of sixty thousand souls," which has been for so long a season the subject of his care. These notes will supply the adequate illustrations for the ode which follows.

Aye, strike with sacrilegious aim
 The temple of the living God;
Hurl iron bolt and seething flame
 Through aisles which holiest feet have trod;
Tear up the altar, spoil the tomb,
 And raging with demoniac ire,
Send down, in sudden crash of doom,
 That grand, old, sky-sustaining spire.

That spire, for full a hundred years,
 Hath been a people's point of sight;
That shrine hath warmed their souls to tears,
 With strains well worthy Salem's height;
The sweet, clear music of its bells,
 Made liquid soft in Southern air,
Still through the heart of memory swells,
 And wakes the hopefuls soul to prayer.

Along the shores for many a mile,
 Long ere they owned a beacon-mark,
It caught and kept the Day-God's smile,
 The guide for every wandering bark;
Averting from our homes the scaith
 Of fiery bolt, in storm-cloud driven,
The Pharos to the wandering faith,
 It pointed every prayer to Heaven!

Well may ye, felons of the time,
 Still loathing all that's pure and free,
Add this to many a thousand crime
 'Gainst peace and sweet humanity:
Ye, who have wrapped our towns in flame,

defiled our shrines, befouled our homes,
But fitly turn your murderous aim
    Against Jehovah's ancient domes.

Yet, though the grand old temple falls,
    And downward sinks the lofty spire,
Our faith is stronger than our walls,
    And soars above the storm and fire.
Ye shake no faith in souls made free
    To tread the paths their fathers trod;
To fight and die for liberty,
    Believing in the avenging God!

Think not, though long his anger stays,
    His justice sleeps—His wrath is spent;
The arm of vengeance but delays,
    To make more dread the punishment!
Each impious hand that lights the torch
    Shall wither ere the bolt shall fall;
And the bright Angel of the Church,
    With seraph shield avert the ball!

For still we deem, as taught of old,
    That where the faith the altar builds,
God sends an angel from his fold,
    Whose sleepless watch the temple shields,
And to his flock, with sweet accord,
    Yields their fond choice, from THRONES and POWERS;
Thus, Michael, with his fiery sword
    And golden shield, still champions ours!

And he who smote the dragon down
    And chained him thousand years of time,
Need never fear the boa's frown,
    Though loathsome in his spite and slime.
He, from the topmost height, surveys
    And guards the shrines our fathers gave;
And we, who sleep beneath his gaze,

May well believe his power to save!

Yet, if it be that for our sin
    Our angel's term of watch is o'er,
With proper prayer, true faith must win
    The guardian watcher back once more!
Faith, brethren of the Church, and prayer—
    In blood and sackcloth, if it need;
And still our spire shall rise in air,
    Our temple, though our people bleed![3]

ANNUS MEMORABILIS
(CONGRESS, 1860–61)
BY HENRY HOWARD BROWNELL

Stand strong and calm as Fate! not a breath of scorn or hate—
    Of taunt for the base, or of menace for the strong—
Since our fortunes must be sealed on that old and famous Field,
    Where the Right is set at battle with the Wrong.

'Tis coming, with the loom of Khamsin or Simoom,
    The tempest that shall try if we are of God or no—
Its roar is in the sky,—and they there be which cry,
    Let us cower, and the storm may over-blow.

Now, nay! stand firm and fast! (that was a spiteful blast!)
    This is not a war of men, but of Angels Good and Ill—
'Tis hell that storms at heaven—'tis the black and deadly Seven,
    Sworn 'gainst the Shining Ones to work their damned will!

How the Ether glooms and burns, as the tide of combat turns,
    And the smoke and dust above it whirl and float!
It eddies and it streams—and, certes, oft it seems

---

[3] William Gilmore Simms, "The Angel of the Church," *War Poetry of the South* (New York: Richardson, 1867) 290–94.

As the Sins had the Seraphs fairly by the throat.

But we all have read, (in that Legend grand and dread,)
How Michael and his host met the Serpent and his crew—
Naught has reached us of the Fight—but, if I have dreamed aright,
'Twas a loud one and a long, as ever thundered through!

Right stiffly, past a doubt, the Dragon fought it out,
And his Angels, each and all, did for Tophet their devoir—
There was creak of iron wings, and whirl of scorpion stings,
Hiss of bifid tongues, and the Pit in full uproar!

But, naught thereof enscrolled, in one brief line 'tis told,
(Calm as dew the Apocalyptic Pen,)
That on the Infinite Shore their place was found no more,
God send the like on this our earth. Amen.[4]

ARKANSIAN BATTLE-HYMN
BY LIEUT.-COL. A. W. BISHOP

Arkansians are rallying round the glorious Stripes and Stars—
We have sworn unceasing vengeance 'gainst the hated stars and bars;
We know no law but justice, though covered o'er with scars,
    As we go marching on.
  CHORUS—Glory! glory! hallelujah,
    Glory! glory! hallelujah,
    Glory! glory! hallelujah,
    As we go marching on.

We were driven from our homes, our wives, and children dear;
Our native hills and valleys no longer gave us cheer—
But now, thank God! forever, we once again are here,
    Where the war goes bravely on.
    Glory, glory, hallelujah, &c.

---

[4] Henry Howard Brownell, "Annus Memorabilis (Congress, 1860–61)," *Lines of Battle* (Boston: Houghton Mifflin, 1912) 56–58.

We remember David Walker, who sought our votes of old,
And linked to ours his "destiny," in voice of utt'rance bold,
But southward drove his "contrabands," a bid for Rebel gold,
  As we came marching on.
  Glory, glory, hallelujah, &c.

We scorn deception ever, we scorn it most of all
In the proud and haughty Rebels, who are seeking still our fall—
But soon they'll hear the shouting, and the trumpet's gath'ring call,
  As we go marching on.
  Glory, glory, hallelujah, &c.

We've fought, bled, and suffered, but gladly sprung to arms,
To trample out the treason that desolates our farms;
We'll bear aloft our banner, and to peace restore her charms,
  As we go marching on.
  Glory, glory, hallelujah, &c.

Let the Union of the fathers be the Union evermore,
Of the sons and the daughters of those who fought of yore;
And moving on the Arkansas, we'll strike the farther shore,
  As we go marching on.
  Glory, glory, hallelujah, &c.

Then JUBILATE DEO! let the welkin ever ring
With the joyous shouts of freemen, attendant now on spring,
And hosannahs loudly shout to God alone, our King,
  As we go marching on.
  Glory, glory, hallelujah, &c.[5]

---

[5] Lieut.-Col. A. W. Bishop, "Arkansian Battle-Hymn," *Songs of the Soldiers*, ed. Frank Moore (New York: G. P. Putnam, 1864) 182–84.

Aurora-Borealis
by Herman Melville

Commemorative of the Dissolution of Armies at the Peace.
(May, 1865.)

What power disbands the Northern Lights
   After their steely play?
The lonely watcher feels an awe
   Of Nature's sway,
      As when appearing,
      He marked their flashed uprearing
In the cold gloom—
   Retreatings and advancings,
(Like dallyings of doom),
   Transitions and enhancings,
      And bloody ray.

The phantom-host has faded quite,
   Splendor and Terror gone—
Portent or promise—and gives way
   To pale, meek Dawn;
      The coming, going,
      Alike in wonder showing—
Alike the God,
   Decreeing and commanding
The million blades that glowed,
   The muster and disbanding—
      Midnight and Morn.[6]

---

[6] Herman Melville, "Aurora-Borealis," in *Battle-Pieces and Aspects of the War* (New York: Harper & Brothers, 1866) 148–49.

A BALLAD FOR THE YOUNG SOUTH
BY JOSEPH BRENNAN

Men of the South! Our foes are up
    In fierce and grim array;
Their sable banner laps the air—
    An insult to the day!
The saints of Cromwell rise again,
    In sanctimonious hordes,
Hiding behind the garb of peace
    A million ruthless swords.
From North, and East, and West, they seek
    The same disastrous goal,
With CHRIST upon the lying lip,
    And Satan in the soul!
Mocking, with ancient shibboleth,
    All wise and just restraints:
"TO SAINTS OF HEAVEN WAS EMPIRE GIVEN,
    AND WE, ALONE, ARE SAINTS!"

A preacher to the pulpit comes
    And calls upon the crowd,
For Southern creeds and Southern hopes
    To weave a bloody shroud.
Beside the prayer-book, on his desk,
    The bullet-mould is seen;
And near the Bible's golden clasp,
    The dagger's stately sheen;
The simple tale of Bethlehem
    No more is fondly told,
For every priestly surplice drags
    Too heavily with gold;
The blessed Cross of Calvary
    Becomes a sign of Baal,
Like that which played when chieftains raised
    The clansmen of the Gael!

Hark to the howling demagogues—
    A fierce and ravenous pack—
With nostrils prone, and bark, and bay,
    That close upon our track:
"Down with the laws our fathers made!
    They bind our hearts no more;
Down with the stately edifice,
    Cemented with their gore!
Forget the legends of our race—
    Efface each wise decree—
Americans must kneel as slaves,
    Till Africans are free!
Out on the mere Caucasian blood
    Of Teuton, Celt, or Gaul!
The stream that springs from Niger's source
    Must triumph over all!"

So speaks a solemn senator
    Within these halls to-day,
That echoed erst, the thunder-burst
    Of Webster, and of Clay!
Look North, look East, look West—the scene
    Is blackening all around;
The negro cordon, year by year,
    Is fast and faster bound;
The black line crossed—the sable flag
    Surrounded by a host—
Our out-post forced, our sentinels
    Asleep upon their posts;
Our brethren's life-blood flowing free,
    To stain the Kansas soil—
And shed in vain, while pious thieves
    Are fattening on our toil!
Look North—look West—the ominous sky
    Is starless, moonless, black,
And from the East comes hurrying up
    A sweeping thunder-rack!

Men of the South! Ye have no kin
    With fanatics, or fools;
Ye are not bound by breed, or birth,
    To Massachusetts rules!
A hundred nations gave their blood
    To feed these healthful springs,
Which bear the seed of JACQUES BONHOMME,
    With those of Bourbon kings.
The Danish pluck and sailor craft—
    The Huguenotic will—
The Norman grace and chivalry—
    The German steady skill—
The fiery Celt's impassioned thought
    Inspire the Southron's heart,
Which has no room for bigot-gloom,
    Or pious plunder's art!

Sons of the brave! The time has come
    To bow the haughty crest,
Or stand alone, despite the threats
    Of North, or East, or West!
The hour has come for manly deeds
    And not for puling words;
The place is passed for platform prate—
    It is the time for swords!
Now, by the fame of John Calhoun,
    To honest truth be true!
And by old Jackson's iron will,
    Now do what ye can do!
By all ye love—by all ye hope—
    Be resolute and proud;
And make your flag a symbol high
    Of triumph, or a shroud!

Men of the South! Look up—behold
    The deep and sullen gloom,
That darkles o'er our sunny land
    With thunder in its womb!

Are ye so blind ye can not see
    The omens in the sky!
Are ye so deaf ye can not hear
    The tramp of foemen nigh?
Are ye so dull ye will endure
    The whips and scorn of men
Who wear the heart of Titus Oates
    Beneath the face of Penn?
Never, I Ween! and foot to foot,
    Ye now will gladly stand
For land and life, for child and wife,
    With naked steel in hand![7]

THE BANNER OF THE SKY
BY E. P. WORTH

Our flag from heaven still waves,
Set up by Him who saves,
    Enthroned above.
Arch of those beauteous rays,
Whose light forever plays
O'er all our clouded days,
    Emblem of love.
CHORUS—The rainbow-flag afar
    Shall float from shore to shore,
    In beauty evermore,
        Forevermore.

Our banner of the sky,
Formed of the light on high,
    Celestial sign;
Ensign of liberty
For all the God made free,
Bright pledge of unity,

---

[7] Joseph Brennan, "A Ballad for the Young South," *South Songs: from the Lays of Later Days*, ed. Thomas Cooper De Leon (New York: Blalock & Co., 1866) 51–55.

From heaven to man.

Standard of victory,
Over earth's misery,
   Triumphant sign
That the eternal word
By all shall yet be heard,
Moving to sweet accord,
   With peace divine.[8]

THE BATTLE-CRY OF THE SOUTH
BY JAMES R. RANDALL

    Arm yourselves and be valiant men, and see that ye be in readiness against the morning, that ye may fight with these nations that are assembled against us, to destroy us and our sanctuary.

For it is better for us to die in battle than to behold the calamities of our
           people and our sanctuary.—*Maccabees 1.*

Brothers! the thunder-cloud is black,
   And the wail of the South wings forth;
Will ye cringe to the hot tornado's rack,
   And the vampires of the North?
Strike! ye can win a martyr's goal,
   Strike! with a ruthless hand—
Strike! with the vengeance of the soul,
   For your bright, beleaguered land!
        To arms! to arms! for the South needs help,
          And a craven is he who flees—
       For ye have the sword of the Lion's Whelp,
          And the God of the Maccabees!

Arise! though the stars have a rugged glare,
   And the moon has a wrath-blurred crown—

---

[8] E. P. Worth, "The Banner of the Sky," *Songs of the Soldiers,* 205–206.

Brothers! a blessing is ambushed there
   In the cliffs of the Father's frown:
Arise! ye are worthy the wondrous light
   Which the Sun of Justice gives—
In the caves and sepulchres of night
   Jehovah the Lord King lives!
          To arms! to arms! for the South needs help,
            And a craven is he who flees—
          For ye have the sword of the Lion's Whelp,
            And the God of the Maccabees!

Think of the dead by the Tennessee,
   In their frozen shrouds of gore—
Think of the mothers who shall see
   Those darling eyes no more!
But better are they in a hero grave
   Than the serfs of time and breath,
For they are the children of the brave,
   And the cherubim of death!
          To arms! to arms! for the South needs help,
            And a craven is he who flees—
          For ye have the sword of the Lion's Whelp,
            And the God of the Maccabees!

Better the charnels of the West,
   And a hecatomb of lives,
Than the foul invader as a guest
   'Mid your sisters and your wives—
But a spirit lurketh in every maid,
   Though, brothers, ye should quail,
To sharpen a Judith's lurid blade,
   And the livid spike of Jael!
          To arms! to arms! for the South needs help,
            And a craven is he who flees—
          For ye have the sword of the Lion's Whelp,
            And the God of the Maccabees!

Brothers! I see you tramping by,

With the gladiator gaze,
And your shout is the Macedonian cry
   Of the old, heroic days!
March on! with trumpet and with drum,
   With rifle, pike, and dart,
And die—if even death must come—
   Upon your country's heart!
            To arms! to arms! for the South needs help,
               And a craven is he who flees—
            For ye have the sword of the Lion's Whelp,
               And the God of the Maccabees!

Brothers! the thunder-cloud is black,
   And the wail of the South wings forth;
Will ye cringe to the hot tornado's rack,
   And the vampires of the North?
Strike! ye can win a martyr's goal,
   Strike! with a ruthless hand—
Strike! with the vengeance of the soul
   For your bright, beleaguered land!
            To arms! to arms! for the South needs help,
               And a craven is he who flees—
            For ye have the sword of the Lion's Whelp,
               And the God of the Maccabees![9]

BATTLE HYMN

Lord of Hosts, that beholds us in battle, defending
   The homes of our sires 'gainst the hosts of the foe,
Send us help on the wings of thy angels descending,
   And shield from his terrors, and baffle his blow.
Warm the faith of our sons, till they flame as the iron,
   Red-glowing from the fire-forge, kindled by zeal;
Make them forward to grapple the hordes that environ,

---

[9] James R. Randall, "The Battle-Cry of the South," *War Poetry of the South*, 37–40.

In the storm-rush of battle, through forests of steel!

Teach them, Lord, that the cause of their country makes glorious
    The martyr who falls in the front of the fight;—
That the faith which is steadfast makes ever victorious
    The arm which strikes boldly defending the right;—
That the zeal, which is roused by the wrongs of a nation,
    Is a war-horse that sweeps o'er the field as his own;
And the Faith, which is winged by the soul's approbation,
    Is a warrior, in proof, that can ne'er be o'erthrown.

And to this oath the dread reply—
Our valiant fathers' sacred ghosts—
These with us, and the God of hosts,
    We will be free or die!
    Then let the drums all roll! etc., etc.[10]

BATTLE HYMN OF THE REPUBLIC
BY JULIA WARD HOWE

Mine eyes have seen the glory of the coming of the Lord:
He is trampling out the vintage where the grapes of wrath are stored;
He hath loosed the fateful lightning of His terrible swift sword:
    His truth is marching on.

I have seen Him in the watch-fires of a hundred circling camps;
They have builded Him an altar in the evening dews and damps;
I can read His righteous sentence by the dim and flaring lamps:
    His day is marching on.

I have read a fiery gospel writ in burnished rows of steel:
"As ye deal with my contemners, so with you my grace shall deal;
Let the Hero, born of woman, crush the serpent with his heel,
    Since God is marching on."

---

[10] "Battle Hymn," reprinted from the *Charleston Mercury, War Poetry of the South,* 97–98.

He has sounded forth the trumpet that shall never call retreat;
He is sifting out the hearts of men before His judgment-seat:
Oh, be swift, my soul, to answer Him! be jubilant, my feet!
    Our God is marching on.

In the beauty of the lilies Christ was born across the sea,
With a glory in his bosom that transfigures you and me:
As he died to make men holy, let us die to make men free,
    While God is marching on.[11]

THE BATTLE OF MANASSAS
BY MRS. CLARKE, WIFE OF COL. CLARKE,
14TH REG. N. CAR.

Dedicated to Gen. Beauregard, C.S.A.

"Now glory to the Lord of Hosts! oh, bless and praise His name,
That He hath battled in our cause and brought our foes to shame,
And honor to our Beauregard, who conquered in His might,
And for our children's children won, Manassas' bloody fight.
Oh, let our thankful prayers ascend, our joyous praise resound,
For God—the God of victory, our untried flag hath crowned!
They brought a mighty army, to crush us with a blow,
And in their pride they laughed to scorn the men they did not know,
Fair women came to triumph, with the heroes of the day,
When "the boasting Southern rebels" should be scattered in dismay.
And for their conquering Generals, a lordly feast they spread.
But the wine in which we pledged them, was all of ruby red!
The feast was like Belshazzar's—in terror and dismay,
Before our conquering heroes, their armies fled away.
God had weighed them in the balance, and His hand Upon the wall,

---

[11] Julia Ward Howe, "Battle Hymn of the Republic," *Atlantic* (February 1862): 1.

At the taking of Fort Sumter, had fore-doomed them to their fall.
But they would not heed the warning, and scoffed in unbelief,
Till their scorn was changed to wailing, and their laughter into grief!

All day the fight was raging, and amid the cannon's peal,
Rang the cracking of our rifles, and the clashing of our steel;
But above the din of battle, our shout of triumph rose,
As we charged upon their batteries, and turned them on our foes.
We staid not for our fallen, and we thought not of our dead,
Until the day was ours, and the routed foe had fled.

But once our spirits faltered—Bee and Bartow both were down,
And our gallant Colonel Hampton lay wounded on the ground;
But Beauregard, God bless him! led the Legion in his stead,
And Johnston seized the colors, and waved them o'er his head!
E'en a coward must have followed, when such heroes led the way.
And no dastard blood was flowing in Southern veins that day!
But every arm was strengthened, and every heart was stirred,
When shouts of "Davis! Davis!" along our lines were heard.
As he rode into the battle the joyful news flew fast—
And the dying raised their voices and cheered him as he passed.
Oh! with such glorious leaders, in Cabinet and field,
The gallant Southern chivalry will die, but never yield!

But from the wings of victory, the shafts of death were sped,
And our pride is dashed with sorrow when we count our noble dead;
Though in our hearts they're living—and our children we will tell
How gloriously our Fisher and our gallant Johnson fell;
And the name of each we'll cherish as an honor to his State,
And teach our sons to envy, and, if need be, meet their fate.
"Then glory to the Lord of Hosts!" oh, bless and praise his name,
For he hath battled in our cause, and brought our foes to shame.
And honor to our Beauregard, who conquered in His might,
And for our children's children, won Manassas' bloody fight.
Oh! let our grateful prayers ascend, our joyous praise resound,
For God—the God of victory our untried flag hath crowned![12]

---

[12] Mrs. Clarke, "The Battle of Manassas," *The Southern Poems of the War*, comp. Emily Virginia Mason (Baltimore: J. Murphy & Co., 1867) 55–58.

BLOOD IS ON THE STAR-SPANGLED BANNER
BY W. B. TAPPAN

Lift up our country's banner high,
 And fling abroad its gorgeous sheen,
Unroll its stripes upon the sky,
 And let its lovely stars be seen!

Blood—blood is on its spangled fold!
 Yet from the battle comes it not;
But all the waters oceans hold
 Cannot wash out the guilty spot.

Up, freemen! up; determine, do
 What Justice claims, what freemen may;
What frowning heav'n demands of you,
 while yet its mutt'ring thunders stay:—
That ye, forever from this soil,
 Bid SLAVERY'S with'ring blight depart,
And to the wretch restore the spoil,
 Though ye can not the broken heart.

Lift up your brother from the dust,
 And speak his long crush'd spirit FREE!
That millions, by your av'rice curst,
 May sharers in your blessings be:
Then to the universe wide spread
 Your glorious stars without a stain;
Bend from your skies, illustrious dead!
 The land ye won is free again.[13]

---

[13] W. B. Tappan, "Blood is on the 'Star-Spangled Banner'" [for July 4], *Freedom's Lyre,* ed. Edwin Francis Hatfield (New York: S. W. Benedict, 1840; reprint, Miami: Mnemosyne Pub. Co., 1969) 186–87.

OF "BULL'S RUN," THE 18TH; AND MANASSEH, THE 21ST JULY, 1861
BY CHARLES CAYLAT

1.
When the Great Judge, Supreme and Just
    Shall once inquire for blood;
The humble soul, who mourns in dust,
    Shall find a faithful God.

2.
He from the dreadful gates of death,
    Does his own children raise;
In "Southern States," where with cheerful breath,
    They sing their Father's praise.

3.
Our foes shall fall with heedless feet,
    Into the Pit, they made;
And Fanatics perish in the act,
    Which their OWN hands had spread.

4.
Thus by Thy judgments, mighty God,
    Are Thy deep Counsels known;
When men of mischief are destroyed,
    The SNARE must be their own.

5.
The wicked shall sink down to hell;
    Thy wrath devour the lands,
That dare forget Thee, or rebel,
    Against Thy known commands.

6.
Though the righteous to sore distress are brought,
    And wait, and long complain,
Their cries shall never be forgot,
    Nor shall their hopes be vain.

7.
Rise, great Redeemer, from Thy seat,
    To judge and save the poor;

Let the North tremble at Thy feet,
    And Man prevail no more.
8.
Thy thunder shall affright the Tyrants,
    And put their hearts to pain,
Made them confess that THOU art GOD.
    And THEY but fanatical wicked men.[14]

THE COMING STORM
BY HERMAN MELVILLE

A Picture by S. R. Gifford, and owned by E. B.
Included in the N. A. Exhibition, April 1865.

All feeling hearts must feel for him
    Who felt this picture. Presage dim—
Dim inklings from the shadowy sphere
    Fixed him and fascinated here.

A demon-cloud like the mountain one
    Burst on a spirit as mild
As this urned lake, the home of shades,
    But Shakespeare's pensive child

Never the lines had lightly scanned,
    Steeped in fable, steeped in fate;
The Hamlet in his heart was 'ware,
    Such hearts can antedate.

No utter surprise can come to him
    Who reaches Shakespeare's core;
That which we seek and shun is there—
    Man's final lore.[15]

---

[14] Charles Caylat, "Of 'Bull's Run,' the 18th, and Manasseh, the 21st July, 1861," *The Glorious Southern Victories*, broadside (Confederate States of America, 25 February 1863).

THE DAWN OF PEACE
BY CHRISTOPHER CRANCH

Four years of war have driven afar the dream
Of union based on hollow compromise.
We wake to see the auroral splendors stream
Across the battle smoke from opening skies.
The demon, shrieking, tears us as he flies
Exorcised from our wrenched and bleeding frame.
O costly ransom! dearly purchased prize!
Release too long delayed! from sin and shame,
From evil compacts and from brutal laws,
Whose iron network all the land encaged.
Force never triumphed in a juster cause,
Nor bloody war was e'er so justly waged.
Henceforth our banner greets a cloudless morn.
Peace dawns at last. The nation is re-born![16]

THE DAY IS AT HAND

Let mammon hold while mammon can,
The bones and blood of living man;
Let tyrants scorn while tyrants dare,
The shrieks and writhings of despair.

THE END WILL COME, IT WILL NOT WAIT,
Bonds, yokes and scourges have their date;
Slavery itself must pass away,
And be a tale of yesterday.[17]

---

[15] Herman Melville, "The Coming Storm," *Battle-Pieces and Aspects of the War* (New York: Harper and Brothers, 1866) 143.

[16] Christopher Cranch, "The Dawn of Peace," *The Bird and the Bell* (Boston: James D. Osgood, 1875) n.p.

[17] "The Day is at Hand," *Songs of the Free, and Hymns of Christian Freedom*, ed. Maria Chapman (Boston: I. Knapp, 1836) 98–99.

DAY OF JUBILEE
BY THOMAS PECK

The following lines, the production of a negro contraband, unable to read
or write, were composed on the Proclamation of President Lincoln.
They were handed to us by Mr. Cornelius Bradford, who has
recently arrived from the hospital at Hampton, having been
discharged on account of sickness.

In 1861 this great and glorious work begun,
    In 1863 brings four millions their liberty;
Glory to God, who spared us to see
    This glorious day of Jubilee.

Moses led the Israelites,
    But Joshua reached the place;
Garrison commenced the glorious work,
    But Lincoln decides the case.

We have suffered long, and were punished wrong,
    But now we see the light;
The time has come, seventy years have won,
    And Lincoln will do all things right.

We'll thank him and praise him,
    And will ever agree
In the great celebration
    Of the day we are free.

Fremont is our friend,
    And that the nation can see
That Hunter is in favor
    Of the day of Jubilee.

Massachusetts has done nobly,
    And Andrew will be
A great man in
    The year of Jubilee.

New York has done well,
   But better she would be
If she were in favor
   Of this great Jubilee.

There is old Pennsylvania,
   She too has shed her blood,
But her sons are opposed
   To the people's being free.

Old England has been growling.
Old Spain has been grouty,
   But they both ought to see
That France is in favor
   Of the people's being free.

Bennet is a Democrat,
   And opposed is he
To the great proclamation
   Of the people's being free,

The Tribune is our friend,
   And ever will be
In favor of the colored man
   Learning his A B C.

Freedom is a good thing;
   Slavery is not fair;—
Thomas Peck was under the yoke
   Twenty-one year.[18]

---

[18] Thomas Peck, "Day of Jubilee," *Zion's Herald and Wesleyan Journal* (18 February 1863): 1.

THE FIEND UNBOUND

No more, with glad and happy cheer,
    And smiling face, doth Christmas come,
But usher'd in with sword and spear,
    And beat of the barbarian drum!
No more, with ivy-circled brow,
    And mossy beard all snowy white,
He comes to glad the children now,
    With sweet and innocent delight.

The merry dance, the lavish feast,
    The cheery welcome, all are o'er:
The music of the viol ceased,
    The gleesome ring around the floor.
No glad communion greets the hour,
    That welcomes in a Saviour's birth,
And Christmas, to a hostile power,
    Yields all the sway that made its mirth.

The Church, like some deserted bride,
    In trembling, at the Altar waits,
While, raging fierce on every side,
    The foe is thundering at her gates.
No ivy green, nor glittering leaves,
    Nor crimson berries, deck her walls:
But blood, red dripping from her eaves,
    Along the sacred pavement falls.

Her silver bells no longer chime
    In summons to her sacred home;
Nor holy song at matin prime,
    Proclaims the God within the dome,
Nor do the fireside's happy bands
    Assemble fond, with greetings dear,
While Patriarch Christmas spreads his hands
    To glad with gifts and crown with cheer.

In place of that beloved form,
    Benignant, bland, and blessing all,
Comes one begirt with fire and storm,
    The raging shell, the hissing ball!
Type of the Prince of Peace, no more,
    Evoked by those who bear His name,
THE FIEND, in place of SAINT of yore,
    Now hurls around Satanic flame.

In hate,—evoked by kindred lands,
    But late beslavering with caress,
Lo, Moloch, dripping crimson, stands,
    And curses where he cannot bless.
He wings the bolt and hurls the spear,
    A *demon loosed*, that rends in rage,
Sends havoc through the homes most dear,
    And butchers youth and tramples age!

With face of Fox—with glee that grins,
    And apish arms, with fingers claw'd,
To snatch at all his brother wins,
    And straight secrete, with stealth and fraud;—
Lo! Mammon, kindred Demon, comes,
    And lurks, as dreading ill, in rear;
He blows the trumpet, beats the drums,
    Inflames the torch, and sharps the spear!

And furious, following in their train,
    What hosts of lesser Demons rise;
Lust, Malice, Hunger, Greed and Gain,
    Each raging for its special prize.
Too base for freedom, mean for toil,
    And reckless all of just and right,
They rage in peaceful homes for spoil,
    And where they cannot butcher, blight.

A Serpent lie from every mouth,
    Coils outward ever,—sworn to bless;

Yet, through the gardens of the South,
   Still spreading evils numberless,
By locust swarms the fields are swept,
   By frenzied hands the dwelling flames,
And virgin beds, where Beauty slept,
   Polluted blush, from worst of shames.

The Dragon, chain'd for thousand years,
   Hath burst his bonds and rages free;—
Yet, patience, brethren, stay your fears;—
   Loosed for "a little season," he
Will soon, beneath th' Ithuriel sword,
   Of heavenly judgment, crush'd and driven,
Yield to the vengeance of the Lord,
   And crouch beneath the wrath of Heaven!

"A little season," and the Peace,
   That now is foremost in your prayers,
Shall crown your harvest with increase,
   And bless with smiles the home of tears;
Your wounds be healed; your noble sons,
   Unhurt, unmutilated—free—
Shall limber up their conquering guns,
   In triumph grand of Liberty!

A few more hours of mortal strife,—
   Of faith and patience, working still,
In struggle for the immortal life,
   With all their soul, and strength, and will;
And, in the favor of the Lord,
   And powerful grown by heavenly aid,
Your roof trees all shall be restored,
   And ye shall triumph in their shade.[19]

---

[19] "The Fiend Unbound," from the *Charleston Mercury*, reprinted in Simms, *War Poetry of the South*, 246–50.

Hymn for Northern People

Great God of Battles, lift we unto Thee
A people's voice in gratitude and praise,
Thou, who, unsearchable in all Thy ways,
    Ordainest victory.

To thee we bow, lend unto us Thine ear,
Clothe us O Lord! with thy protecting power,
And unto us in this our thankful hour,
    Great God in heaven, draw near!

Bend down upon us Thine all-seeing eyes,
Thou who in ages past Thy throne didst set
With myriad stars, and see our altars wet
    With blood of sacrifice!

Reach unto us, O God! Thy bounteous hand
Full of all blessings with the closing year,
And scatter them like good seed far and near,
    Throughout our bleeding land!

Forgive our foes, restore to them their sight,
Cleanse us from guilt; allay our many fears;
Wipe from the people's eyes the scalding tears,
    O turn our night to day!

Announce thy coming, Lord! show us that sign
Seen in the prophet's vision long ago;
How long, O Lord! from out the press must flow
    The nation's blood-red wine?

Give unto them, the rulers of our land,
A love of Truth, of Justice, and of Right:
May they be upright in thine own pure sight:
    Give each a firm right hand!

Let War, and Pestilence, and Famine cease
From off the earth; Great God! we fain would hear,
Ere yet the Christmas chimes sound sweet and clear,
    The voice of Christ say "Peace"![20]

JACKSON
BY HARRY FLASH

Not 'mid the lightning of the stormy fight,
Not in the rush upon the vandal foe,
Did kingly Death, with his resistless might,
    Lay the Great Leader low.

His warrior soul its earthly shackles broke
In the full sunshine of a peaceful town.
When all the storm was hushed, the trusty oak
    That propped our cause went down.

Though his alone the blood that flecks the ground,
Recording all his grand, heroic deeds,
Freedom herself is writhing with the wound,
    And all the country bleeds.

He entered not the Nation's Promised Land,
At the red belching of the cannon's mouth;
But broke the House of Bondage with his hand—
    The Moses of the South!

O gracious God! not gainless is the loss:
A glorious sunbeam gilds thy sternest frown;
And, while his country staggers with the Cross,
    He rises with the Crown![21]

---

[20] "Hymn for Northern People," *Zion's Herald and Wesleyan Journal* (5 October 1864): 1.

[21] Harry Flash, "Jackson," *South Songs*, 29.

JOHN BROWN

John Brown's body lies a mouldering in the grave,
John Brown's body lies a mouldering in the grave,
John Brown's body lies a mouldering in the grave,
His soul's marching on!

Glory, Hally, Hallelujah!
Glory, Hally, Hallelujah!
Glory, Hally, Hallelujah!
His soul's marching on!

He's gone to be a soldier in the army of our Lord, etc.
His soul's marching on!

John Brown's knapsack is strapped upon his back, etc.
His soul's marching on!

His pet lambs will meet him on the way—, etc.
They go marching on.

They will hang Jeff Davis to a tree!, etc.
As they march along!

Now, three cheers for the Union! etc.
As we go marching on.

Hip, Hip, Hip, Hip, Hurrah![22]

---

[22] "John Brown" (Boston: J. F. Nash, 1860).

LINES TO THE MEMORY OF FATHER TURGIS
BY T. WHARTON COLLINS

March weaponless and think of God,
Muffle the roll of war's tambour,
Dig me a grave beneath the sod,
And have me buried with the poor.

So spoke the holy priest and died.
Let no mausoleum rise in pride
O'er where his sacred bones repose,
But mark the humble grave he chose
With the Redeemer's cross of wood—
Glorious, though 'tis low and rude.

No sword bore he 'midst battling hosts;
Yet when the lines of bayonets
Met with their deadly clash and thrust,
When howling balls and whizzing bullets
Swept, gathering harvest o'er the plain,
There, 'mong the wounded and the slain,
While boomed the deep artillery,
While blazed the rattling musketry,
While fire and smoke rose round the brave,—
While mingled blood of friend and foe
Gushed out with groans of death and woe,—
There went the Christian priest to save,
To save—to bring the bread of life:
Reclaim a soul from hell and strife.
From bleeding form to bleeding form,
Resigned, devoted, through the storm,
Seeking God's own, here, there he ran,
This gentle one, this unarmed man;
Fearless he strove, nor prayed release,
This Chieftain of the Prince of Peace.

Father! haste thee from this deadly field:
Leave us in our blood—there is no shield
To screen thy holy breast. Farewell!
    —Nay, nay! my son, for here I tell
Of him who lifts a living soul
From dying flesh; and to the goal
Of heaven's glory bears it up
To drink of His eternal cup.
Come! list of Christ the pressing call!
Think not of me; for, if I fall,
Our comrades, flushed with victory,
On morrow's dawn, in triumph's glee,
Will bear us hence with thoughts of God.
Muffle the clang of war's tambour,
Dig us a grave beneath the sod,
And leave us buried with the poor.
    Yea, with the poor, the blessed ones,
Whose hearts yearned not for worldly wealth;
But cheerful hoped for heavenly thrones,
And died unknown to all the earth.
    No records here their memories keep,
Their graves deserted none can tell;
But when on clouds comes Jesus bright,
When the proud men shall sink to hell,
The levelled ground where now they sleep
Will burst with rays of dazzling light,
And let their shining bodies rise
To meet their Saviour in the skies.
    Follow this humble corpse, ye braves,
With whom 'twas once a tender, cheering friend—
A voice that told the truth that saves—
A hand that led where honour could attend.
Follow! ye chiefs and men of fame,
Follow! ye mothers of the dead,
Follow! his name outshines your name—
His meek and venerable head
Has won a fairer wreath than yours:
Yours of country, his of heaven!

Follow! while forth his spirit soars
Triumphant, to its higher haven.
Follow unarmed, and think of God.
Muffle the beat of war's tambour,
Dig him a grave beneath the sod,
And leave him buried with the Poor.[23]

THE LORD WILL COME

The Lord will come! the earth shall quake,
The hills their lasting seat forsake;
And with'ring from the vault of night,
The stars withdraw their feeble light.

The Lord will come! but not the same,
As once in lowly form he came,
A silent lamb to slaughter led—
The bruis'd, the suff'ring, and the dead.

The Lord will come! a dreadful form,
With wreath of flame and robe of storm:
Then slaves and masters both shall find
An equal judge of human kind.[24]

THE MARCH OF THE REGIMENT
BY HENRY HOWARD BROWNELL

Here they come!—'tis the Twelfth, you know—
    The Colonel is just at hand—
The ranks close up, to the measured flow
    Of music cheery and grand.
Glitter on glitter, row by row,
The steady bayonets, on they go
    For God and the Right to stand—

---

[23] T. Wharton Collens, "Lines to the Memory of Father Turgis," *The Living Writers of the South*, ed. James Wood Davidson (New York: Carleton, 1869)103–104.

[24] "The Lord Will Come," *Lyre*, ed. Hatfield, 102.

Another Thousand to front the Foe!
And to die—if it must be even so—
    For the dear old Fatherland!

O, trusty and true! O gay, warm heart!
    O, manly and earnest brow!
Here, in the hurrying street, we part—
    To meet—ah, where and how?
O, ready and staunch! who, at war's alarm,
On lonely hill-side and mountain-farm
    Have left the axe and the plow!
That every tear were a holy charm,
To guard, with honor, some head from harm,
    And to quit some generous vow!
For, of valiant heart and of sturdy arm
    Was never more need than now.

Never a nobler Morn to the bold
    For God and for Country's sake!
Lo, a Flag, so haughtily unrolled
On a hundred foughten fields of old,
    Now flaunts in a pirate's wake!
The lion coys in each blazoned fold,
    And leers on the blood-barred Snake!

O, base and vain! that, for grudge and gain,
    Could a century's feud renew—
Could hoard your hate for the coward chance
When a Nation reeled in a wilder Dance
    Of Death, than the Switzer drew!
We have borne, and borne—and may bear again
    With wrong, but if wrong from *you.*

Welcome the sulphury cloud in the sky!
    Welcome, the crimson rain!
Act but the dream ye dared to form,
Strike a single spark!—and the storm
Of serried bayonets sweeping by,

Shall swell to a hurricane!

Dree your weird!—though an hour may blight,
 In treason, a century's fame—
Trust Greed and Spite!—(sith Reason and Right
 Lie cold, with Honor and Shame)—
And learn anon—as on that dread night
When, the dead around and the deck aflame,
From John Paul's lip the fierce word came—
 "We have only *begun* to fight!"

O, blind and bitter! that could not know,
Even in fight, a caitiff blow,
(Foully dealt on a hard-set foe,)
 Ever is underwise—
Ever is ghosted with after Fear—
Ye might lesson it—year by year,
 Looking, with fevered eyes,
For sail or smoke from the Breton shore,
Lest a Land, so rudely wronged of yore,
 In flamy revenge should rise!

Office at outcry!—ah, wretched Flam!
 Vile Farce of hammer and prate!
Trade! bids Derby—and blood! smirks Pam—
Little ween they, each courtly Sham,
 Of the Terror lying in wait!
Little wot of the web he spins,
Their Tempter in purple, that darkly grins
 'Neath his stony visor of state,
O'er Seas, how narrow!—for, whoso wins,
At yon base Auction of Outs and Ins,
 The rule of his Dearest Hate—
Her point once flashing athwart her Kin's,
And the reckoning, ledgered for long, begins—
The galling Glories and envied Sins
 Shall buzz in a mesh like fate!

Aye, mate your meanest!—ye can but do
That permitted—when Heaven would view
How wrong, self-branded, her rage must rue
In wreck and ashes!—(such scene as you,
    If wise, shall witness afar)—
How Guilt, o'erblown, her crest heaves high,
And dares the injured, with taunt, to try
    Ordeal of Fire in war—
Blindfold and brazen, on God doth call—
Then grasps, in horror, the glaring ball,
    Or treads on the candent bar!

Yet a little!—and men shall mark
This our Moloch, who sate so stark,
(These hundred winters through godless dark
    Grinning o'er death and shame)—
Marking for murder each unbowed head,
Throned on his Ghizeh of bones, and fed
Still with hearts of the holy dead—
Naught but a Spectre foul and dread,
    Naught but a hideous Name!
At last!—(ungloom, stern coffined frown!
Rest thee, Gray-Steel!—aye, dead Renown!
In flame and thunder by field and town
The Giant-Horror is going down,
    Down to the Home whence it came!)

Deaf to the Doom that waits the Beast,
Still would ye share the Harlot's Feast,
    And drink of her blood-grimed Cup!
Pause!—the Accursed, on yon frenzied shore,
Buyeth your merchandise never more!
Mark, 'mid the Fiery Dew that drips,
Redder, faster, through black Eclipse,
    How Sodom, to-night, shall sup!
(Thus the Kings, in Apocalypse,
The traders of souls and crews of ships,
Standing afar, with pallid lips,

While Babylon's Smoke goes up!)

Aye, 'tis at hand!—foul lips, be dumb!
Our Armageddon is yet to come!
But cheery bugle, and angry drum,
    With volleyed rattle and roar,
And cannon thunder-throb, shall be drowned,
That day, in a grander, stormier sound—
    The Land, from mountain to shore,
Hurling shackle and scourge and stake
Back to their Lender of pit and lake—
    ('Twas Tophet leased them of yore)—
Hell, in her murkest hold, shall quake,
As they ring on the damned floor!
O mighty Heart! thou wast long to wake—
'Tis thine, to-morrow, to win or break
    In a deadlier close once more—
If but for the dear and glorious sake
    Of those who have gone before.

O Fair and Faithful! that, sun by sun,
Slept on the field, or lost or won—
Children dear of the Holy One!
    Rest in your wintry sod.
Rest, your noble Devoir is done—
Done—and forever!—ours, to-day,
The dreary drift and the frozen clay
    By trampling armies trod—
The smoky shroud of the War-Simoom,
The maddened Crime at bay with her Doom,
    And fighting it, clod by clod.
O Calm and Glory!—beyond the gloom,
Above the bayonets bend and bloom
    The lilies and palms of God.

February 1862[25]

---

[25] Henry Howard Brownell, "The March of the Regiment," *War-Lyrics* (Boston: Ticknor and Fields, 1866) 74–79.

Marching Song of the First Arkansas
by Captain Lindley Miller

This song was written by Captain Lindley Miller, of the First Arkansas
Colored Regiment. Captain Miller says the "boys" sing the song on
dress-parade with an effect which can hardly be described; and he
adds that "while it is not very conservative, it will do to fight with."

Oh! we're de bully soldiers ob de "First of Arkansas,"
We are fightin' for de Union, we are fightin' for de law,
We can hit a Rebel furder dan a white man eber saw,
   As we go marchin' on.
   Glory, glory, hallelujah, &c.

See dar! above de centre, where de flag is wavin bright;
We are goin' out of slavery; we are bound for Freedom's light,
We mean to show Jeff. Davis how de Africans can fight!
   As we go marchin' on.

We hab done wid hoein' cotton, we hab done wid hoein' corn,
We are colored Yankee soldiers now, as sure as you are born;
When de massas hear us yellin' dey'll tink its Gabriel's horn,
   As we go marchin' on.

Dey will hab to pay us wages, de wages ob their sin,
Dey will hab to bow their foreheads to their colored kith and kin,
Dey will hab to gib us house-room, or de roof shall tumble in!
   As we go marchin' on.

We heard de proclamation, massa hush it as he will;
De bird he sing it to us, hoppin' on de cotton-hill,
And de possum up de gum-tree, he couldn't keep it still,
   As he went climbing on.

Dey said, "Now colored bredren, you shall be forever free,
From de first ob January, eighteen hundred sixty-three;"
We heard it in de riber goin' rushin' to de sea,
   As it went soundin' on.

Father Abraham has spoken, and de message has been sent,
De prison-doors he opened, and out de pris'ners went,
To join de sable army ob de "African descent,"
      As we go marchin' on.

Den fall in, colored bredren, you'd better do it soon;
Don't you hear de drum a beatin' de Yankee Doodle tune?
We are wid you now dis mornin', we'll be far away at noon,
      As we go marchin' on.[26]

THE MARTYR
BY CHRISTOPHER CRANCH

No, not in vain he died, not all in vain,—
Our good, great President. This people's hands
Are linked together in one mighty chain,
Knit tighter now in triple woven bands,
To crush the fiends in human mask, whose might
We suffer, O, too long! No league or truce
Save *men* with *men.* The devils we must fight
With fire. God wills it in this deed. This use
We draw from the most impious murder done
Since Calvary. Rise, then, O countrymen!
Scatter these marsh-light hopes of union won
Through pardoning clemency. Strike, strike again!
Draw closer round the foe a girdling flame!
We are stabbed when'er we spare. Strike, in God's name![27]

---

[26] Captain Lindley Miller, "Marching Song of the First Arkansas," *Songs of the Soldiers*, 206–208.

[27] Christopher Cranch, "The Martyr," *The Bird and the Bell*, n. p.

The Martyr
by Herman Melville

Indicative of the passion of the people on the 15th of April 1865.

Good Friday was the day
   Of the prodigy and crime,
When they killed him in his pity,
   When they killed him in his prime
Of clemency and calm—
        When with yearning he was filled
        To redeem the evil-willed,
And, though conqueror, be kind;
   But they killed him in his kindness,
   In their madness and their blindness,
And they killed him from behind.

There is sobbing of the strong,
   And a pall upon the land;
But the People in their weeping
        Bare the iron hand:
Beware the people weeping
   When they bare the iron hand.

He lieth in his blood—
   The father in his face;
They have killed him, the Forgiver—
   The avenger takes his place,
The Avenger wisely stern,
        Who in righteousness shall do
        What the heavens call him to,
And the parricides remand;
   For they killed him in his kindness,
   In their madness and their blindness,
And his blood is on their hand.

There is sobbing of the strong,

And a pall upon the land;
But the People in their weeping
      Bare the iron hand:
Beware the People weeping
   When they bare the iron hand.[28]

THE MASSACHUSETTS JOHN BROWN SONG

Old John Brown's body is a-mouldering in the dust,
Old John Brown's rifle's red with blood-spots turned to rust,
Old John Brown's pike has made its last, unflinching thrust,
      His soul is marching on!

    Glory! Glory! Hallelujah!
    "Forward!" calls the Lord, our Captain:
    Glory! Glory! Hallelujah!
      With him we're marching on.

For treason hung because he struck at treason's root,
When soon palmetto-tree had ripened treason's fruit,
His dust, disquieted, stirred at Sumter's last salute—
      His soul is marching on!

Who rides before the army of martyrs to the word?
The heavens grow bright as He makes bare his flaming sword,
The glory fills the earth of the coming of the Lord—
      His soul is marching on!

"Thou soul the altar under, white-robed by martyrdom!
Thy cry, 'How long, O Lord?' no longer finds me dumb;
'Come forth!' calls Christ, 'the year of my redeemed is come'—
      His soul is marching on!

"And ye on earth, my army! tread down God's grapes till blood

---

[28] Herman Melville, "The Martyr," *Battle-Pieces*, 141–42.

Unto your horses' bridles hath out His wine-press flowed!
The day of vengeance dawns,—the day of wrath of God"—
His soul is marching on!

His sacrifice we slay! our sword shall victory crown!
For God and country strike the fiend Rebellion down!
For Freedom and the Right remember Old John Brown!
His soul is marching on!

"Glory! Glory! Hallelujah!"
Sings that army in the skies;
"Glory to the Lord, our Captain!"
His army here replies.
Glory rings through heaven's arches,
Earth takes on the grand accord;
"Glory!" on to glory marches
The army of the Lord.[29]

ODE–"DO YE QUAIL?"
BY WILLIAM GILMORE SIMMS

Do ye quail but to hear, Carolinians,
The first foot-tramp of Tyranny's minions?
Have ye buckled on armor, and brandished the spear,
But to shrink with the trumpet's first peal on the ear?
Why your forts now embattled on headland and height,
Your sons all in armor, unless for the fight?
Did ye think the mere show of your guns on the wall,
And your shouts, would the souls of the heathen appal?
That his lusts and his appetites, greedy as Hell,
Led by Mammon and Moloch, would sink at a spell;—
Nor strive, with the tiger's own thirst, lest the flesh
Should be torn from his jaws, while yet bleeding afresh.

---

[29] L. Holbrook, "The Massachusetts John Brown Song," *Songs of the Soldiers*, 125–27.

For shame! To the breach, Carolinians!—
To the death for your sacred dominions!—
Homes, shrines, and your cities all reeking in flame,
Cry aloud to your souls, in their sorrow and shame;
Your greybeards, with necks in the halter—
Your virgins, defiled at the altar,—
In the loathsome embrace of the felon and slave,
Touch loathsomer far than the worm of the grave!
Ah! God! if you fail in this moment of gloom!
How base were the weakness, how horrid the doom!
With the fiends in your streets howling paeans,
And the Beast o'er another Orleans!

Do ye quail, as on yon little islet
They have planted the feet that defile it?
Make its sands pure of taint, by the stroke of the sword,
And by torrents of blood in red sacrifice pour'd!
Doubts are Traitors, if once they persuade you to fear,
That the foe, in his foothold, is safe from your spear!
When the foot of pollution is set on your shores,
What sinew and soul should be stronger than yours?
By the fame—by the shame—of your sires,
Set on, though each freeman expires;
Better fall, grappling fast with the foe, to their graves,
Than groan in your fetters, the slaves of your slaves.

The voice of your loud exultation
Hath rung, like a trump, through the nation,
How loudly, how proudly, of deeds to be done,
The blood of the sire in the veins of the son!
Old Moultrie and Sumter still keep at your gates,
And the foe in his foothold as patiently waits.
He asks, with a taunt, by your patience made bold,
If the hot spur of Percy grows suddenly cold—
Makes merry with boasts of your city his own,
And the Chivalry fled, ere his trumpet is blown;
Upon them, O sons of the mighty of yore,
And fatten the sands with their Sodomite gore!

Where's the dastard that cowers and falters
In the sight of his hearthstones and altars?
With the faith of the free in the God of the brave,
Go forth; ye are mighty to conquer and save!
By the blue Heaven shining above ye,
By the pure-hearted thousands that love ye,
Ye are armed with a might to prevail in the fight,
And an aegis to shield and a weapon to smite!
Then fail not, and quail not; the foe shall prevail not:
With the faith and the will, ye shall conquer him still.
To the knife—with the knife, Carolinians,
For your homes, and your sacred dominions.[30]

     Our Men are Marching on.
     Air—"GLORY HALLELUJAH."

The day our fathers waited for is dawning on us now;
I see the mantle falling on the prophet at the plough;
I hear the trumpet ringing where the victors strike the blow,
    CHORUS—Our men are marching on,
  Glory, glory, Hallelujah, glory, glory Hallelujah,
     Our men are marching on.

Niagara shouts the chorus of the rivers to the sea;
Each wave swells like the bosom that is panting to be free.
The stars are lit in heaven for the nation's jubilee.
    CHORUS—Our men are marching on,
  Glory, glory, Hallelujah, etc. /

Sweet promises are written on the soft leaves of the flowers;
The birds of spring are jubilant within their leafy towers;
A rainbow ahs been woven in the shuttle of the showers.
    CHORUS—Our men are marching on,
  Glory, glory, Hallelujah, etc.

---

[30] William Gilmore Simms, "Ode—"Do Ye Quail?" *War Poetry of the South*, ed. Simms, 252–55.

God bless our gallant President, and grant him length of days,
Let all the people crown him, with fame's unfading lays,
And generations yet unborn perpetuate his praise.
    CHORUS—Our men are marching on,
  Glory, glory, Hallelujah, etc.[31]

A PRAYER FOR PEACE
BY GEORGE HERBERT SASS

Look forth, look forth from the pale hills of Time
    Which, deepening in the distance, rise and swell
In shadowy surges to the great Sublime.
    Look forth from those grey heights, look forth, and tell
If the Deliverer comes! Long have we striven
    And toiled, and waited—darker to our view
Grows the horizon of yon lowering heaven,
    And the chill blasts blow menacingly through;
Closer the shadows crouch around our path—
The billowy storm-clouds of impending wrath.

Look forth, pale Sentry of the Eastern hills,
    Wan with long watching, gaunt with vigil sore;
Speak the wild thought which through my bosom thrills.
    Comes the Good Master never, never more?
Hath He forgot His people in their woes?
    Is the Great Ruler impotent to save?
Are these sharp pangs but Life's expiring throes,
    And tend our blood-stained footsteps to the grave?
When comes of all our ills the blest surcease?
Where loitereth, prison-bound, sweet-featured Peace?

For two long years the wine-press have we trodden,
    Sure Thou wilt hearken as we turn to Thee,
Lifting our bridal-robes, all stained and sodden
    With the red tears of wounded Purity!

---

[31] "Our Men are Marching On," *Encyclopedia of Popular Songs (Touch the Elbow Songster)* (New York: Dick & Fitzgerald, 1864) 68–69.

Sure Thou wilt bare Thine arm's avenging might,
    Till in Thy glorious kingdom upon earth
We stand a nation of the nations, bright
    In all the grandeur of heroic birth,
Clad in the purple, yet with mourning weeds,
The proud heart throbbing, even while it bleeds.

Ah, yes! triumphant still, though stricken sore—
    Like some fair barque, whose prow hath wooed the wave
Which leaps in maddening surges on the shore,
    Where foam-crowned eddies lure her to her grave,—
Yet still hath borne her proudly on her way,
    Though tempests rage, and billows roar and swell,
Into the haven of eternal day
    Hath passed, and is at rest, and all is well!
Ay, even though the lordly mast hath bowed,
And the breeze murmurs through a storm-rent shroud.

With wistful glance the dying western sun
    Looks down upon a lone and peaceful grave;
Full lovingly the shadows, pale and dun,
    Guard the last home of him who died to save
His fair fame from foul slander's blighting breath—
    His country from the foe's polluting tread;
Bright smiling in the phantom arms of death,
    With no vain sigh or throb of craven dread,
Where weeps the wave of that calm western river,
Fell the true knight, a hero now forever.

Once more the shadows darken through the land;
    Once more goes forth that wild, despairing cry;
The bright blade falleth from the nerveless hand,
    The light of battle fadeth from the eye!
A moan of woe in Shenandoah's vale;
    One quick, short sigh on Rappahannock's shore,
And then outswelleth proudly on the gale
    The grand old shout, the battle-cry of yore!
Still Jackson's name the foremost charge hath led,

Still Jackson's war-cry thunders at their head!

Yes, all unshaken is the patient trust,
    The steadfast heart, the calm, undaunted will,
And now we lift us to Thee from the dust
    Of penitence, and pray that Thou wilt still
The raging of the waters, till the calm
    Of peace shall brood upon the troubled deep,
And the soft billows, murmuring a psalm
    Of love and glory, gently charm to sleep
The storm-tossed mariner, soft as the chime
Of distant home bells in a fairy clime.

And so, as some rich-freighted Argosie
    Which glides in swan-like grandeur o'er the main
While all the treasures of a tropic sea
    Flash round her prow and glitter in her train,
In triumph o'er the waves our Ship of State
    Shall proudly ride, while yet the soft breeze fills
Her sails, until at last the crystal gate,
    Deep-bosomed 'mid the Everlasting Hills,
Shall open to her prow, her wanderings cease,
And o'er her decks shall brood love-crowned Peace.[32]

RESTORATION OF ISRAEL

Daughter of Zion, from the dust
    Exalt thy fallen head;
Again in thy Redeemer trust,
    He calls thee from the dead.

Awake, awake, put on thy strength,
    Thy beautiful array;
The day of freedom dawns at length;
    The Lord's appointed day.

---

[32] George Herbert Sass, "A Prayer for Peace," *Living Writers of the South*, 496–98.

Rebuild thy walls, thy bounds enlarge,
    And send thy heralds forth;
Say to the south, 'Give up thy charge,
    And keep not back, O north!'

They come, they come;—thine exiled bands
    Where'er they rest or 'roam,
Have heard thy voice in distant lands,
    And hasten to their home.

King of the dead! how long shall sweep
Thy wrath! how long thy outcasts weep!
Two thousand agonizing years
Has Afric steeped her bread in tears;
The vial on her head been poured—
Flight, famine, shame, the scourge, the sword!

'Tis done! Has breathed thy trumpet blast;
The tribes at length have wept their last!
On rolls the host! From land and wave
The earth sends up the unransomed slave
There rides no glittering chivalry,
No banner purples in the sky;
The world within their hearts has died;
Two thousand years have slain their pride!
The look of pale remorse is there,
The lip's involuntary prayer;
The form still marked with many a stain—
Brand of the soil, the scourge, the chain;
The serf of Afric's fiery ground;
The slave, by Southern suns embrowned;
The weary drudges of the oar,
By the swart Arab's poisoned shore,
The gatherings of earth's wildest trace—
On bursts the living cataract!
What strength of man can check its speed?
They come—the nation of the FREED!

Who leads their march? Beneath his wheel
Back rolls the sea, the mountains reel!
Before their tread the trump is blown,
Who speaks in thunder, and 'tis done!
King of the dead! Oh, not in vain
Was thy long pilgrimage of pain;
Oh not in vain arose thy prayer,
When pressed the thorn thy temples bare;
Oh, not in vain the voice that cried,
To spare thy maddened homicide!

Even for this hour thy heart's blood streamed!
They come!—the host of the redeemed!
What flames upon the distant sky?
'Tis not the comet's sanguine dye,
'Tis not the lightning's quivering spire,
'Tis not the sun's ascending fire.
And now, as nearer speeds their march
Expands the rainbow's mighty arch;
Though there has burst no thundercloud
No flash of death the soil has ploughed,
And still ascends before their gaze,
Arch upon arch, the lovely blaze;
Still as the gorgeous clouds unfold,
Rise towers and domes, immortal mould,
Whose city this? What potentate
Sits there the king of Time and Fate,
Whom glory covers with a robe,
Whose sceptre shakes the solid globe,
To Whom archangels bow the knee?—
The weeper of Gethsemane!
Down in the dust! ay, Christian kneel!
For now thy withered heart must feel!
Ay, let thy wan cheek burn like flame;
there sits thy glory and thy shame![33]

---

[33] "Restoration of Israel," *Songs*, ed. Chapman, 17–19.

SHERMANIZED
BY L. VIRGINIA FRENCH

In this city of Atlanta, on a dire and dreadful day,
'Mid the raging of the conflict, 'mid the thunder of the fray,
In the blaze of burning roof-trees, under clouds of smoke and flame,
Sprang a new word into being from a stern and dreaded name;
Gaunt and grim and like a spectre, rose that WORD before the world,
From a land of bloom and beauty into ruin rudely hurled,
From a people scourged by exile, from a city ostracised,
Pallas-like it sprang to being, and that WORD is—SHERMANIZED.
And forevermore hereafter, where the fierce Destroyer reigns,
Where Destruction pours her lava over cultivated plains,
Where want and woe hold carnival—where bitter blight and blood
Sweep over prosperous nations in a strong relentless flood;
Where the golden crown of harvest trodden into ashes lies,
And Desolation stares abroad with famine-phrenzied eyes;
Where the wrong with iron-sceptre crushes every right we prized,
There shall people groan in anguish—"GOD! THE RIGHT, IS
    SHERMANIZED!"

Man may rule the raids of ruin, lead the legions that despoil,
From the lips of honest labor dash the guerdon of his toil,
"Sow with salt" the smiling valleys, and on every breezy height
Kindle bale-fires of destruction, lurid on the solemn night;
He may sacrifice the aged, and exult when woman stands
'Mid the sunken, sodden ashes of her home, with palsied hands
Drooping over hungered children—man may thus immortalize
His name with haggard infamy—his watchword—"SHERMANIZE!"
Nobler deeds are Woman's province—she must not destroy, but build.
She must bring the urns of Plenty, with the wine of Pleasure filled;
She must be the "sweet restorer" of this sunny Southern land,
Fill our schools, rebuild our churches, take the feeble by the hand,
Aid the press, befriend the teacher, give to Want, its daily bread,
And never, NEVER fail to weave above our "noble dead"
The laurel garland due to deeds of Valor's high emprise,
And won by men whom FAILURE could not sink, or—SHERMANIZE!
With her wakened love of labor, let her labor on in love,

Still, in softness and in stillness, as the starry circles move,
Bearing light, and bringing gladness, from the leaden clouds unfurled,
As the soft rise of the sunlight bringeth morning to the world;
Grandly urging on Endeavor, as the gates of Day unclose,
Till the "solitary place again shall blossom as the rose,"
And WOMAN, THE REBUILDER, shall be freely eulogized
By the triumph of her people, then no longer SHERMANIZED!
God bless our noble Georgia! though her soil was overrun,
And her lands in desolation laid, beneath an autumn's sun;
With her signal shout "To action!" like the boom of signal guns,
She has roused the lion mettle of her strong and stalwart sons,
May her daughters aid that effort to rebuild and to restore,
Working on for SOUTHERN FREEDOM as they never worked before!
May Georgia as a laggard never once be stigmatized,
And her PEOPLE, PRESS OR PULPIT, never more
     be—SHERMANIZED![34]

THE SOUTHERN CROSS
BY ST. GEORGE TUCKER

Oh! say can you see, through the gloom and the storm,
More bright for the darkness, that pure constellation?
Like the symbol of love and redemption its form,
As it points to the haven of hope for the nation.
How radiant each star, as the beacon afar,
Giving promise of peace, or assurance in war!
'Tis the Cross of the South, which shall ever remain
To light us to freedom and glory again!

How peaceful and blest was America's soil
'Til betrayed by the guile of the Puritan demon,
Which lurks under Virtue and springs from its coil
To fasten its fangs in the life-blood of freemen.
Then boldly appeal to each heart that can feel,
And crush the foul viper neath Liberty's heel!
And the Cross of the South shall in triumph remain

---

[34] L. Virginia French, "Shermanized," *Southern Poems*, ed. Mason, 360–63.

To light us to freedom and glory again!

'Tis the emblem of peace, 'tis the day-star of hope,
Like the sacred LABARUM that guided the Roman;
From the shore of the Gulf to the Delaware's slope,
'Tis the trust of the free and the terror of foemen.
Fling its folds to the air, while we boldly declare
The rights we demand or the deeds that we dare!
While the Cross of the South shall in triumph remain
To light us to freedom and glory again!

And if peace should be hopeless and justice denied,
And war's bloody vulture should flap its black pinions,
Then gladly to arms! while we hurl in our pride,
Defiance to tyrants and death to their minions!
With our front in the field, swearing never to yield,
Or return like the Spartan in death on our shield!
And the Cross of the South shall triumphantly wave
As the Flag of the free or the pall of the brave![35]

THE STONEWALL BANNER

Old Stonewall's banner in triumph waving
So oft has flash'd on the foeman's sight
That grand-Sires hoary in future story
Shall tell their children his deeds of might.
The corps advances
Each eye up glances
That flag recalls brave comrades dead
But proudhearted swell as bright mem'ries dwell
On Vic'tries countless in which it led.

The fiery pillar to Israel's children,
Was less sure guide to their wand'ring feet
Than that old flag on whose every ray
Bright faith sits pointing to vic'try sweet.

---

[35] St. George Tucker, "The Southern Cross," *Southern Poems*, 13.

That Banner o'er us
The foe before us
Our watch word Jackson and our trust in God
We'll free our land from the base born band
or sleep in death neath our native sod.[36]

STONEWALL JACKSON MORTALLY
WOUNDED AT CHANCELLORSVILLE (MAY 1863)
BY HERMAN MELVILLE

The Man who fiercest charged in fight,
    Whose sword and prayer were long–
        Stonewall!
Even him who stoutly stood for Wrong,
How can we praise? Yet coming days
    Shall not forget him with this song.

Dead is the Man whose Cause is dead,
    Vainly he died and set his seal–
        Stonewall!
Earnest in error, as we feel;
True to the thing he deemed was due,
    True as John Brown or steel.

Relentlessly he routed us;
    But *we* relent, for he is low–
        Stonewall!
Justly his fame we outlaw; so
We drop a tear on the bold Virginian's bier,
    Because no wreath we owe.[37]

---

[36] "The Stonewall Banner!" (Richmond: J. W. Randolph, n.d.).

[37] Herman Melville, "Stonewall Jackson Mortally Wounded at Chancellorsville (May 1863)" in *The Collected Poems of Herman Melville*, ed. Howard P. Vincent (Chicago: Packard and Company, 1947) 52–53.

STONEWALL JACKSON'S WAY

Found on a Confederate Sergeant of the old Stonewall
Brigade taken at Winchester, Va.

Come, stack arms, men! pile on the rails,
    Stir up the camp fire bright,
No matter if the canteen fails,
    We'll make a roaring night!
Here Shenandoah brawls along,
    There burly Blue Ridge echoes strong,
To swell the Brigade's rousing song
    Of Stonewall Jackson's way.

We see him now, the old slouch'd hat
    Cock'd o'er his eye askew,
The shrew'd dry smile, the speech so pat,
    So calm, so blunt, so true:
"The Blue Light Elder," knows 'em well
    Says he "that's Banks, he's fond of shell,
Lord save his soul! we'll give him—" well,
    That's Stonewall Jackson's way.
Silence! ground arms! kneel all! caps off!
    Old Blue Light's going to pray,
Strangle the fool that dares to scoff!
    Attention! 'tis his way!
Appealing from his native sod
    In FORMA PAUPERIS to God,—
"Lay bare thine arm, stretch forth thy rod,"
    "Amen!" That's Stonewall's way.

He's in the saddle now, "Fall in!
    Steady! the whole brigade!
Hill's at the ford, cut off; we'll win
    His way out, ball and blade.
What matter if our feet are torn?
    Quick step! we're with him before dawn!"
That's Stonewall Jackson's way.

The sun's bright lances route the mists
    Of morning—and by George!
Here's Longstreet, struggling in the lists
    Hemmed in an ugly gorge.
Pope and his Yankees, whipped before
    "Bay'nets and grape!" hear Stonewall roar
"Charge, Stewart! pay off Ashby's score!"
    In Stonewall Jackson's way.

Ah! maiden, wait, and watch, and yearn,
    For news of Stonewall's band!
Ah! widow, read with eyes that burn,
    That ring upon thy hand!
Ah! wife, sew on, pray on, hope on!
    Thy life shall not be all forlorn;
The foe had better ne'er been born
    That gets in "Stonewall's way!"[38]

THE THUNDER-CLOUD
BY MISS CHANDLER

Thy thunder pealeth o'er us,
    God of the earth and sky!
And o'er the gloomy heavens,
    The clouds roll dark and high;
But oh! there lieth brooding
    A cloud more dark and dread,
Above our guilty nation,
    In fearful portent spread.

Though broad our fertile borders
    All smilingly expand,
The curse of blood is on us,
    And on our pleasant land;
For we have sinn'd before thee,

---

[38] "Stonewall Jackson's Way!" (Richmond: J. W. Randolph, 1863).

And caus'd dark floods to roll,
Of tyranny and anguish,
   Across our brother's soul.

But let not yet thine anger
   Consume our blood-stain'd sod;
Extend a little longer
   Thy mercy, O our God!
And touch our flinty bosoms,
   With thy dissolving grace,
That we may hate our vileness,
   And weep before thy face.[39]

THE WAR-CHRISTIAN'S THANKSGIVING
BY S. TEACKLE WALLIS

Respectfully dedicated to the War-Clergy of the United States, bishops,
   priests, and deacons.

Cursed be he that doeth the work of the Lord negligently, and cursed be
   he that keepeth back his sword from blood.—JEREMIAH 48:10

O God of Battles! once again,
   With banner, trump, and drum,
And garments in Thy wine-press dyed,
   To give Thee thanks, we come!

No goats or bullocks, garlanded,
   Unto thine altars go—
With brothers' blood, by brothers shed,
   Our glad libations flow.

From pest-house and from dungeon foul
   Where, maimed and torn, they die;
From gory trench and charnel-house,
   Where, heap on heap, they lie:

---

[39] Miss Chandler, "The Thunder-Cloud," *Freedom's Lyre*, 203–204.

In every groan that yields a soul,
    Each shriek a heart that rends—
With every breath of tainted air—
    Our homage, Lord, ascends.

We thank thee for the sabre's gash,
    The cannon's havoc wild;
We bless Thee for the widow's tears,
    The want that starves her child.

We give Thee praise, that Thou hast lit
    The torch and fanned the flame;
That lust and rapine hunt their prey,
    Kind Father! in Thy name;

That, for the songs of idle joy
    False angels sang of yore,
Thou sendest War on Earth, Ill Will
    To Men, for evermore.

We know that wisdom, truth, and right
    To us and ours are given—
That thou hast clothed us with the wrath
    To do the work of Heaven.
We know that plains and cities waste
    Are pleasant in Thine eyes;
Thou lov'st a hearthstone desolate,
    Thou lov'st a mourner's cries.

Let not our weakness fall below
    The measure of Thy will,
And while the press hath wine to bleed,
    Oh! tread it with us still!

Teach us to hate—as Jesus taught
    Fond fools, of yore, to love—
Grant us Thy vengeance as our own,

Thy Pity, hide above.

Teach us to turn, with reeking hands,
    The pages of Thy word,
And hail the blessed curses there,
    On them that sheathe the sword.

Where'er we tread, may deserts spring,
    Till none are left to slay;
And when the last red drop is shed,
    We'll kneel again—and pray![40]

Words that Can Be Sung to the
Hallelujah Chorus

Old John Brown lies a-mouldering in the grave,
Old John Brown lies slumbering in his grave—
But John Brown's soul is marching with the brave,
        His soul is marching on.
        Glory, glory, hallelujah!
        Glory, glory, hallelujah!
        Glory, glory, hallelujah!
        His soul is marching on.

He has gone to be a soldier in the army of the Lord,
He is sworn as a private in the ranks of the Lord—
He shall stand at Armageddon with his brave old sword—
        When Heaven is marching on
        Glory, glory, hallelujah, &c.
        For heaven is marching on.

He shall file in front where the lines of battle form, He shall face to front
    when the squares of battle form—
Time with the column, and charge in the storm,
        Where men are marching on.
        Glory, glory, hallelujah, &c.

---

[40] S. Teackle Wallis, "The War-Christian's Thanksgiving," *South Songs*, 75–77.

True men are marching on.

Ah! foul tyrants! do ye hear him where he comes?
Ah! black traitors! do ye know him as he comes?
In thunder of the cannon and roll of the drums,
        As we go marching on.
        Glory, glory, hallelujah, &c.
  We all are marching on.

Men may die, and moulder in the dust,
Men may die, and arise again from dust,
Shoulder to shoulder, in the ranks of the just,
        When Heaven is marching on.
        Glory, glory, hallelujah, &c.
        The Lord is marching on.[41]

YANKEE-DOODLE-DOO!

BY AN ALABAMIAN

Curse on the canting, whining race,
    The peddling, meddling crew,
Whose hearts are vile, and spirits base,
    And backs and bellies blue!
They brag, they lie, they cheat, they steal,
    In every place and time;
Their souls are bloat with bigot zeal,
    And crusted o'er with crime!
A curse upon their menial crew,
The sniffling, whiffling, Yankee-doodle-doo!

They've been the pest of all the world,
    Since Cromwell's bloody days;
From Holland's quagmires they were hurled,
    For their pragmatic ways.
The Mayflower ship, that brought them o'er,

---

[41] Henry Howard Brownell, "Words That Can be Sung to the 'Hallelujah Chorus,'" *Songs of the Soldiers*, 168–69. The date accompanying these words is 17 April 1862.

Conveyed a felon flock,
And spewed the vermin on the shore,
    By Plymouth's "blarney rock."
Then curse the Puritanic crew,
The ranting, canting, Yankee-doodle-doo!

In Northern snows their souls congealed
    To ice lumps in their breasts,
Their hearts became like ING-UNS peeled,
    And by the devil possessed.
Each mother's son, ere he could run,
    His daddy learned to cheat,
And thus a graduate became,
    With peddlers to compete!
Then curse upon the pilfering crew,
The shuffling, snuffling, Yankee-doodle-doo!

They swarmed, like bilge-flies, thro' the land,
    With saintly, drawling speech;
They claimed to be God's missioned band,
    To edit, teach and preach!
With wooden nutmegs, saw-dust seed,
    And pinchbeck ware, they strayed,
And made even little NIGGERS "bleed,"
    When they could "strike a trade."
Then curse upon the cheating crew,
The peddling, meddling Yankee-doodle-doo!

You know them by their coffin face,
    Their pallid lantern jaws,
Their smirking lips, their sneaking ways,
    Their clumsy feet and paws!
With hypocritic eyes they leer,
    And sycophantic smile;
With nasal twang they utter prayer,
    And rob the church the while!
Then curse the pharisaic crew,
The robbing, jobbing, Yankee-doodle-doo!

They're cowards in their hollow hearts,
    Nor dare an equal field;
In battle, on their hinder-parts,
    They wisely put the shield;
With iron ship, and long, long gun,
    They keep beyond our shots;
Get near, and every mother's son
    In double quick-time trots!
Then curse upon the dastard crew
The shunning, running, Yankee-doodle-doo!

Soon from our land we'll drive them all,
    To their dark holes afar;
Thank God we've broke the Northern thrall,
    And see the rising star!
Yes, Yankee-doodle-doodle-doo,
    We've done with you at last;
Go eat your onions, spin and spew,
    Your "occupation's" passed!
Yet curse upon your cringing crew,
Poor shrieking, sneaking, Yankee-doodle-doo![42]

ZOLLICOFFER

BY HARRY FLASH

First in the fight, and first in the arms
    Of the white-winged angels of glory,
With the heart of the South at the feet of God,
    And his wounds to tell the story;

For the blood that flowed from his hero heart,
    On the spot where he nobly perished,

---

[42] "Yankee-Doodle-Doo!" *The Southern Soldier's Prize Songster, Containing Martial and Patriotic Pieces* (Mobile AL: W. F. Wisely, 1864) 19–21.

Was drunk by the earth as a sacrament
   In the holy cause he cherished!

In Heaven a home with the brave and blessed,
   And for his soul's sustaining
The apocalyptic eyes of Christ—
   And nothing on earth remaining,

But a handful of dust in the land of his choice,
   A name in song and story—
And fame to shout with immortal voice:
   DEAD ON THE FIELD OF GLORY![43]

---

[43] Harry Flash, "Zollicoffer," *South Songs*, Ed. De Leon, 83.

SELECTED BIBLIOGRAPHY

PRIMARY SOURCES: NORTH

Adams, John Quincy. *Memoirs of John Quincy Adams.* Edited by Charles Francis Adams. 12 Volumes. Philadelphia: J. B. Lippincott and Co., 1874–1877.

Aikman, William. *The Future of the Colored Race in America.* Philadelphia: William S. Young, 1862.

Arnold, Isaac Newton. *The History of Abraham Lincoln and the Overthrow of Slavery.* Chicago: Clarke & Co., 1866.

Barlow, Joel. *The Columbiad.* Philadelphia: Fry and Kammerer, 1807.

Pierpoint, John, ed. *Anti-Slavery Poems.* Boston: Oliver Johnson, 1843.

Beecher, Henry Ward. *The American Rebellion.* Manchester UK: Union & Emancipation Society, 1864.

———. *Freedom and War: Discourses in Topics Suggested by the Times.* Boston: Ticknor & Fields, 1863.

———. *Lectures and Orations.* Edited by Newell Dwight Hills. New York: Fleming H. Revell Co., 1913.

———. *War and Emancipation.* Philadelphia: T. B. Peterson, 1861.

Beman, Nathan Sydney Smith. *Our Civil War: the Principles Involved, Its Cause and Cure.* Troy NY: W. W. Scribner, 1863.

Botts, John Minor. *The Great Rebellion: Its Secret History.* New York: Harper & Brothers, 1866.

Bowen, C. *The Bible on the Present Crisis.* New York: Sinclair Toucey, 1863.

Boynton, Charles Brandon. *God's Hand in the War.* Cincinnati: "Free Nation" Office, 1862.

Brimblecomb, Nicholas [pseud.], *Uncle Tom's Cabin in Ruins!* Boston: Charles Waite, 1853.

Brownell, Henry Howard. *Lines of Battle.* Boston: Houghton Mifflin, 1912.

———. *War-Lyrics.* Boston: Ticknor and Fields, 1866.

Brownson, Orestes Augustus. *Babylon is Falling.* 2nd ed. Boston: I. R. Butts, 1837.

Burleigh, George S. "Our First Ten Years in the Struggle for Liberty." *Liberty Bell* 5 (1843): 45–46, 48.

Bushnell, Horace. *Reverses Needed: A Discourse Delivered on the Saturday after the Disaster of Bull Run.* Hartford CT: L. E. Hunt, 1861.

Chapman, Maria, ed. *Songs of the Free, and Hymns of Christian Freedom.* Boston: I. Knapp, 1836.

Cheever, George B. *The Fire and Hammer of God's Word Against the Sin of Slavery.* New York: American Abolition Society, 1858.

———. *God's Hand in America.* New York: M. W. Dodd, 1841.

———. *The Sin of Slavery, the Guilt of the Church, and the Duty of the Ministry.* Boston: John P. Jewett & Co., 1860.

Christ in the Army: A Selection of Sketches of the Work of the U. S. Christian Commission. Philadelphia: Ladies of the Christian Commission, 1865.

Clarke, James Freeman. *Discourse on the Aspects of the War.* Boston: Walker, Wise, & Co., 1863.

Conway, Moncure Daniel. *Addresses and Reprints 1850–1907.* Boston: Houghton Mifflin, 1909.

———. *The Rejected Stone: or, Insurrection vs. Resurrection in America.* 2nd ed. Boston: Walker, Wise & Co., 1862.

Corby, William. *Memoirs of Chaplain Life: Three Years with the Irish Brigade in the Army of the Potomac.* New York: Fordham University Press, 1992.

Cranch, Christopher. *The Bird and the Bell.* Boston: James D. Osgood, 1875.

Davies, E. "Watchman, What of the Night?" *Zion's Herald and Wesleyan Journal* (22 April 1863): 1.

Drew, Thomas, ed. *The John Brown Invasion: an Authentic History of the Harper's Ferry Tragedy.* Boston: James Campbell, 1860.

Dye, John Smith. *History of the Plots and Crimes of the Great Conspiracy to Overthrow Liberty in America.* New York: the author, 1861. Reprint, Freeport NY: Books for Libraries Press, 1969.

Ellis, George Edward. "Our Civil War." *Bunker Hill Aurora,* 11 May 1864, 1.

The Encyclopedia of Popular Songs. New York: Dick & Fitzgerald, 1864.

Fast Day Sermons, or, the Pulpit on the State of the Country. New York: Rudd & Carleton, 1861.

Garrison, William Lloyd. *William Lloyd Garrison.* Edited by George M. Frederickson. Great Lives Observed Series. Englewood Cliffs NJ: Prentice-Hall, 1968.

Grierson, Francis. *Abraham Lincoln, the Practical Mystic.* New York: John Lane Co., 1918.

———. *The Valley of Shadows: The Coming of the Civil War to Lincoln's Midwest, A Contemporary Account.* Edited by Bernard De Voto. New York: Harper & Row, 1966.

Hardinge, Emma. *America and Her Destiny: Inspirational Discourse through E. H., by the Spirits.* New York: Robert M. DeWitt, 1863.

Hatfield, Edwin Francis, ed. *Freedom's Lyre.* New York: S. W. Benedict, 1840. Reprint, Miami: Mnemosyne Pub. Co., 1969.

Haven, Gilbert. *National Sermons: Sermons, Speeches and Letters on Slavery and Its War.* Boston: Lee & Shepard, 1869.

Hedge, Frederick Henry. *The National Entail.* Boston: Wright & Potter, 1864.

Holmes, Daniel. *Dialogue on Slavery.* Dayton: Gazette Book & Job Rooms, 1854.

Hopkins, Samuel. *A Dialogue Concerning the Slavery of the Africans.* Norwich: Judah P. Spooner, 1776. Reprint, n.p.: Robert Hodge, 1785.

———. *Timely Articles on Slavery.* Edited by Edwards Amasa Parks. Boston: Congregational Board of Publication, 1854.

———. *The Works of Samuel Hopkins.* 3 Volumes. Boston: Doctrinal Tract and Book Society, 1852.

Howe, Julia Ward. "The Battle Hymn of the Republic." *The Atlantic Monthly* (February 1862): 1.

———. *Reminiscences 1819–1899.* Boston: Houghton Mifflin, 1900.

"A Hymn for Northern People." *Zion's Herald and Wesleyan Journal* (5 October 1864): 1.

John Brown. Boston: J. F. Nash, [1860?]

Johnson, Herrick. *The Shaking of the Nations.* Pittsburgh: W. S. Haven, 1864.

Lincoln, Abraham. *The Collected Works of Abraham Lincoln.* 9 Volumes. Edited by Roy P. Basler. New Brunswick NJ: Rutgers University Press, 1953.

———. *The Literary Works of Abraham Lincoln.* Edited by Carl Van Doren. New York: Readers Club, 1942.

Melville, Herman. *Battle-Pieces and Aspects of the War.* New York: Harper & Brothers, 1866.

———. *The Collected Poems of Herman Melville.* Edited by Howard P. Vincent. Chicago: Packard and Company, 1947.

Moore, Frank, ed. *Songs of the Soldiers.* New York: G. P. Putnam, 1864.

Moore, Henry D. *Our Country—Its Sin and Its Duty.* Portland ME: H. Packard, 1861.

Parker, Theodore. *John Brown's Expedition.* Boston: The Fraternity, 1860.

———. *A Sermon of the Dangers Which Threaten the Rights of Man in America.* Boston: Benjamin B. Mussey, 1854.

Parks, Edwards Amasa. *Memoir of the Life and Character of Samuel Hopkins, D.D.* Boston: Doctrinal Tract and Book Society, 1852.

Peck, Thomas. "The Day of Jubilee." *Zion's Herald and Wesleyan Journal* (18 February 1863): 1.

Phillips, George Searle. *The American Republic and Human Liberty Foreshadowed in Scripture.* Cincinnati: Poe and Hitchcock, 1864.

Quint, Alonzo Hall. *National Sin Must be Expiated by National Calamity.* New Bedford: Mercury Press, 1865.

Sears, Edmund H. "Signs in the Sky—Beautiful Incident." *Monthly Religious Magazine,* April 1862, 267.

Seiss, Joseph Augustus. *Last Times and the Great Consummation*. Rev. ed. Philadelphia: Smith, E. & Co., 1863.

Sherman, William T. *Memoirs of General William T. Sherman*. 2 Volumes. New York: D. Appleton, 1875.

Simpson, Matthew. *Funeral Address Delivered at the Burial of President Lincoln at Springfield, Illinois, May 4, 1865*. New York: Carlton & Porter, 1865.

Stanley, E. S. "National Fast Day Sermon on "The Times."" *Zion's Herald and Wesleyan Journal* (9 October 1861): 1.

Stanton, R. L. *The Church and the Rebellion*. New York: Derby & Miller, 1864.

Stedman, Edmund Clarence. *The Poems of Edmund Clarence Stedman*. Boston: Houghton Mifflin, 1908.

Stowe, Harriet Beecher. *Dred: A Tale of the Great Dismal Swamp*. Boston: Houghton Mifflin, 1889.

———. *A Key to Uncle Tom's* Cabin. Boston: J. P. Jewett & Co., 1854.

———. *The Minister's Wooing*. 21st Edition. Boston: Houghton Mifflin, 1885.

———. "The Story of 'Uncle Tom's Cabin.'" *Old South Leaflets*, No. 82. Boston: Directors of the Old South Work, 1897.

———. *Uncle Tom's Cabin*. Edited by Philip Van Doren Stern. New York: Paul S. Eriksson, 1964.

Torrey, Jesse. *A Portraiture of Domestic Slavery in the United States*. Philadelphia: 1817.

Victor, Orville James. History of American Conspiracies. New York: J. D. Torrey, 1863.

"The War—When Shall it End?" *Zion's Herald and Wesleyan Journal* (18 February 1863): 1.

Whitman, Walt. *Leaves of Grass*. Edited by Sculley Bradley and Harold W. Blodgett. New York: W. W. Norton, 1973.

Willson, James Renwick. *Tokens of the Divine Displeasure*. Newburgh NY: Charles U. Cushman, 1836.

Wilson, Henry. *History of the Rise and Fall of the Slave Power in America*. 3 Volumes. Boston: J. R. Osgood and Co., 1873–1877.

Wisner, William Carpenter. *The Biblical Argument on Slavery*. New York: Leavitt, Trow & Co., 1844.

PRIMARY SOURCES: SOUTH

Allan, Francis D., ed. *Allan's Lone Star Ballads*. Galveston TX: J. D. Sawyer, 1874.

Armstrong, George D. *The Good Hand of God is Upon Us*. Norfolk: J. D. Gillselin, Jr., 1861.

Barrows, J. L. *"Nationality Insured!" Notes of a Sermon Delivered at the First Baptist Church, Augusta, GA, Sept. 11, 1864*. Augusta: Jas. Nathan Ells, 1864.

Bennett, William W. *A Narrative of the Great Revival.* Philadelphia: Claxten, 1877.

Berry, Harrison. *Slavery and Abolitionism as Viewed by a Georgia Slave.* Atlanta: Franklin Printing House, 1861.

Birch, Edmund Pendleton. *The Devil's Visit to Old Abe.* La Grange GA: n.p., [1862?].

Caylat, Charles E. *The Glorious Southern Victories!* Confederate States of America, 25 February 1863.

Chestnut, Mary. *Mary Chestnut's Civil War.* Edited by C. Vann Woodward. New Haven: Yale University Press, 1981.

Davidson, James Wood. *The Living Writers of the South.* New York: Carleton, 1869.

De Leon, Thomas Cooper, ed. *South Songs: from the Lays of Later Days.* New York: Blelock & Co., 1866.

Doggett, David Seth. *The War and Its Close.* Richmond: Macfarlane & Fergusson, 1864.

Eastman, Mary. *Aunt Phillis's Cabin, or Southern Life as It Is.* Philadelphia: Lippincott, Grambo and Co., 1852. Reprint, New York: Negro University Press, 1968.

Elliott, E. N. *Cotton is King and Pro-Slavery Arguments Composing the Writings of Hammond, Harper, Christy, Stringfellow, Hodge, Bledsoe, and Cartwright.* n.p.: Pritchard, Abbott, & Loomis, 1860. Reprint, New York: Negro Universities Press, 1969.

Elliott, Stephen, Bishop of Georgia. *Ezra's Dilemma.* Savannah: George N. Nichols, 1863.

———. *Funeral Services at the Burial of the Right Rev. Leonidas Polk, D.D.* Columbia SC: Evans & Cogswell, 1864.

———. *God's Presence with Our Army at Manassas!* Savannah: W. Thorne Williams, 1861.

———. *New Wine Not to be Put into Old Bottles.* Savannah: John M. Cooper, 1862.

———. *Our Cause in Harmony with the Purposes of God in Christ Jesus.* Savannah: Power Press of John M. Cooper & Co., 1862.

———. *Vain is the Help of Man.* Macon GA: Burke, Boykin & Co., 1864.

Gammage, W. S. *The Camp, the Bivouac, and the Battle Field.* Selma AL: Cooper & Kimball, 1864.

Grady, Benjamin Franklin. *The Case of the South Against the North.* Raleigh NC: Edwards & Broughton, 1899.

Grayson, William John. *The Hireling and the Slave, Chicora, and Other Poems.* Charleston SC: McCarter, 1856.

Harrison, William Pope. *The Gospel Among the Slaves: A Short Account of Missionary Operations among the African Slaves of the Southern States.*

Nashville: Publishing House of the Methodist Episcopal Church, South, 1893.

How, Samuel Blanchard. *Slaveholding Not Sinful.* New York: John A. Gray, 1855.

Introduction to a History of the Second American War for Independence or the Civil War in the United States. Confederate States of America, n.p., June 1863.

Jones, Charles Colcock, Sr. *Religious Instruction of the Negroes.* Richmond: Presbyterian Committee of Publication, [1862?].

Jones, John William. *Christ in the Camp: Or, Religion in Lee's Army.* Richmond: B. F. Johnson & Co., 1888.

———. *The Southern Soldier's Duty.* Rome GA: D. H. Mason, 1861.

Ker, Leander. *Slavery Consistent with Christianity.* Jefferson City MO: W. Lusk, 1842.

Mason, Emily Virginia, ed. *The Southern Poems of the War.* Baltimore: J. Murphy & Co., 1867.

McDonald, Angus W. *The Two Rebellions: Or, a Treason Unmasked.* Richmond: Smith, Bailey, & Co., Sentinel Office, 1865.

McDonald, Cornelia. *A Diary with Reminiscences of the War and Refugee Life in the Shenandoah Valley 1860–1865.* Nashville TN: Hunter McDonald, 1934.

McTyeire, Holland Nimmons. *Duties of Christian Masters.* Nashville: Southern Methodist Publishing House, 1859.

Miles, James Warley. *God in History.* Charleston: Steam Power Press of Evans and Cogswell, 1863.

Mitchell, J. C. *A Bible Defense of Slavery, and the Unity of Mankind.* Mobile: J. Y. Thompson, 1861.

Myers, Robert Manson, ed. *Children of Pride: A True Story of Georgia and the Civil War, Selected Letters of the Family of the Rev. Dr. Charles Colcock Jones.* New Haven: Yale University Press, 1984.

Palmer, Benjamin Morgan. *A Vindication of Secession and the South.* Columbia: Southern Guardian Steam-Power Press, 1861.

Pannill, D. H. Letter to the *Richmond Dispatch*, 17 August 1891.

Philpott, J. P. *The Kingdom of Israel.* Fairfield TX: Pioneer Office Print, 1864.

Quintard, Charles Todd. *Doctor Quintard, Chaplain CSA and Second Bishop of Tennessee, Being His Story of the War.* Edited by Arthur Howard Noll. Sewanee TN: The University Press, 1905.

Ross, Frederick Augustus. *Slavery Ordained of God.* Philadelphia: J. B. Lippincott & Co., 1857. Reprint, Miami FL: Mnemosyne Publishing Co., 1969.

Seat, W. H. *The Confederate States of America in Prophecy.* Nashville TN: Methodist Publishing House, 1861.

Simms, William Gilmore. *The Morals of Slavery.* Charleston: 1838. Reprint, New York: Negro Universities Press, 1968.

———. *Slavery in America.* Richmond: T. W. White, 1838.

————. *Southward Ho! A Spell of Sunshine.* Caxton ed. Chicago: Donohue, Henneberry & Co., 1890.

————. *War Poetry of the South.* New York: Richardson, 1867.

The Southern Soldier's Prize Songster, Containing Martial and Patriotic Pieces. Mobile AL: W. F. Wisely, 1864.

The Stonewall Banner. Richmond: J. W. Randolph.

Stonewall Jackson's Way! Richmond: J. W. Randolph, 1863.

Thornwell, James Henley. *The Rights and Duties of Masters.* Charleston: Walker & James, 1850.

Thrasher, John B. *Slavery a Divine Institution.* Port Gibson MS: Southern Reveille Book & Job Office, 1861.

Tucker, Nathaniel Beverly. *The Partisan Leader: A Novel, and an Apocalypse of the Origin and the Struggles of the Southern Confederacy.* Edited by Thomas A. Ware. Richmond: West & Johnston, 1862.

Warren, Ebenezer W. *Nellie Norton: or Southern Slavery and the Bible.* Macon GA: Burke, Boykin & Co., 1864.

Wiley, C. H. *Scriptural Views of National Trials: or the True Road to the Independence and Peace of the CSA.* Greensboro NC: Sterling, Campbell & Albright, 1863.

Williams, James. *Letters on Slavery from the Old World: Written During the Canvass for the Presidency in 1860.* Nashville TN: Southern Methodist Publishing House, 1861.

Wright, Henry Clarke. *Self-Convicted Violaters of Principle.* N.p., [184?].

PRIMARY SOURCES: SLAVES

Allen, William Francis. *Slave Songs of the US.* New York: John Ross & Co., 1871.

Higginson, Thomas Wentworth. *Slave Life in a Black Regiment.* Boston: Fields, Osgood & Co., 1870.

Rawick, George P., ed. *The American Slave: A Composite Autobiography.* 42 Volumes. Westport CT: Greenwood Press, 1972, 1979.

SECONDARY SOURCES

Aaron, Daniel. *The Unwritten War: American Writers and the Civil War.* New York: Oxford University Press, 1973.

Alter, Robert. "The Apocalyptic Temper." *Commentary* 41 (1966): 61–66.

Altizer, Thomas J. J. *History as Apocalypse.* SUNY Series in Religion. Albany: State University of New York Press, 1985.

Ammons, Elizabeth, and Dorothy Berkson, eds. *Critical Essays on Harriet Beecher Stowe.* Boston: G. K. Hall, 1980.

Bates, Samuel P. *History of the Pennsylvania Volunteers, 1861–1865.* 4 Volumes. Harrisburg PA: B. Singerly, 1870.

Benners, Alfred H. *Slavery and Its Results.* Macon GA: J. W. Burke, 1923.

Bennett, Gaymon Lamont. "Melville's *Battle-Pieces* and Whitman's *Drum-Taps:* Two Northern Poets Interpret the Civil War." Ph.D. dissertation, Washington State University, 1981.

Bercovitch, Sacvan. *The American Jeremiad.* Madison: The University of Wisconsin Press, 1978.

Blassingame, John W. "Using the Testimony of Ex-Slaves: Approaches and Problems." *The Journal of Southern History* 41/4 (November 1975): 473–92.

Brugger, Robert J. *Beverly Tucker: Heart over Head in the Old South.* Baltimore: Johns Hopkins University Press, 1978.

Bull, Malcolm, ed. *Apocalypse Theory and the Ends of the World.* Oxford: Blackwell, 1995.

Burke, Edmund. *Philosophical Inquiry into the Origin of Our Ideas of the Sublime and Beautiful.* London: R. and J. Dodsley, 1759. Reprint, New York: John B. Alden, 1885.

Case, Shirley Jackson. *The Millennial Hope.* Chicago: University of Chicago Press, 1918.

Caskey, Marie. *Chariot of Fire: Religion and the Beecher Family.* New Haven: Yale University Press, 1978.

Catton, Bruce. "A Southern Artist on the Civil War." *American Heritage* 9/6 (1958): 117–20.

Chambers, Bruce William. "David Gilmour Blythe (1815–1865): An Artist at Urbanization's Edge." Ph.D. dissertation, University of Pennsylvania, 1974.

———. "The Southern Artist and the Civil War." *Southern Quarterly* 24/1-2 (1985): 71–94.

———. *The World of David Gilmour Blythe: 1815–1865.* Washington, DC: Smithsonian Institution Press, 1980.

Chesebrough, David B. *Clergy Dissent in the Old South, 1830–1865.* Carbondale: Southern Illinois University Press, 1996.

Cherry, Conrad. *God's New Israel: Religious Interpretations of American Destiny.* Englewood Cliffs NJ: Prentice-Hall, 1971.

Clebsch, William A. "Baptism of Blood: A Study of Christian Contributions to the Interpretation of the Civil War in American History." Ph.D. dissertation, Union Theological Seminary, New York, 1957.

———. *Christian Interpretations of the Civil War.* Philadelphia: Fortress Press, 1969.

———. *From Sacred to Profane America: The Role of Religion in American History.* New York: Harper & Row, 1968.

Clifford, Deborah Pickman. *Mine Eyes Have Seen the Glory.* Boston: Little, Brown, 1979.

Cohn, Norman. *The Pursuit of the Millennium: Revolutionary Millenarians and the Mystical Anarchists of the Middle Ages.* 2nd ed. New York: Oxford University Press, 1970.

Colbenson, Pamela Elwyn Thomas. "Millennial Thought Among Southern Evangelicals, 1830–1885." Ph.D. dissertation, Georgia State University, 1980.

Collins, Adela Yarbro. *Crisis and Catharsis: The Power of the Apocalypse.* Philadelphia: The Westminster Press, 1984.

Cross, Whitney. *The Burned-Over District: the Social and Intellectual History of Enthusiastic Religion in Western New York 1800–1850.* Ithaca: Cornell University Press, 1950.

Davis, Charles T. and Henry Louis Gates, Jr., eds. *The Slave's Narrative: Texts and Contexts.* New York: Oxford University Press, 1984.

Davis, Richard Beale. *Intellectual Life in the Colonial South 1585–1763.* 3 Volumes. Knoxville: University of Tennessee Press, 1978.

Dennard, David Charles. "Religion in the South: A Study of Slave Preachers in the Antebellum South, 1800–1860." Ph.D. dissertation, Northwestern University, 1983.

Doyle, Bertram Wilbur. *The Etiquette of Race Relations in the South: A Study in Social Control.* New York: Schocken Books, 1971.

Dunham, Chester Forrester. *The Attitude of the Northern Clergy Toward the South, 1860–1865.* Philadelphia: Porcupine Press, 1974.

Early, Gerald Lyn. "'A Servant of Servants Shall He Be...': Paternalism and Millennialism in American Slavery Literature, 1850–1859." Ph.D. dissertation, Cornell University, 1982.

Escott, Paul D. *Slavery Remembered: A Record of Twentieth-Century Slave Narratives.* Chapel Hill: University of North Carolina Press, 1979.

Farmer, James O., Jr. *The Metaphysical Confederacy: James Henley Thornwell and the Synthesis of Southern Values.* Macon GA: Mercer University Press, 1986.

Farwell, Byron. *Stonewall: A Biography of General Thomas J. Jackson.* New York: W. W. Norton, 1992.

Fisher, Miles Mark. *Negro Slave Songs in the United States.* Ithaca NY: Cornell University Press, 1953.

Frederickson, George. *The Inner Civil War: Northern Intellectuals and the Crisis of the Union.* New York: Harper & Row, 1965.

Furness, Clifton Joseph. "Communal Music Among Arabians and Negroes." *Musical Quarterly* 16/1 (1930): 48–51.

Garner, Stanton. *The Civil War World of Herman Melville.* Lawrence: The University Press of Kansas, 1993.

Genovese, Eugene. *A Consuming Fire: The Fall of the Confederacy in the Mind of the White Christian South.* Athens: University of Georgia Press, 1998.

————. *Roll, Jordan, Roll: The World the Slaves Made.* New York: Pantheon, 1974.

Grant, Mary H. *Private Woman, Public Person: An Account of the Life of Julia Ward Howe from 1819 to 1868.* New York: Carlson Publishing, 1994.

Gravely, William B. *Gilbert Haven, Methodist Abolitionist.* New York: Abingdon Press, 1973.

Hareven, Tamara K., ed. *Anonymous Americans: Explorations in Nineteenth-Century Social History.* Englewood Cliffs NJ: Prentice-Hall, 1971.

Hatch, Nathan O. "The Origins of Civil Millennialism in America: New England Clergymen, the War with France, and the Revolution." *William and Mary Quarterly.* 31 (July 1974): 407–30.

Hedin, Raymond. "Muffled Voices: The American Slave Narrative." *Clio* 10/2 (1981): 129–42.

Hedrick, Joan. *Harriet Beecher Stowe: A Life.* New York: Oxford University Press, 1994.

Herndon, William H. and Jesse W. Weik. *Herndon's Life of Lincoln: The History and Personal Recollections of Abraham Lincoln.* New York: Albert & Charles Boni, 1936.

Hertz, Emmanuel. *The Hidden Lincoln: From the Letter and Papers of William H. Herndon.* New York: The Viking Press, 1938.

Holzer, Harold. "Confederate Caricature of Abraham Lincoln." *Illinois Historical Journal* 80/1 (Spring 1987): 23–36.

Huntington, David C. *The Landscapes of Frederic Edwin Church: Vision of an American Era.* New York: George Braziller, 1966.

Husch, Gail. "'Something Coming': Prophecy and American Painting, 1848–1854." Ph.D. dissertation, University of Delaware, 1992.

Jackson, Mary Anna. *Life and Letters of General Thomas J. Jackson.* New York: Harper & Brothers, 1892.

Jenkins, William Sumner. *Pro-Slavery Thought in the Old South.* Chapel Hill: University of North Carolina Press, 1935. Reprint, Gloucester MA: Peter Smith, 1960.

Kammen, Michael. *A Season of Youth: The American Revolution and the Historical Imagination.* New York: Oxford University Press, 1978.

Kaplan, Justin. *Mr. Clemens and Mark Twain: A Biography.* New York: Simon and Schuster, 1966.

Keller, Catherine. *Apocalypse Now and Then: A Feminist Guide to the End of the World.* Boston: Beacon Press, 1996.

Kelly, Franklin, et al., *Frederick Edwin Church.* Washington, DC: National Gallery of Art, 1989.

Kermode, Frank. *The Sense of an Ending: Studies in the Theory of Fiction.* New York: Oxford University Press, 1967.

Ketterer, David. "Epoch-Eclipse and Apocalypse: Special 'Effects' in *A Connecticut Yankee*," *PMLA* 88 (1973): 1104–114.

Levine, Lawrence. *Black Culture and Black Consciousness: Afro-American Folk Thought from Slavery to Freedom*. New York: Oxford University Press, 1977.

Lewis, R. W. B. *Trials of the Word: Essays in American Literature and the Humanistic Tradition*. New Haven: Yale University Press, 1965.

Manthorne, Katherine. *Creation and Renewal: Views of Cotopaxi by Frederic Edwin Church*. Washington, DC: National Museum of American Art, 1985.

Marty, Martin E. *Righteous Empire: The Protestant Experience in America*. New York: The Dial Press, 1970.

Mathews, Donald G. *Religion in the Old South*. Chicago: University of Chicago Press, 1977.

May, John R. *Toward a New Earth: Apocalypse in the American Novel*. Notre Dame: University of Notre Dame Press, 1972.

McGinn, Bernard, John J. Collins, and Stephen J. Stein, eds. *The Encyclopedia of Apocalypticism*. 3 Volumes. New York: The Continuum Publishing Company, 1999.

McKivigan, John R. *The War Against Proslavery Religion: Abolitionism and the Northern Churches, 1830–1865*. Ithaca NY: Cornell University Press, 1984.

Milder, Robert. "The Rhetoric of Melville's *Battle-Pieces*." *Nineteenth Century Literature* 44/2 (September 1989): 173–200.

Miller, Angela. *The Empire of the Eye: Landscape Representation and American Cultural Politics, 1825–1875*. Ithaca: Cornell University Press, 1993.

Miller, Dorothy. *The Life and Work of David G. Blythe*. Pittsburgh: University of Pittsburgh Press, 1950.

Miller, Edwin Havilland. *Melville*. New York: George Braziller, 1975.

Miller, Randall M., Harry S. Stout, and Charles Reagan Wilson, eds. *Religion and the American Civil War*. New York: Oxford University Press, 1998.

Moorhead, James. *American Apocalypse: Yankee Protestants and the Civil War 1860–1869*. New Haven: Yale University Press, 1978.

Morgan, David. *Protestants and Pictures: Religion, Visual Culture, and the Age of American Mass Production*. New York: Oxford University Press, 1999.

Neely, Mark E., Jr., Harold Holzer, and Gabor S. Boritt, eds. *The Confederate Image: Prints of the Lost Cause*. Chapel Hill: University of North Carolina Press, 1987.

Niebuhr, H. Richard. *The Kingdom of God in America*. Chicago: Willet, Clark, 1937.

O'Leary, Stephen D. *Arguing the Apocalypse: A Theory of Millennial Rhetoric*. New York: Oxford University Press, 1994.

Parrington, Vernon Louis. *Main Currents in American Thought*. 3 Volumes. New York: Harcourt Brace Jovanovich, 1930.

Pressly, Thomas J. *Americans Interpret Their Civil War*. Princeton: Princeton University Press, 1954.

Raboteau, Albert J. *Slave Religion: The "Invisible Institution" in the Antebellum South*. New York: Oxford University Press, 1978.

Robertson, James I., Jr. *The Stonewall Brigade*. Baton Rouge: Louisiana State University Press, 1963.

Robinson, Douglas Jack. "American Apocalypses: The Image of the End of the World in American Literature." Ph.D. dissertation, University of Washington, 1983.

Rossbach, Jeffrey. *Ambivalent Conspirators: John Brown, the Secret Six, and a Theory of Slave Violence*. Philadelphia: The University of Pennsylvania Press, 1982.

Sandeen, Ernest Robert. *The Roots of Fundamentalism: British and American Millenarianism 1800–1930*. Chicago: University of Chicago Press, 1970.

Sanford, Charles L. *The Quest for Paradise: Europe and the American Moral Imagination*. Urbana: University of Illinois Press, 1961.

Sears, Stephen W. *Landscape Turned Red: The Battle of Antietam*. Boston: Ticknor & Fields, 1983. Reprint, New York: Warner Books, 1985.

Sharp, Richard Dale. "*The Poet's Witness:* A Comparative Study of the Civil War Poetry of Walt Whitman and Herman Melville." Ph.D. dissertation, University of California, Santa Cruz, 1978.

Smith, David. "Millenarian Scholarship in America." *American Quarterly* 17 (1965): 535–49.

Smith, Timothy. *Revivalism and Social Reform in Mid-Nineteenth Century America*. New York: Abingdon Press, 1957.

Snay, Mitchell. *Gospel of Disunion: Religion and Separatism in the Antebellum South*. Chapel Hill: University of North Carolina Press, 1993.

Snyder, Edward D. "The Biblical Background of the 'Battle Hymn of the Republic.'" *New England Quarterly* 24 (1951): 231–38.

Strout, Cushing. *The New Heavens and the New Earth: Political Religion in America*. New York: Harper & Row, 1974.

Tandy, Jeanette Reid. "Pro-Slavery Propaganda in American Fiction in the 1850s." *South Atlantic Quarterly* 20 (June–March 1922): 41–50.

Tanner, Robert G. *Stonewall in the Valley: Thomas J. "Stonewall" Jackson's Shenandoah Valley Campaign, Spring 1862*. Garden City NY: Doubleday, 1976.

Tharp, Louise Hall. "The Song That Wrote Itself." *American Heritage* 8/1 (December 1956): 10–13.

Trent, William P. *William Gilmore Simms*. American Men of Letters Series. Boston: Houghton Mifflin, 1892. Reprint, New York: Greenwood Press, 1969.

Treuttner, William H. "The Genesis of Frederic Edwin Church's 'Aurora Borealis.'" *Art Quarterly* 81 (Autumn 1968): 267–83.

Trilling, Lionel. *The Liberal Imagination: Essays on Literature and Society.* New York: The Viking Press, 1951.

Turner, Lucille Price. "Negro Spirituals in the Making." *Musical Quarterly* 17/4 (1931): 480–85.

Tuveson, Ernest Lee. *Millennium and Utopia: A Study in the Background of the Idea of Progress.* Berkeley: University of California Press, 1949. Reprint, New York: Harper & Row, 1964.

———. *Redeemer Nation: The Idea of America's Millennial Role.* Chicago: University of Chicago Press, 1968.

Twain, Mark. *A Connecticut Yankee in King Arthur's Court.* Edited by Allison R. Ensor. New York: W. W. Norton, 1982.

Tyler, Alice Felt. *Freedom's Ferment: Phases of American Social History to 1860.* Minneapolis: The University of Minnesota Press, 1944.

Voss, Frederick S. "Adalbart Volck: The South's Answer to Thomas Nast." *Smithsonian Studies in American Art* 2/3 (1988): 67–87.

Wagar, W. Warren. *Terminal Visions: The Literature of Last Things.* Bloomington: Indiana University Press, 1982.

Wakelyn, Jon L. *The Politics of a Literary Man: William Gilmore Simms.* Westport CT: Greenwood Press, 1973.

Wills, Garry. *Inventing America: Jefferson's Declaration of Independence.* Garden City NY: Doubleday, 1978.

Wilmerding, John, ed. *American Light: The Luminist Movement 1850–1875.* Washington, DC, National Gallery of Art, 1980.

Wilson, Charles Reagan. *Baptized in Blood: The Religion of the Lost Cause 1865–1920.* Athens: University of Georgia Press, 1980.

Wilson, Edmund. *Patriotic Gore: Studies in the Literature of the American Civil War.* New York: Oxford University Press, 1962.

Woodward, C. Vann. *The Burden of Southern History.* Baton Rouge: Louisiana State University Press, 1968.

Yetman, Norman R. "Ex-Slave Interviews and the Historiography of Slavery." *American Quarterly* 36/2 (1984): 181–210.

INDEX

abolitionists, 17: as infidels, 66; as portrayed by proslavery Southerners, 53; critique of Southern slavery by, 53

Adams, John Quincy, 22

Adger, John, 52

Advent, First, 28

Advent, Second. *See* Second Coming, The

Africa, evangelization of, 71

Aikman, William, 89

American Revolution: apocalyptic interpretation of, 3, 17, 51; Civil War as second, 60; criticism of slavery during, 14, 18; supporters of slavery and, 23, 24

Anaconda Plan, 131

Antichrist, The, 65

Antietam, Battle of, 14, 90: Confederate religious interpretation of the war and, 59; emancipation and, 75, 89, 109

antislavery movement 51. *See also* abolitionism

Apocalypse, the, 3, 6, 11, 22, 120, 128, 135; and "Battle Hymn of the Republic," 82; associated with the Civil War, 78, 120; as interpreted by slaves, 128; as motif for American mythmakers, 3; as secular event, 10-11, as "unveiling," 9-10; *Cotopaxi* and *Twilight in the Wilderness* as depictions of, 7-8; hastened by moral laxity, 23; language of, as encouragement to war effort, 120; regional attitudes toward, 34, 126

Apocalypse Now. See Coppola, Francis Ford

apocalypse, secular expressions of, 145: *Apocalypse Now*, 146; *Connecticut Yankee in King Arthur's Court, A*, 141-144; *Crying of Lot 49, The*, 145; *Curse of the Starving Class, The*, 145; *Day of the Locust, The*, 145; *End of the Road, The*, 145; *Mysterious Stranger, The* 145; *Octopus, The*, 145

apocalyptic belief: antislavery and, 51; as part of mainstream American culture, 19; Christian, 4-5, 9-10; Jewish, 4-5, 9-10

apocalyptic imagery, 5-6, 7-8, 11, 22, 38, 83, 120, 131, 146: as aesthetic and rhetorical device, 14-15, 141; as vindication of the status quo in the North, 120; associated with death of Uncle Tom, 38; employed by abolitionists, 27; employed in North during war, 75; in "Battle Hymn of the Republic," 83; postwar, 141-148; the sublime and, 140

apocalyptic interpretations, 101, 120: of Lincoln, 113; of military events by Northern Christians, 77-79; of slavery by antebellum Northern Protestants, 16-17; of American wars, 3, 17-19; of Lincoln's death, 117; of World Trade Center and Pentagon events, 148

apocalyptic literature, 146n.: *Connecticut Yankee and King Arthur's Court, A*, 141; in the South, 3; poetic aspects of, 13, 14; postwar, 141-148